THE DOOMED EXPEDITION

THE DOOMED EXPEDITION

The Norwegian Campaign of 1940

JACK ADAMS

Leo Cooper
London

First published 1989 by Leo Cooper Ltd

Leo Cooper is an independent imprint of
the Octopus Publishing Group
Michelin House, 81 Fulham Road, London SW3 6RB

LONDON MELBOURNE AUCKLAND

ISBN 0 85052 0363

Printed and bound in Great Britain by
Butler & Tanner Ltd, Frome and London

CONTENTS

ILLUSTRATIONS

MAPS

Drawn by Chester Read *Page*

FOREWORD

Unsuccessful military campaigns tend to be forgotten, particularly by the losers. Such is the ill-fated campaign fought by the Allies in Norway in the Spring of 1940.

Years later the distinguished German historian, Professor Walther Hubatsch, insisted that: 'The Norwegian campaign occupies a special place among the campaigns and operations of the Second World War.' He points out that its duration was relatively short, its theatre restricted and the forces engaged limited. Why 'special'?

Because it was the first example of a modern combined operation by land, sea and air. It was the first modern trial of strength between air and sea power.

Here the 'experts' are divided. Some maintain that it was the first real conclusive proof we have had of the undermining of sea-power by air power. Others say that the main effect of Germany's superiority in the air was 'psychological'. Dr T.K. Derry, whose *Campaign in Norway*, written with full access to official papers, was published in 1952, formed the opinion that the effect of German air superiority was the most obvious lesson of the campaign, although 'no degree of foresight could at that time have prevented us from defeat'. He goes on to say that the campaign 'was in many respects a novelty'. Lieutenant-General Sir Adrian Carton de Wiart, VC, who commanded the Allied forces in the Namsos area, reinforces this view by saying that 'this was a campaign for which the book does not cater'.

The weather conditions ranged from unpleasant to impossible, faced by the soldiers, sailors and airmen on both sides with courage and fortitude. They met with new and unusual problems. Most did not understand the strategic, economic, technical and political dilemmas besetting the field commanders and their staffs.

On the Allied side this was mainly due to an overwhelming lack of communication, aggravated by personality clashes among some of the top commanders, (notably at Narvik between Admiral of the Fleet the Earl of Cork and Orrery and Major-General P. J. Mackesy, who commanded the Allied troops on the ground).

This book does not profess to be a full and comprehensive history of the campaign in Norway. In the space allotted there is, regrettably, no room for a full account of the famous sea fights, such as the first and second naval battles in the Narvik fiords. However, these are well documented and easily available. Furthermore, in a book of this kind a detailed analysis of higher strategy and the political in-fighting which caused changes of course, sometimes leading to catastrophe, may be of marginal interest to the general reader.

The book is concerned with the events on land in the geographic areas of Narvik and Bodö-Mosjöen, Namsos and Aandalsnes. The sea-borne operations which covered these confrontations are recorded as, without this naval back-up, movement on land could not have been sustained. Emphasis is strongly on unit action, and the participation of individuals and small groups.

Many of the troops taking part were specialized and well-trained. The French put in the Chasseurs Alpins as ski troops but failed to deliver the vital equipment needed to perform their role. With them came the Foreign Legion, swapping their semi-tropical station for the rigours of the Arctic.

The Poles sent their Highland Brigade (under French command), some of whom had already fought against the Germans. The scattered units of the Norwegian forces fought doggedly on their home ground, at first without allies. Their two brigades in the north, under the determined command of General Fleischer, played a crucial role in the recapture of Narvik.

Britain provided two first-class, well-trained Regular Brigades, together with five Territorial Army battalions. The latter had neither the training nor equipment and weapons to carry out the exacting task thrust upon them at such short notice.

The Germans sent General Dietl's Mountain Division to the Narvik front. Having secured the Oslo area and the port of Trondheim on 9 April 1940, they poured a steady stream of reinforcements into Norway. The ground had been well-prepared beforehand with the help of German residents and 'tourists'.

The Norwegian traitor, Quisling, helped to undermine the authority of the legitimate Norwegian government, who were forced to evacuate to the North, together with King Haakon and the Crown Prince.

The scene was set for the first significant land encounter of the war. The outcome for the Allies can perhaps be summed up in the words of Desmond Fitzgerald, the Historian of the Irish Guards '... hopes and plans ended in failure and depression. The campaign was a tragedy, made more grievous by the endurance of the few troops who did the fighting with inadequate material. From the beginning of May a sense of ineluctable fate hung over Norway.'

JACK ADAMS
Freshford
October 1988

ACKNOWLEDGEMENTS

I owe a special debt of gratitude to Kingston Derry, OBE, who, with full access to official papers, wrote a definitive history of the campaign in Norway, which was published in 1952. From his home in Oslo he read and commented on the text of my manuscript. His familiarity with the Norwegian language (of which I am dismally ignorant) and his wider knowledge of the scattered operational areas, enabled him to offer advice and guidance which have been most helpful.

Professor Olav Riste, the Director of the Research Centre for Defence History at the Norwegian College in Oslo, kindly provided background material and helped with the compilation of the list of Norwegian units shown in Appendix A. He also found time to read and comment on Part Seven of the book.

The British Embassy in Oslo was particularly co-operative. The Military Attaché, Lieutenant-Colonel Robin Gamble, Royal Green Jackets, opened the door to sources that may otherwise have been out of my reach.

The Director of the Red Cross War Museum at Narvik, Mr Nils Ryeng, went out of his way personally to guide me around the battlegrounds and, by translating German Army documents into English, threw new light on the operations in which 24th Guards Brigade took part.

Further south, at Bodö, Captain Knut Störe of the Royal Norwegian Air Force acted as my guide through the still recognizable operational areas as well as allowing me access to his extensive collection of Norwegian, British and German photographs and documents relating to the campaign.

The Curator of the South Wales Borderers Museum at Brecon, Major R.P. Smith, readily provided archive material and published an appeal for help in the *Regimental Journal* of the Royal Regiment of Wales. The response brought in anecdotes and personal accounts, some of which are used and acknowledged in the book. The foremost contributor is Brigadier C.F. Cox, OBE, who, in addition, read and commented on Part Three of the manuscript. My thanks are also due to Lieutenant-Colonel Ian Hywell-

Jones MC, Mr Tom Flower, Colonel Peter Martin, Mr Leslie Morgan, Mr T. G. Morgan, Major J. G. Morgan-Owen CB, MBE, QC, Mr A. A. Williams, Mr Kenneth Williams and Lieutenant-Colonel P. A. Worrall OBE.

I received help from the Royal Artillery Association at Woolwich, the Royal Engineers Corps Library at Chatham and the Institution of the Royal Corps of Transport (for the RASC). As ever, the Regimental Secretaries of the British Regiments mentioned in the book were prompt and generous in supplying material. The Commando Association provided me with information about their forerunners, the Independent Companies who fought in the campaign. The Clifton Park Museum at Rotherham made available documents of the now-disbanded York and Lancaster Regiment.

I paid several visits to the Imperial War Museum, where my friend, Dr Conrad Wood, was particularly helpful. The Public Records Office at Kew made available primary material, such as War Diaries, and the Army Historical Branch of the MOD provided a list of relevant published sources.

Lieutenant-Colonel J. Dezaunay, the French Army Liaison Officer at the School of Infantry, Warminster, kindly obtained documents from the *Service Historique de l'Armée de Terre* in Paris which plotted the movements of the Chasseurs Alpins, the Foreign Legion and the Polish Highland Brigade. Further information about the Poles came from the Polish Institute and Sikorski Museum in London. The most important document, the official history of the *Samodzielna Brygada Strzelcow Podhalanskich*, was translated into excellent English for me by Mrs Teresa Mundziel-Staniszewska, Associate of the Institute of Linguists. From Germany, Captain W. Heinemann of the *Militärgeschichtliches Forschungsamt* kindly forwarded a list of useful German sources.

My wife Ellen accompanied me on my Norwegian researches. Later, while typing and retyping (and retyping!) the manuscript, she developed a forthright interest in the story of the campaign from the viewpoint of the general reader. Acting on their behalf, she became their devil's advocate, insisting on a reduction of jargon and obscure military terminology. The cliché that 'the book would not have been written without her help' tells the truth.

Finally, I must thank all those who have given me permission to quote them or to use sketch maps and photographs. At the same time I would apologise for errors of omission or commission in the execution of a task which has given me much enjoyment.

NORWAY
Scale of Sea Miles
0
60
120
180
240
TROMSÖ
Vaagsfiord
Andfiord
LOFOTEN Is.
Harstad
NARVIK
Vestfiord
Skjelfiord
Allied Mines
BODO
Lillesjona
Mo
Elsfiord
Mosjöen
Fellingfors
SWEDEN
NAMSOS
Grong
Steinkjer
TRONDHEIM
Stören
Molde
Kristiansund
Aalesund
Aandalsnes
Lillehammer
Lake Mjösa
Elverum
Hamar
Randsfiord
SHETLAND Is.
BERGEN
OSLO
Oscarborg
Mysen
Telemark
Setesdal R.
ORKNEY Is.
Scapa
Stavanger
Sola
Egersund
Arendal
Lillesand
Kristiansand
Skagerrak

PART ONE

Scandinavian Prelude
3 September 1939 to 8 April 1940

The autumn of 1939 declined into a severe winter as the year wore out. Hitler's armies faced the Allies across the Maginot line at the start of what was now called the phoney war. The governments of both Britain and France were accused in some sections of the Press of having a 'First War Mentality'. In this static phase none of the protagonists seemed anxious to extend the theatre of operations.

Adolf Hitler, in conferring with his Italian associates, had been reported as saying that Scandinavia should not fear an attack from *any* source. Nor would the Scandinavians, in his view, attack Germany. They valued their neutrality too highly, with Russia on one flank and the powerful Reich on the other.

The Second World War was two weeks old when the British Government declared that an attack on Norway would meet with the same resistance as an attack on Britain itself. It seemed obvious that both sides wanted to preserve Norway's neutrality, hoping to benefit from it in some way. Britain wanted to blockade Germany's sea-borne supplies, hoping that Norway would offer no serious resistance to British naval measures for controlling the passage of the long, narrow stretch of water known as the 'Leads'.

The Leads lie between the Norwegian off-shore islands and the mainland, running for hundreds of miles southward along the deeply-indented coastline towards the Skagerrak. Kept clear of ice by the Gulf stream, they were an asset to Norway's large, modernised merchant fleet.

They also provided one of the two sea-routes by which Germany received high-grade Swedish iron ore for her armaments. This travelled by rail from large deposits in North Sweden, either to Lulea for shipment across the Baltic or to Narvik for passage along the Norwegian sea lane. The latter route was the only one available in winter months, when Lulea was closed by ice. Reliable sources estimated that out of the yearly German intake of eight million tons of iron ore, six million tons came from Sweden.

If this supply could be interrupted or cut off, the German war economy would be seriously affected. In September, 1939, Winston Churchill, now First Lord of the Admiralty and a member of the War Cabinet, proposed mining the northern approaches to the Leads with a view to preventing the flow of ore to Germany.

The German leaders were well aware of this danger. Their senior naval advisers, Admirals Raeder and Doenitz, privately disagreed with Hitler's view of the Scandinavian problem. On 9 October Doenitz submitted a paper to Raeder, now Chief of the Naval War Staff, proposing the establishment of a naval base in north Norway, hopefully with the concurrence, albeit reluctantly, of the Norwegian government.

This base should have good port facilities, be a railhead and remain ice-free throughout the winter. Two areas only met these requirements, Trondheim and Narvik. The latter was considered too far north. It stretched communications and it was outside the range of German fighter planes in the event of trouble. At this planning stage Trondheim was selected.

Hitler was preoccupied with events on the Western front, where the possibility of a German break-through in the Low Countries was already being considered. He shelved the plan for Norway, promising to give it his personal consideration. This project was later to form part of the German *Weserübung*, the invasion of Denmark and Norway.

Churchill's plan was also postponed. The Foreign Office took the view that the practical difficulties were insurmountable at this stage of the war. They pointed out the necessity of complying with International Law. But in November, 1939, the Cabinet decided to lay a barrage of anti-submarine mines across the North Sea and this led to a tacit understanding that mine-laying in the Leads would eventually follow.

The First Lord received unexpected support on 19 December, when, at a meeting of the Allied Supreme War Council, the French produced a memorandum from Herr Fritz Thyssen, one of Hitler's earliest supporters among German industrialists but now living as an anti-Nazi exile in Switzerland. Thyssen, formerly a successful steel manufacturer on a large scale, stated authoritatively that Swedish iron ore was absolutely essential to the German war economy.

This eased the pressure on Churchill from old political enemies and some Cabinet colleagues who were against direct involvement in Scandinavia. The spectre of Gallipoli, which had haunted Churchill for so long, reappeared. British public opinion would never accept the enormous losses for so little gain suffered in the First World War. The Narvik fiords were being compared with the hazardous beaches of the Gallipoli Penninsula. Churchill himself wrote, 'I also pondered a good deal on the lessons of the Dardanelles' (*The Second World War*, Vol 1, p. 490).

Prior to the Thyssen disclosure, the Ministry of Economic Warfare had informed the Supreme War Council that the stoppage of Narvik ore alone was of doubtful value. They now changed their stance, saying that if the supply of ore was cut off the Germans would be caused acute embarrassment. Such ambiguity irritated Churchill, who was already hampered by the uneasy relationship between the Chiefs of Staff and their civilian masters.

The position of the Chiefs of Staff was itself ambiguous. Their dual function was to act as individual and collective advisers to the War Cabinet and its Military Co-ordination Committee. But, in Civil Service terms, they were 'high departmental officials serving their three respective Ministers'. And, in the nature of things, they held the welfare of their own particular Service to be paramount.

In reality they worked as a separate and largely independent body. They received no guidance from Prime Minister Neville Chamberlain, nor did they have effective guidance from the supreme executive power directing the war. On page 495 of his book Churchill explains the dilemma:

> The leaders of the three Services had not yet got the conception of the war as a whole, and were influenced unduly by the departmental outlook of their own Services. They met together, after talking things over with their respective Ministers, and issued aide-memoires or memoranda which carried enormous weight. Here was the fatal weakness of our system of conducting war at this time.

This situation changed shortly before Churchill became Prime Minister. He reduced the power of the Chiefs of Staff and brought them more directly under his control by using Major-General H. L. Ismay as a Senior Staff Officer co-ordinating the Chiefs of Staff Committee. Ismay reported directly to Churchill in his capacity as deputy to Chamberlain in the chair of the Military Co-ordination Committee.

On 30 November, 1939, Russia launched an unprovoked attack on Finland. This event pushed the Allies towards the Scandinavians. The Supreme War Council met on 19 December and agreed on positive steps to materially assist Finland. A force of one hundred thousand was envisaged, including one hundred and fifty RAF planes from the sparse Home Defence quota. The French were particularly keen to set up a field of operations around Scandinavia and proposed a naval blockade of the Russian port of Murmansk.

But it was not until the Council's meeting on 5 February, 1940, that the British finalized their plans. The advance elements of the equivalent of two Allied brigades were to leave for the Finnish front in mid-March. Significantly, they were to land at Narvik and advance along the railway through the heart of the Swedish ore fields to the Baltic port of Lulea.

A separate force would occupy Bergen and Trondheim. Stavanger would also be taken and held until Sola airfield was put out of action. This force would consist of five British Territorial battalions who would defend the Norwegian bases against a possible German attack. A considerable build-up would follow with the British contributing up to one hundred thousand men and the French half that number. A strong naval contingent would sustain the land forces.

The British public in general sympathized with the Finns and this interest was intensified on 16 February when HMS *Cossack*, commanded by Captain P. L. Vian, RN, attacked the German auxiliary *Altmark*, which was suspected of carrying British prisoners.

Acknowledging that the *Altmark* was within Norwegian territorial waters, Vian parleyed briefly with the commander of an escorting Norwegian torpedo boat before boarding the German vessel. Almost three hundred British prisoners, mainly Merchant Navy men, were freed. The British public, bored with the phoney war, was ecstatic. A popular song, 'The Navy's here', was written about the incident and Vian was the hero of the hour.*

Churchill's supporters, numerically weak, now pressed for quick action in aid of Finland. The French strongly advocated an immediate landing at Narvik. But the British Cabinet, under Neville Chamberlain, feared active resistance from the Swedes and Norwegians. They claimed that an uninvited invasion would push the Scandinavians towards the Germans and that the latter would seize the opportunity of marching into Norway and Sweden.

About this time (21 March) M. Paul Reynaud replaced M. Daladier as Prime Minister of France. Adopting a more aggressive stance he demanded positive action, pointing out that Allied inactivity provided good propaganda for the enemy. The Finns had surrendered to the Russians on 13 March and a new initiative was needed.

Predictably, the first move was diplomatic. The Allies delivered to the Swedish and Norwegian legations in London and Paris a strongly-worded note protesting against the brazen violation of Scandinavian waters by German warships and merchant vessels. There was a sting in the tail; the note warned that steps would now be taken to lay mines in Norwegian territorial waters.

Paul Reynaud, urged on by French 'hawks' hoping to shorten the war, offered the immediate services of the *Corps Expéditionnaire Français en Scandinavie*, a special force which had been standing by in France since 16 February. Some fifty thousand strong, it contained elements of the

*As Commander-in-Chief, Home Fleet, in 1950–2, Admiral Vian wished to revisit the scene, but the Norwegian authorities refused him access.

Chasseurs Alpins, the Poles and the Foreign Legion, with full supporting arms. Churchill and the Chiefs of Staff welcomed this offer but the Cabinet turned it down.

But the tide of war was running towards Scandinavia. The mining of the northern approaches to the Leads, (christened Operation Wilfred by Churchill as it was 'minor and innocent'), was now scheduled for early April. Linked with this was a military plan, code-named R4, set to be activated 'the moment German forces set foot on Norwegian soil, or there is clear evidence that they intend to do so'.

The so-called 'Big Plan', for which the British Fifth Division, (a Regular force), had been earmarked, was much modified as the two main Allies moved towards agreement. It seemed that the major thrust would come from the Navy and the Royal Marines in the initial stages.

Since severing their Union with Sweden in 1905 the Norwegian nation had looked inwards to its own particular problems. Professor Riste* has written of the obsessive concern with neutrality that flourished between the two world wars. The popular catchphrase was 'We want no foreign policy'. This seemed apposite enough, as, apart from the inevitable interruption of trade, the Norwegians were relatively unaffected by the 1914–18 war. Her merchant fleet had been chartered to Britain and, although it suffered devastating losses, had revived between the wars and was the fourth largest in the world. (This agreement was repeated in November, 1939, when the Norwegian Shippers' Association chartered their merchant ships to Britain).

Friendship with Britain over many years had been cemented by the closeness of the respective Royal Families. Britain's continuing naval presence in the North Sea (Scapa Flow was 'just across the water' from Stavanger) kept alive the belief that Britain still ruled the waves.

These rather naive convictions lessened the latent fear of Germany as the ever-present aggressor. But as the winter of 1939 waned the incessant pro-German propaganda in the Quisling-owned newspaper *The Free Nation*, and the added anxieties caused by the Russo-German pact, caused Norway to look to her defences.

When Russia invaded Finland the Norwegians aligned themselves with Britain and France to support the Finns. But when the Allies sought permission to take the short route into Finland both Norway and Sweden refused to allow Allied forces to cross their territories. Suspicion of the Allies was deepened by the *Altmark* incident on 16 February, 1940.

Preparation for defence centred around the Royal Norwegian Navy,

*Professor Olav Riste, *Norway and the Second World War.*

which had been mobilized at the outbreak of war. Resources were scarce as the defence budget had always been modest (one pound sterling per head in 1938). Most of the ships were obsolescent and the training of the conscript sailors had been reduced to just thirteen weeks in the year, the lowest in Europe.

Unlike Britain, Norway had no independent airforce. There were five airfields scattered around the country and on these were eighteen scout aircraft and just six fighters.* At the seven naval coastal stations there were thirty seaplanes, used primarily for the co-ordination of naval vessels. Since November, 1939, a brigade of the Norwegian Army's 6th Division had been stationed along the border with Russia, establishing a military presence as far south as Narvik. Partial mobilization was ordered in the early morning of 9 April, 1940, when the Germans were already occupying the chief mobilization centres. Some thirteen thousand soldiers stood-to in defence of Norway's neutrality. Many Norwegians now looked to their British friends for help.

In October, 1939, the German Naval War Staff instructed Grossadmiral Raeder to place before Hitler a strongly-worded recommendation that (with the Russians) Germany should put pressure on Norway in order to obtain bases for 'a fundamental improvement in our strategic and operational situation'. They named certain ports which were ice-free, including Narvik and Trondheim.

Raeder reported that Hitler, though hesitant, had shown some interest. The Service chiefs bided their time. They knew too well that the Führer preferred to dictate his own strategy and regarded any initiative other than his own with suspicion. His current obsession was a breakthrough in the West involving a surprise attack through Luxembourg and the Low Countries.

The aim was to capture northern France, thus providing the necessary bases for an attack on Britain. At this stage Hitler, on the advice of Ribbentrop, (the former German Ambassador to Britain), was convinced that the British lacked the will to fight, leaving him to concentrate on the Masterplan, the subjugation of Russia.

But in mid-December his attention was re-directed to Norway through a visit to Berlin by Vidkum Quisling, a former Norwegian Minister of Defence. On the 11th he was interviewed by Admiral Raeder, who knew that Quisling was an ardent disciple of National-Socialism and had founded a political party called *Nasjonal Samling*, based on the Nazi philosophy.

*A consignment of nineteen newly-arrived Curtis Pursuit fighter planes from America was destroyed in their crates by the Germans at Oslo airport on 9 April.

Quisling occupied a position in Norway in the 1930s somewhat similar to Sir Oswald Mosley's in Britain. His aim was to establish a Hitler-type régime but his followers were few.

Raeder reported to Hitler next day in the presence of Generals Keitel and Jodl, when he claimed that Quisling appeared to be a reliable person, though caution was needed. It was always difficult with such (unsolicited) offers of co-operation to know how far the persons concerned were pushing their own interests or to what extent they had Germany's interests at heart. On the other hand, Norway must not fall into the hands of the British. Accordingly, on 13 December a working party was set up for '*Studie Nord*', (a *Besetzung* [occupation] of Norway by peaceful or other means). This secret study was restricted to fewer than ten participants at its inception.*

Quisling in person was brought before Hitler on 14 December and again on the 18th. It appeared that the Führer considered the occupation of Norway as a preventative measure, preferably with the consent of the Norwegians. Hitler publicly professed his admiration for this Nordic race, stressing the long-standing friendship and trade links between the two peoples. In private he despised them for their 'spineless neutrality'. But Quisling seriously considered himself to be the saviour of Norway and seemed confident that its people would, in the event, prefer his leadership to that of King Haakon and his democratically elected government.

By the end of January, 1940, '*Studie Nord*' had developed into a project with a very small planning staff, a code name (*Weserübung*), and a scope which might include action against Denmark. But Hitler's naval advisers wanted quick action in Norway which, to them, posed a worsening political, military and economic problem. In this their thinking paralleled that of Churchill and the British Chiefs of Staff, (but not Prime Minister Chamberlain and the majority of the Cabinet).

The German Naval War Staff were determined to keep the Leads clear for the transport of Swedish ore. Privately they criticized Hitler's reluctance to move against Scandinavia. They accused him of following a strategy opposed to the great German tradition of Bismarck, of lack of experience, of wishful thinking. Professor Walther Hubatsch, the German historian, lecturing at London University in 1958 on the problems of the Norwegian Campaign said: 'Hitler behaved in a fashion which the entire system of European states had persistently combated since the days of William of Orange'. That is to say that the Führer believed in the Divine Right of Kings, seeing himself privately as the Kaiser incarnate.

On 1 March, 1940, possibly influenced by the famous *Altmark* incident, Hitler issued a formal directive for the occupation of Norway and Denmark. Two days later, acting in character and against the advice of Hermann

*See article by Professor Magne Skodvin in *Aftenposten*, Oslo 24 December 1987.

Goering, the Luftwaffe chief, he reversed his military priorities and decreed that *Weserübung* should now precede any German initiative in the West.

General Nikolaus von Falkenhorst, an apolitical Infantry commander in his early sixties, was appointed as overall co-ordinator of the top three Service directors. As far as Norway was concerned Falkenhorst's brief was to occupy Oslo, Kristiansand, Stavanger, Bergen, Trondheim and Narvik, employing six divisions. The Luftwaffe now emerged, for the first time, as a fully independent branch of the Wehrmacht, with its own operational role. This included the mass transportation of troops for the initial assault.

For reasons probably connected with scarce resources, Falkenhorst was specifically debarred from occupying certain minor ports, including Namsos and Aandalsnes, (ironically, weeks later, both ports became British beach-heads). Transportation of such a huge mass of men and material presented the German Staff with a major problem. Speed and secrecy were essential. Falkenhorst decided against slow and vulnerable troop transports in favour of naval vessels. Complementing the air-lift the first nine thousand men would travel in warships, accepting the risk of a handicap if a sea-fight developed.

The bulk of the vast amount of equipment, ammunition and stores needed in Norway would be ferried in by merchant vessels. Narvik, in the far north, was served by the German tanker, *Jan Willem*, working out of Murmansk with Russian connivance. She would provide fuel oil for the warships and supplies for the German garrison when it arrived. In a largely sea-borne enterprise of this kind much thought was given to the selection of the commander but it was not until two days before the first echelon sailed that Admiral Carls was chosen. He summed up the chances of success in these words:

> I think we can achieve the vital part of our task, and therefore we shall achieve it if we carry it through with ruthless determination and unrestrained vigour. The risk is considerable, bad enough during the first part of the operation and even greater in the second, on the return journey home. We shall incur losses. But the operation is so important that they would not be too heavy even if the greater part of the surface fleet were lost. We must reckon from the outset on a total loss of 50 per cent unless particularly favourable conditions obviate both Norwegian and British intervention. (Hubatsch, 1958)

The warship echelon to transport the maritime operation was organized with Teutonic thoroughness. There were six groups. Group One was for Narvik, escorted by the warships *Gneisenau* and *Scharnhorst*. It carried two thousand men of the 3rd Mountain Division. The next group was meant for Trondheim, in central Norway, carrying the remainder of the Mountain Division. The escort was the heavy cruiser *Hipper*, accompanied by four destroyers. They would travel with group one until the latitude of Trondheim was reached. The third group headed for Bergen, carrying almost two thousand men of the 69th Division. Their main escort was the light cruiser *Köln* and also the *Königsberg*, supported by fast patrol boats.

The fourth group, having less seaway to cover, had a lighter escort, the cruiser *Karlsruhe* and five fast patrol boats. The troops came from the 163rd Division and were to land at Kristiansand and Arendal. The attacking force for the Oslo area came from the same division and was about two thousand men with a strong escort because the fort at Oscarborg in Oslofiord had to be passed. There were the pocket battleship *Lutzow*, the heavy cruiser *Blücher* and the light cruiser *Emden* with eight minesweepers and two torpedo boats. The last group was a small force with the task of taking the cable station at Egersund. It carried a company of bicycle troops about 150 strong and was escorted by minesweepers.*

Many of the troops had been assembled at short notice. With the exception of the Mountain battalions they were not fully trained. In quality they can perhaps be compared with the best of the British Territorial Divisions, for example the 51st Highland or the 53rd Welsh. Like their British counterparts they were woefully short of equipment and heavy support weapons. In contrast the German 3rd Mountain Division was fully trained for snow and mountain warfare, with some battle experience in Poland.

Although inexperienced in combined operations, the Germans carried out their preparations for the invasion with efficiency and guile. The three Services conformed to the overall provisions of *Weserübung* free of many of the constraints experienced by the Allied planners. In the propaganda war, with an eye to the implications of international law, they justified their invasion by referring to the mining of the Leads by the British. They stressed 'the necessity of forestalling an Anglo-French action against Norway'.

The German intelligence build-up in Scandinavia had been going on long before the outbreak of war in September, 1939. A scattering of German refugees had found temporary homes in Norway after 1918. Some of their children had grown up speaking Norwegian. Later, after suitable training, some of these had returned to Norway as 'tourists' with intelligence-gathering as their main role.† German merchant seamen were familiar with the main Norwegian port facilities.

The German invasion plans included elaborate and ingenious arrangements for using the names of British warships when communicating by

*Adapted from *The Norwegian Campaign of 1940* by Major-General J. L. Moulton, pp. 63–4.

†Some sources maintain that the alleged return of the *Wienerbarn* to spy out the land smacks of wartime propaganda.

wireless in Norwegian waters. To further confuse port officials some of the German ships were to fly the British flag. German naval representatives actively paved the way for the invaders, working with Quisling's sympathizers, while the German Air Attaché at Oslo, having requisitioned the necessary transport for the first wave of parachutists, actually guided them to their first objective.

Herr Hagelin, a Norwegian accomplice of Quisling based in Berlin, used his widespread trading activities to observe and report on the British military build-up after the Russo-Finnish war. In retrospect the value to Germany of the traitor Quisling's 'Fifth column' was much exaggerated. But in the days preceding the invasion their activities added to the uncertainties that beset the Norwegian people, who were totally unprepared for war.

At 8.15 p.m. on 7 April, 1940, the Home Fleet, keeping strict wireless silence, sailed from Scapa Flow in the north of Scotland for Norwegian waters. That same evening the First and Second Cruiser Squadrons left Rosyth and turned north. The destroyer *Glowworm*, part of the screen for the battle cruiser *Renown*, was forced to stop in heavy weather to pick up a seaman fallen overboard. She had been alerted by signal to look out for a German expedition believed to be heading for Narvik. She sighted and engaged two German destroyers, who broke off and wirelessed the *Glowworm*'s position to the German heavy cruiser, *Hipper*.

The *Glowworm* was hopelessly outmatched. The German warship opened fire at about ten thousand yards, hitting the *Glowworm* squarely on the bridge. The British destroyer replied with a salvo of torpedoes, putting up a smoke screen as part of her defence. The *Hipper* came through the smoke into the destroyer's path and the ships collided, tearing away about a hundred and forty feet of *Hipper*'s outer armour. *Glowworm* was able to signal the enemy ship's position to the main flotilla before blowing up and sinking with heavy loss of life.*

Further south the Polish submarine *Orzel* was patrolling the mouth of the Skagerrak. She sighted and challenged the German transport *Rio de Janeiro* off Lillesand. When the transport failed to stop, the *Orzel* sunk her. About one hundred survivors were picked up by Norwegian fishermen. On landing, they turned out to be uniformed German soldiers, who, when interrogated, said that they were part of a fully armed expedition sent to 'protect' the Norwegian port of Bergen.

This information alerted the British ships guarding the mine-layers off

*The *Glowworm*'s Captain, Lieutenant-Commander G. Broadmead Roope, was later posthumously awarded the Victoria Cross.

Bodö, near the Vestfiord. Among them was HMS *Renown*. In the early dawn of 9 April she sighted 'two heavy German warships'. They turned out to be the *Scharnhorst* and the *Gneisenau*, two of the enemy's most formidable armoured ships. Hampered by poor light and heavy seas the *Renown* engaged both enemy ships at a range of some ten miles. As the range shortened *Gneisenau*'s main gunnery control centre was hit by a 15-inch shell from *Renown*. In the running fight which followed the *Gneisenau* sustained further damage while the *Renown*, though hit by three of the German ship's heavy shells, came through comparatively undamaged. At about 6.15 a.m. the enemy ships broke off the engagement and ran for cover. The *Gneisenau* eventually got to Wilhelmshaven where she was repaired.

Conflicting intelligence reports were flooding in to the Admiralty on 8 April, 1940. When analysed, checked and verified there was no doubt that the expected German invasion of Norway was under way. The dispositions of the Home Fleet were quickly revised in the hope of locating and bringing to battle the German warships heading for Narvik. Yet, when the Chiefs of Staff were roused from their beds for an early meeting, it was decided that we could still 'peacefully occupy' Narvik, but not until 'the naval situation had been cleared up'.

The Allied Supreme War Council, with its committees, revised their own military organization to cope with the new emergency. Meanwhile the Germans had achieved that most important element, surprise.

The British preparation for events in Scandinavia roughly paralleled that of Germany. But a democracy, by its very nature, lacks the clear-cut direction of a dictatorship. The alliance with France had its centre on the Western front. The French were regarded as equal partners in the Supreme War Council, but in Scandinavian matters seem to have delegated executive power to the British. Nevertheless, they pressed strongly for quick action in Norway.

The Expeditionary Force of Chasseurs, Poles and Foreign Legionnaires, originally assembled for service in Finland, stood ready for action. On 28 March, 1940, the Council, without enthusiasm, agreed to assemble a force in readiness to act against a possible German attack on Norway. Churchill expressed the hope that the German battle fleet, if it emerged, would be promptly engaged and decisively defeated. At this stage of the war the Allied command structure was inexperienced, unwieldy and complicated. In any organization where uncertainty exists, a form of leadership, either individual or collective, will emerge. In this case the Admiralty, with Churchill as First Lord, acted impulsively when intelligence reports confirmed that elements of the German fleet had left Kiel and other northern ports on 4 April. Orders were issued by the First Sea Lord, by-passing the Commander-in-Chief, Home Fleet.

The Admiralty continued to get intelligence reports of German naval activity in the Wilhelmshaven Roads, including a sighting by the RAF of the *Gneisenau* and the *Scharnhorst*. On 7 April the Admiralty sent a telegram to the Commander-in-Chief, Home Fleet:

> Recent reports suggest a German expedition is being prepared; Hitler is reported from Copenhagen to have ordered unostentatious movement of one division in ten ships by night to land at Narvik, with simultaneous occupation of Jutland. Sweden to be left alone. Moderates said to be opposing the plan. Date given for arrival at Narvik was 8 April.
>
> All these reports are of doubtful value and may well be only a further move in the war of nerves.

In fact the first two groups of German warships had left port and at 8 p.m. on 7 April were off the Norwegian coast between Egersund and Bergen. Within twenty-four hours *HMS Glowworn* had been sunk and the long-awaited encounter with the German fleet had begun.

The British plan R4 was abandoned. New dispositions, both naval and military, were set in motion. The four cruisers lying at Rosyth, packed with troops for Bergen and Stavanger, hastily disembarked the soldiers and sailed north to rejoin the fleet. The proposed frontal attack on Trondheim was off and the third phase of the minelaying operation in the Leads was abandoned.

> This critical step, which involved the abandonment of a carefully considered military expedition, seems to have been taken by the Admiralty independently and to the surprise of the Prime Minister. The First Sea Lord issued the order; the Commander-in-Chief, Home Fleet, who already had superior forces at his disposal, was not consulted. Thus the measures adopted to secure the traditional object of a decisive encounter at sea, which was not secured, deprived us of our last chance to restore the position on land.*

The forces earmarked for Norway were again re-shuffled. The 24th Guards Brigade, made up of the 1st Scots Guards, 1st Irish Guards and 2nd South Wales Borderers, were still in the Clyde, awaiting sailing instructions. This Regular Brigade was experienced and well trained, having seen service in either the Palestine 'troubles' or the insurrections on the North-West Frontier of India. It was commanded by Brigadier the Hon. W. Fraser, and destined for Narvik.

The French contingent, who were to join them later, included the 13th

*Dr T. K. Derry, *The Campaign in Norway*, p. 26.

Demi-Brigade of the Foreign Legion (two battalions); the 13th, 53rd and 67th Battalions of Chasseurs Alpins, trained as ski-troops; and the Polish Highland Brigade of mountain troops. In the event, the Chasseurs were diverted to Namsos, where they were commanded by the French General Audet.

The British attempt to capture Trondheim was now envisaged as a pincer movement coming from Namsos, in the north, and Aandalsnes, to the south of Trondheim. The force to land at Namsos was 146 Brigade, consisting of 1/4th Royal Lincolns, 1/4th King's Own Yorkshire Light Infantry and 1/4th York and Lancasters (the Hallamshire battalion). The Territorial soldiers who made up this brigade had been denied the training and experience of the Regular force earmarked for Narvik. They were poorly equipped and lacked the essential support of tanks and artillery. The 5th Demi-Brigade, Chasseurs Alpins, would join them later. 146 Brigade was commanded by Brigadier C. G. Phillips with the legendary hero, Major-General Sir Adrian Carton de Wiart, VC, in overall command of the force.

Another Territorial force provided the troops to land at Aandalsnes. 148 Brigade had only two battalions, 1/5th Royal Leicesters and 1/8th Sherwood Foresters. Their commander, Brigadier H. de R. Morgan, had transformed them in a few months from ill-trained amateurs into someting resembling a competent fighting force. Again, they were unsupported by heavy weapons and, in common with the others, lacked anti-aircraft cover. This contingent was later to be joined by 15 Brigade, then serving in France. They were the 1st Green Howards, 1st King's Own Yorkshire Light Infantry and 1st York and Lancasters, all Regular soldiers, commanded by Brigadier H. E. F. Smyth.

The Chiefs of Staff, under pressure from the French to continue to reinforce the British Expeditionary Force in France, were unable to find the resources to back up the expedition to Norway. The Territorial brigades were from the start looked upon as second-line troops, responsible for garrison and line of communication duties, and they were equipped accordingly.

Churchill had been at odds with most of the planning staff over the dispersion of the limited forces available for Norway. To him Narvik seemed to be the focal point of the Allied attack and he had consistently opposed an attack on Trondheim. 'Left to myself I would have stuck to my first love, Narvik ...' Then, later, 'Although Narvik was my pet I threw myself with increasing confidence into this daring adventure, and was willing that the Fleet should risk the petty batteries (at Trondheim).'

But, as we have seen, the direct assault on Trondheim was dropped and the very ports that the German Staff had forbidden General von Falkenhorst to occupy (Namsos and Aandalsnes) were chosen instead. In the event what appeared at the time to be a logical choice turned out to be disastrous. Both landings were short-lived.

PART TWO

The German Invasion, Norwegian Resistance and Allied Countermeasures 9 to 15 April 1940

On 9 April, 1940, the 2nd Battalion of the South Wales Borderers was on stand-by to move from Barnard Castle, in County Durham, to an unknown destination. The author, who was then the battalion Signals Sergeant, remembers the preceding three months as the worst winter he had ever encountered in his young life:

> After the wet, mild weather of Londonderry the bitter, persistent north wind and the deep snow were depressing. We spent long, arduous days and sub-zero nights training on the moors high above the town. We were billeted in public halls and, occasionally, private houses. We were about eight hundred strong and could have swamped the little town.
>
> The soldiers could have drunk the local pubs dry but were advised to 'top up' in their own wet canteens before going out on the town. A rapport quickly grew up between the cheerful Geordie inhabitants and the Welshmen. There were many coal pits in the neighbourhood and the small mining villages sustained the close community spirit so familiar to the young soldiers from the Valleys. Among other things this later led to several marriages, and to this day the Welsh survivors of the Norwegian Campaign speak of Barnard Castle with great affection.
>
> Earlier, the Russo-Finnish war had started a spate of rumours that the battalion was earmarked for that conflict. Why else were we training so hard in the snow? The tracks across the moors were criss-crossed with icy ruts and as I slithered across them on my heavy BSA motorbike I sometimes wondered how we would cope against the Russians. In retrospect the prolonged bitterness of the weather and the spartan conditions under which we lived and trained can be seen as a providential opportunity to fit ourselves for the Arctic ordeal that we were to undergo.
>
> When, in March, the Finns capitulated, many of us heaved sighs of relief. But on 1 April the Commanding Officer attended a conference in London and strange Staff officers and representatives of other units began to arrive. Then 2/Lieutenant Petch, a Norwegian Interpreter, was posted in by the War Office. So we were going to Norway! It was never officially confirmed but everyone was quite certain of our destination. 'Expert' information and advice on the Norwegian people, the climate and practically everything else now became readily available for the asking.

The only available genuine expert, the Norwegian interpreter, was lured to the Sergeants' Mess, plied with beer and pumped. But 2/Lieutenant Petch was the soul of discretion. The weather in Barnard Castle was much worse than Norway, he said. Also, the Norwegian people were very pro-British and many of them spoke English. More sighs of relief.

Rumours abounded. Place names were picked up from the Press. Everyone knew Oslo, we were *not* going there. We were going to storm ashore at Trondheim, or some other fancied beachhead. As I remember it, Narvik was not a front runner in my own small, but well-informed circle. One of the rumours grew persistently, we were to be part of a Guards Brigade. 'Oh aye,' said the wags, 'do you think they'll be able to keep up with us?' 'Well, they were OK in Palestine. Let's hope it's the Welsh Guards.' In the outcome they were the Scots and the Irish Guards.

The battalion was now streamlined. The Reservists were welcomed back by their old mates. The low-category men had been sent to the Depot. Wives, who had surreptitiously slipped into convenient lodgings in the town, were sent weeping away. Weapons were oiled and equipment was overhauled. Morale was high.

It would take two trains to haul the battalion away from Barnard Castle. The last one pulled out at 2310 hours on 9 April. There was, I was told later, a sense of sadness and loss the next day in Barnard Castle.*

Once launched, the German attack on Norway went forward with ruthless determination. Their navy was the dominant force until the landing of the troops, while the Luftwaffe had the dual role of transporting soldiers and providing fighter cover in case of air attack. Once landed, the Army's task was to occupy and subdue all centres of resistance. The Norwegian people were bewildered by the widespread co-ordination of air and sea landings and the speed with which the German forces reached their objectives.

Running parallel with the military operations was a strong German 'diplomatic' offensive to force King Haakon and his government to capitulate. A Note in the form of an ultimatum demanded immediate total surrender. This was handed to Dr Koht, the Norwegian Minister of Foreign Affairs, by the German representative, Dr Braüer, at 4.30 a.m. on 9 April. The memorandum contained a list of conditions, which the Norwegian Cabinet rejected out of hand. In order to clarify the situation in the critical early stages of the invasion, some explanation of the tactical position must be attempted before continuing with the reactions of the Norwegian government.

The German preparations were far from perfect. The Naval forces were overstretched. Submarines reported unexplained faults in their torpedoes which may have been caused by magnetic interference common to polar regions. The tactical handling of destroyers resulting in their concentration

*From notes for a Tape made for the Imperial War Museum, October, 1985.

in narrow fiords, deprived of fuel and ammunition (as at Narvik), was disastrous. Yet, the landing of the main assault force was carried out on time, with far fewer casualties than had been forecast.

The Luftwaffe suffered from a lack of technical equipment for effective intercommunication. This was common to all three services and one of the many repercussions of this was the failure of front line information to reach Command level. Instances of this kind of frustration will occur throughout this book and it can be seen that the Allies also suffered. Professor Hubatsch comments:

> In the Norwegian Campaign more than in any other theatre of war we see the fascinating problem of how different the impressions gained by men at the front could be from those held by the High Command ... but in this too the will to co-operate in essentials overcame the difficulties and mastered the crisis..*

In general the Luftwaffe proved less effective against Allied naval targets than expected. But on land, particularly in the forward areas, the Luftwaffe had almost unchallenged superiority. Their constant low-level patrolling and effective message-dropping techniques restricted the mobility of the Allied infantry, particularly in the area of Namsos, where the lack of anti-aircraft support was most apparent.

The eventual success of the Wehrmacht seems, in retrospect, to have been assured from the start. But in the early stages of the invasion, when it was most vulnerable, the German Army suffered serious setbacks. The Norwegian defences, particularly in Oslofiord, inflicted losses in men and material which reduced the Army's effectiveness as a fighting force. The sinking of the *Rio de Janeiro* by the Polish submarine *Orzel* on 8 April contributed to the confusion caused when units, weakened by casualties, were made up to strength from untrained second-line troops.

This improvisation gives an imbalance which field commanders are often faced with in war. We have already seen that there was a shortage of artillery, and the lack of mortars, particularly in mountain country, was a serious hindrance. At first the small number of tanks available worried the forward commanders but as the terrain worsened it was obvious that they would have been useless anyway. Despite these drawbacks credit must be given where it is due. The German Army was able to achieve its ultimate purpose of subjugating most of Norway. Professor Hubatsch comments that this was largely due to:

*The British classical example of this during the First World War was when the (alleged) message, 'Send reinforcements: we are going to advance', arrived at Headquarters as 'Send three and fourpence: we are going to a dance.'

> The uniformity of training, the efficient command organization, and the standardized communications (within field organizations) which made rapid decisions possible. And this was to prove decisive. Finally, hardly ever in the recent history of wars have intermediate commanders enjoyed so much scope for initiative as they did in this spacious but minor theatre.

Until they were ashore with weapons and essential supplies, the troops were dependent on the navy for protection. Admiral Raeder wanted his warships clear of the Norwegian ports as quickly as possible because of the danger of an attack by the British fleet. He relied upon a surprise approach under cover of darkness, using ruse and deception to get past the Norwegian outer defences. After a rapid disembarkation the navy would withdraw. Hitler disagreed with the plan, saying that the navy's firepower must support the soldiers if the Norwegians resisted. But Raeder convinced the Führer that the loss of a large part of the German fleet in the narrow coastal waters was inevitable if the warships stayed on. It was decided that, once they were landed, the Luftwaffe would supply protection and support for the troops.

In the event the Norwegian defences were not entirely deceived. At midnight on 8 April the German warships approached the narrow entrance to Oslofiord. The heavy cruiser *Blücher* spearheaded Group 5, carrying two battalions of the 169th Division commanded by Major-General Engelbrecht. With him were the Staff officers of the Wehrmacht and the Luftwaffe who were to direct and control the taking of Oslo. The moon was down and the ships were darkened.

On watch was a Norwegian patrol boat, *Pol III*, which at once alerted its base. The Norwegian boat, barely two hundred tons, rammed one of the German torpedo boats, only to be machine-gunned and set on fire.

There has been some controversy over this incident, in which the captain of *Pol III* was killed. The German orders made it clear that Norwegian vessels were not to be fired on unless they fired first. One version (Major-General Moulton's) states that *Pol III* fired a warning shot, while the official historian (Dr Derry) says that the Norwegian ship 'challenged', and raised the alarm. There had been a shouted conversation, in German, before the machine guns opened up, and it has been suggested that this was a demand for surrender, which was refused.

As the German warships nosed cautiously past the island fort of Rauöy it opened fire on the leading enemy ship, with no apparent effect. Knowing that the Norwegian defences were now fully alerted, the Germans stopped long enough to detach torpedo boats and minesweepers to take Rauöy, and its sister fort of Bolaerne on the other side of the channel. The same force subdued Horten, the naval base further up the fiord, where the Norwegian minelayer *Olav Tryggvason* tried ineffectually to halt the invaders.

The main German convoy steamed on towards the Dröbak narrows, moving into the restricted 500-yard passage before Oscarborg fort. The main defences of Oslofiord lay ahead. It was now about 5 a.m. and Colonel Eriksen, Oscarborg's sixty-five-year-old commander, made ready his gun batteries and torpedo tubes. The fort searchlights were temporarily out of action but a beam from the mainland lit up the leading warship long enough for Eriksen to recognise the *Blücher*.

He opened fire with two of his ageing 28 cm Krupp guns, hitting the *Blücher* below the bridge and further aft, in the area of the aircraft hangars. This started a raging petrol fire and the flames provided a target for the smaller weapons of the fort. One of the *Blücher*'s engines was out of action and the heavy turret guns were unusable. The German ship retaliated with her anti-aircraft weapons but soon came within range of the torpedo batteries and was hit twice.

The fires were now out of control and caused one of the main magazines to explode. The *Blücher* sank in deep water with the loss of a thousand men. Among them were most of the staff specially trained to secure control of the King and Government. Five hundred soldiers of the 163rd Division went down, with their weapons and equipment. The pocket battleship *Lutzow* was hit by shells from a shore battery and damaged. With the light cruiser *Emden*, she pulled into the bank and disembarked her troops. It was now about 8 a.m. and they were well behind schedule as they forced their way on foot up the fiord towards Oslo.

At about the same time (8 a.m. on the morning of 9 April), German parachute soldiers should have dropped at Fornebu, the airport for Oslo. Fog delayed them and the air-transported element of 163rd Division landed first. Norwegian anti-aircraft gunners brought down three of the JU52's and damaged four. The nearby military airfield at Kjeller capitulated, and within four hours of landing the airborne troops were at the centre of Oslo.

After consultation among the politicians the capital surrendered as an Open City. But, swift though the attack had been, it was not quick enough to prevent the Norwegian government from using the radio to attempt to mobilize the armed forces. Quisling, as we shall see later, had already tried in vain to establish an alternative administration and when, a few hours later, he announced over the air that he was now the head of the 'legal government' he was largely ignored, although confusion deepened.

The legitimate government's call to mobilize was only partially effective. The navy was already fully committed but the army reservists were waiting for the official letter which would confirm the call-up by allocating them to units and depots. This was not expected until 11 April but in response to the government's broadcast thousands of young Norwegians headed for the nearest military centre, impeded by the stream of civilians pouring out of Oslo.

In the very early hours of 9 April the Norwegian Foreign Minister, Dr Koht, after conferring with the British Embassy, realized that 'this was war' and that Oslo was indefensible. It was decided that the Royal Family and key members of the government should be evacuated from the capital to Hamar, a good communications centre, about seventy-five miles to the north. In their absence rumours spread and Quisling began to consolidate his shaky position.

The fog-bound spearhead of parachutists, drawn from the 1st Parachute Regiment, landed four hours late at 12 noon. Waiting for them was the German Air Attaché, Captain Spiller, with requisitioned buses to take them immediately towards Hamar where the Norwegian parliament was holding an emergency session. News of a German attempt to kill or capture the King and his government reached the assembled Ministers and they started out for Elverum, some miles to the east. The Germans got wind of this move and the two companies of parachutists were re-routed to Elverum. On the way they were spotted by a party of Norwegian soldiers, who telephoned a warning to the government.

A company of Norwegian partly-trained recruits, helped by civilian volunteers, set up a road block south of Elverum, near Midtskogen. As the Germans approached they were fired on and a brisk action developed, but movement off the road was restricted by thick snow. After sustaining some casualties, the parachutists withdrew, taking with them Captain Spiller, who was mortally wounded.* The parliament completed its session at Elverum, where the Assembly President, Carl J. Hambro, with great presence of mind, secured a unanimous resolution granting the King plenary power. Five momentous years were to pass before their next meeting.

Elsewhere in the country the Germans, using the threat of indiscriminate bombing as a weapon, had occupied their main objectives. The major ports and population centres were in their hands, as were most airfields. Although much of the hoped-for surprise had been lost, the sheer audacity and speed of the attack carried them forward with a momentum which was hardly checked. By the evening of 9 April, 1940, Hitler was congratulating Admiral Raeder on the auspicious start to *Weserübung*. There were few violent acts of retaliation from the ordinary Norwegians, partly because of their peaceful, unmilitary way of life and partly because they had been engulfed

*Why the Luftwaffe parachutists carried out this attack caused some speculation as Dr Braüer knew that a party of Gestapo aboard the *Blücher* had been detailed to arrest the King. The affair was later labelled 'Spiller's private war'. (Moulton, p. 99).

by the impetus of the German advance. But this state of affairs was not going to last.

Meanwhile, the light cruiser *Karlsruhe*, leading the fourth group of the German invasion fleet, arrived off Kristiansand in thick fog. At 4 a.m. on 9 April it was impossible to distinguish the navigation channel and the commander, Captain Rieve, decided to wait. After two hours the fog cleared but it was now daylight and a Norwegian seaplane had spotted the group. The original orders had called for the soldiers of the 163rd Division to be disembarked by fast patrol vessels. But Rieve ignored this and decided to use torpedo boats to land his troops close to the Norwegian shore batteries, which were now firing at his ship.

Air support was called for and the Luftwaffe bombed the fort at Odderöya in an attempt to silence the guns. The air attack was unsuccessful and the first attempt to force the passage was called off. The next two attempts also failed and then the situation suddenly changed in the Germans' favour. The Norwegian commander received a message to the effect that British and French warships were approaching and should be allowed to enter the harbour. At 11 a.m. a small group of warships approached the harbour and an observer reported that one of them was flying the French flag. The Norwegian gunners were ordered to hold their fire.

But it was German soldiers in patrol boats who landed at the batteries, without opposition. Shortly afterwards the *Karlsruhe* entered, followed by the main force, and by 3 p.m. Kristiansand was in enemy hands. Whether the flag incident was a genuine mistake or whether the Germans used deceit is not clear. One account says that a German signal flag, resembling the French tricolour, had been hoisted. Others stated that German destroyers had been sighted, flying the French flag.

However, there were no destroyers in number four group. What is clear is that British Intelligence had received sound information that German ships had orders to use the old ruse of flying their enemies' flags to gain an advantage.

In the course of that afternoon two further battalions of troops reinforced the 163rd Division. The Germans were now sure of securing the small airfield at Kjevik and the poorly defended port of Arendal was at their mercy. The situation was now well under control and the light cruiser and her consorts were ordered to put to sea that evening. One hour after leaving port the *Karlsruhe* was torpedoed by the British submarine *Truant* and was damaged so badly that she had to be sunk. The following night the pocket battleship *Lutzow*, her task at Oslofiord completed, was caught in the Kattegat by the British submarine *Spearfish*. She was hit by torpedos and badly damaged but managed to make her home port. From this point on, the Germans routed their invasion troops in small vessels from the coast of Jutland to southern Norwegian ports in an attempt to reduce attacks by Allied submarines.

The German aim of striking simultaneously at vital targets along the coast proceeded to plan. The task force for Egersund, some hundred miles west of Oslo, was comparatively weak. The target was the cable station which linked the small Norwegian port to Peterhead in Scotland. Light resistance failed to stop the 150 cyclists from the 69th Division and the station was soon secured.

Stavanger, with its airfield at Sola, was taken by air assault. Shortly after 8 a.m. on 9 April six Messerschmitt 110's attempted to destroy the aircraft on the ground, thus paving the way for the JU88 bombing force. Luckily, most of the Norwegian pilots had already taken off and only two aircraft were destroyed. The large airfield was poorly defended and the German parachute troops sustained only light losses from machine-gun fire. They quickly captured the airfield and moved on to their next objective.

Stavanger was an unfortified port although the area was one of the few allotted a fully mobilized infantry battalion. After the German parachutists had cleared the barbed wire obstructions from the runways the 69th Division was flown in, using 180 aircraft, to establish a strong German presence in case of counterattack.

The previous night a Norwegian destroyer had sunk a 'suspicious looking' German freighter, found to be loaded with anti-aircraft guns. The Norwegians were hitting back at sea as strongly as their limited resources allowed. Off Stavanger, on the morning of 9 April, the torpedo boat *Aegir* attacked and sunk the 6000 ton *Roda*, one of the German Export Echelon ships.

But this did not stop the enemy bringing in reinforcements, and during the afternoon three ships landed the 193rd Regiment to garrison the city and the Sola area. The Norwegian 'neutrality watch' battalion, hopelessly outnumbered, withdrew to Oltedal, some fifteen miles inland, without offering resistance.

Bergen, Norway's second city, lies at the head of North Byfiord, fifteen miles from the open sea. There was a complex of small, rather ineffective forts guarding the outer defences with two stronger outposts, Kvarven and Hellen, nearer to the city. The commander of the German convoy, Admiral Schmundt, knew that several German cargo ships carrying war material and flying foreign flags, were anchored in the fiord. He also knew, from intercepted messages, that the Norwegians suspected his approach.

At 2 a.m. on 9 April, flying his flag in the light crusier *Koln*, he warned her sister ship *Königsberg* and the auxiliaries acting as troop carriers to douse all lights as he entered the fiord. The moonless night still held a trace of fog as they passed undetected through the outer ring of forts. The searchlights at Kvarven had only just become operational after generator problems. As their beams swept the fiord the *Koln* was picked out and challenged.

> She promptly made the recognition signal in English: 'HMS *Cairo* proceeding to Bergen for a short visit'.* She was allowed to proceed.

But not for long. The ruse was detected and the guns at Kvarven and Hellen opened up, hitting the *Königsberg* three times. The auxiliaries *Bremse* and *Karl Peters* were damaged, but the *Koln* sailed on and the forts were overpowered by soldiers of the 69th Division. Two German trawlers, supported by fast patrol craft, landed almost two thousand troops in Bergen. Some carried white flags tied to their bayonets and all claimed to be friends of the Norwegians coming to protect them from the British. A curious incident happened here. A German boy, studying at a grammar school in Bergen, was woken up by the firing from the forts. He must have assumed that it was his fellow-countrymen who were arriving, and was on the quay in time to direct the first landing party to one of the forts.

Mobilization in Bergen had progressed swiftly and Major-General Steffens, the local military commander, had called for reinforcements. The Norwegian troops withdrew in good order to their centre inland at Voss. The light cruiser *Koln*, her mission completed, was preparing to leave Bergen in the early evening of 9 April when twenty-four RAF bombers, (Hampdens and Wellingtons), raided the harbour. Little damage was done to the German warships and an hour later *Koln* put to sea with two torpedo boats.

The following morning, 10 April, the *Konigsberg*, immobilized by Norwegian gunfire, was attacked by fifteen Skuas of the Fleet Air Arm. Flying at extreme range from Hatston in the Orkneys, they dive-bombed the damaged cruiser, leaving her to sink three hours later. This German cruiser was the first major naval vessel to be destroyed from the air by either side.

Apart from the threat from the air, the increasing aggressiveness of the British fleet worried the Germans. Immediately their own synchronized convoys had left port, German air reconnaissance plotted the movements of Allied warships. The results were ineffectual because of poor visibility, although in some areas the bad weather favoured the Germans.

The task force heading for the port of Trondheim crept towards the Norwegian coast under low cloud, led by the heavy cruiser *Hipper*, handicapped by the damage inflicted during her encounter with HMS *Glowworm* the previous day. Her escort of four destroyers provided a protective screen for the seventeen hundred men of the 3rd Mountain Division who were her seasick passengers.

*Christopher Buckley, *Norway, the Commandos, Dieppe*, p. 20. Dr Derry has a different version in his book, *The Campaign in Norway*, saying that a signal, in English, was sent to the forts 'Stop firing! We are friends.'

Trondheim was regarded as an important objective by both sides. Churchill had been prepared to accept heavy naval losses to secure it, and Admiral Raeder had recommended it to Hitler as the ideal Norwegian base for the German navy. It was a defended port, sited some thirty miles from the sea on Trondheimfiord. Two forts, Brettingen and Hysnes, armed with 150-mm and 210-mm guns, stood side by side on the eastern edge of the fiord, facing the fort of Hambaara on the other side. Hambaara was temporarily unoccupied, due to be manned on 9 April – too late by twelve hours.

The *Hipper*'s commander, Captain Heye, was ahead of schedule and headed west, away from the coast. He was spotted by a British Sunderland flying boat on the afternoon of 8 April and, in consequence, expected an Allied attack. But his own reconnaissance seaplane reported the Trondheim area clear of enemy ships and he turned east towards the Norwegian coast. He reached the entrance to Trondheimfiord at about 2.30 a.m., 9 April, knowing from intercepted messages that the defenders were aware of an imminent attack.

Led by two of the destroyer escort, the group forced the entrance at 25 knots. A lucky first salvo from the *Hipper* destroyed the cable connecting the defenders' searchlights but almost immediately the cruiser was challenged by a Norwegian patrol boat. Captain Heye used morse code to reply in English: 'Have orders from the government to go to Trondheim. No hostile intentions.'* Using her powerful searchlights to blind the small patrol boats and the batteries of the fort, *Hipper* forged ahead at full speed.

The German warship had just turned away from the forts towards Trondheim when both defences opened fire. Captain Heye ordered one of his destroyers to silence the forts while he made for his objective with the remaining escort. Shortly before 6 a.m. the German warships reached Trondheim and immediately landed two companies of the 138th Mountain Regiment from motor boats. Colonel Weiss, the German commander, using the Hitler formula of 'We come in peace to protect you from the British', soon established himself in the city. There was no resistance. Many of the young men of military age had left the port, seeking their mobilization units.

The two forts continued to put up a fight, damaging one enemy destroyer which was beached. The *Hipper* turned back to help her escort as the entrance had to be cleared for the following supply ships. At 5 p.m. the stubborn forts were silenced and by the evening of 9 April the port and its environs were in German hands. The airfield at Vaernes held out until 12 noon on the following day. This did not delay the expected transport planes as the Germans improvised a landing strip on the ice.

With these reinforcements the Germans were now able to consolidate

*Moulton, p. 85.

their hold on the Trondheim area. Its importance to them was its nearness to the Swedish border and they could now effectively divide Norway into two parts. Some resistance still had to be overcome, notably that of Major Holtermann at the old fort of Hegra, about twenty-five miles to the east. With a force of 260 young Norwegians, mixed soldiers and civilians, he repulsed several determined enemy attacks, despite the fact that his guns pointed away from the sea towards the Swedish frontier. Against all odds they held out until 5 May, starved of food. But this did not delay the main German advance to the north.

The northernmost objective of the German invasion was Narvik, 200 miles inside the Arctic Circle and 900 from Oslo. The risk element was high, no fighter cover could be provided until Norwegian airfields were secured. Hitler, infuriated by the action against the *Altmark* and fearing that Britain might block the Leads south of Narvik, insisted that the port must be secured for Germany.

Admiral Raeder ordered the well-armoured *Scharnhorst* and *Gneisenau* to escort the ten destroyers destined for Narvik, carrying two thousand men of the 3rd Mountain Division. The convoy, aided by atrocious weather, eluded the British warships searching for them. At 8 p.m. on 8 April, as they reached the approaches to the Vestfiord, the battleships veered off to the west and the ten destroyers pushed on, unescorted, towards Narvik.

This apparent disregard for the safety of the unescorted destroyers is puzzling. The Germans were aware of the strong British naval presence, led by the capital ships *Repulse* and *Renown*, in the seas around the Vestfiord. But the Germans' luck held and the destroyers, almost out of fuel, arrived off Ofotfiord in the early hours of 9 April.* They had been battered by heavy seas and the soldiers were cold and seasick in their narrow quarters below deck. One destroyer, the *Erich Giese*, lay fifty miles behind, suffering from compass trouble.

As they entered the narrows at the fiord entrance two destroyers, one each side, dropped off troops to search for the coast defence batteries that Vidkum Quisling had warned the Germans about. Floundering through six feet of thick, wet snow the soldiers could find no trace of the defences. In fact they were non-existent. The convoy commander, Commodore Bonte, continued up the fiord towards Narvik until sighted by an old Norwegian coastal defence ship, the *Eidsvold*, which fired a warning shot.

One of the German destroyers, the *Wilhelm Heidekamp*, sent out a boat with two officers to parley, with a signaller to keep communication. Captain

*When the Prime Minister, Neville Chamberlain, was informed that this enemy convoy, depending on communications hundreds of miles long, and hunted by the RAF and the British navy, was heading for Narvik, he refused to believe it. 'This is highly improbable,' he told Parliament. 'A mistake has arisen. The mention of Narvik is meant to be the small port of Larvik, situated just outside Oslofiord.' (Christopher Buckley, *Norway, the Commandos, Dieppe*, p. 22).

Willoch, the *Eidsvold's* commander, had earlier been warned of hostile intruders, and was in touch with Captain Per Askim (the senior naval officer at Narvik) in the defence ship *Norge*, moored in the harbour. The German officers courteously explained that they had come to protect Narvik from a British landing. When Willoch asked for time to consult his superior officer the Germans returned to their ship.

Captain Askim's reply was firm and clear: 'Resist the enemy!'

The Germans were invited back to the *Eidsvold* and told that the Norwegians intended to fight. The German officers saluted and left. On the way back to their destroyer they made a pre-arranged Very-light signal, alerting the other German ships. Before the gunners on the *Eidsvold* could train their weapons the enemy opened fire and the Norwegian vessel was hit by a salvo of torpedoes. Her magazine exploded and she sank almost at once. Of her crew of 175 only six survived.

A snowstorm was in progress and the *Norge* could not see her sister ship. But Captain Askim heard the explosions and opened fire on the nearest destroyer, the *Bernd von Arnim*. The *Norge* was promptly sunk and the German mountain soldiers began to disembark. Three of the enemy destroyers had already crossed the fiord and landed their troops at Bjerkvik, going on to take the Norwegian army base at Elvegaardsmoen. The harbour was crowded with merchant ships and amid the confusion Norwegian resistance ceased.

General Dietl had landed with the first wave of troops. He and his staff officers assured the Norwegians that they had come in peace to protect Norway and her neutrality. The German Commander-in-Chief was taken to the Norwegian garrison headquarters hoping to meet the local commander, Colonel Sundlo, whose role in the taking of Narvik has causd some controversy.

Theodor Broch, who was Mayor of Narvik at the time, says in his book *The Mountains Wait* (pp. 79–80) that he was told by General Dietl 'Your Colonel (Sundlo) showed good sense in not offering any resistance. He surrendered the city to me.' Later, at the City Hall in the centre of Narvik, Broch asked Sundlo, who was 'calm and impassive', to explain his actions. The Colonel said that he had been taken by surprise when the attack came. He found it useless to resist after the Norwegian warships had been sunk. He had from three to four hundred men ashore. The Germans were said to have ten thousand. When asked if he had received power to surrender the town he said 'Yes.' Colonel Sundlo then added, 'It seems that the Norwegian military authorities did not completely understand the situation.'

The author of the official history, Dr Derry, says (p. 41):

> The garrison of about 450 men, which was being hurriedly reinforced at the moment of the German arrival, (in the early hours of 9 April), could still have

made some defence with the help of its two newly constructed pillboxes; but its commander, Colonel Sundlo, who was one of the very few followers of Quisling in occupation of a key post, at the critical moment refused to fight. By the time he had been superseded at the order of Divisional Headquarters the Germans were in the town, and it was too late for his successor to do more than extricate one half of the garrison by a bold act of bluff.

The implication here is that Sundlo was a 'Quisling', a traitor who willingly served the German purpose by surrendering the port of Narvik. Major-General Moulton comments on this version in his book *The Norwegian Campaign of 1940* (footnote, pp. 83–84):

Derry, p. 41, says that Sundlo was a follower of Quisling and refused to fight, and this line is usually followed in British accounts. The full story in 'Norges Sjökrig', however, reads more like that of an elderly, and perhaps rather incompetent officer, drifting into disobedience of orders which were certainly not easy for him. At his post-war court martial Sundlo was found not guilty of treason in the surrender of Narvik, but for his collaboration with Quisling later, (during the German occupation), was sentenced to lose his commission and to hard labour for life.

A more detailed story is told by John Waage in his book *The Narvik Campaign*. Waage frankly states that it was never his intention to write military history, and offers no specific sources to authenticate incidents in his book. But his account, including the names of Norwegian officers cited by him (e.g. Majors Spjeldnaes and Omdahl), is confirmed in Norwegian records. Waage's version was published in English in 1964.

On 8 April, when invasion seemed imminent, the Norwegian deputy commander of the 6th District at Harstad ordered the 1st/13th Infantry battalion at Elvegaardsmoen to concentrate at Narvik, where it already had one company on detachment. At the same time Colonel Sundlo, the garrison commander, was ordered to stand by to resist the expected German invasion. The commanding officer of the 1st/13th, Major Spjeldnaes, marched his battalion eight miles through a heavy snowstorm and crossed the ferry into Narvik.

Spjeldnaes reported to Colonel Sundlo at 2 a.m., 9 April, and was told to put his cold and tired men into billets. Sundlo emphasized that he had no precise information about German movements and ordered the troops to be prepared to move at short notice. He had already alerted the machine-gunners overlooking the bay and posted his four Bofors guns at strategic points around the harbour.

At 4.30 a.m., 9 April, 6th District received orders from Oslo that 'Norwegian forces will not open fire on British or French warships in Narvik'. Sundlo received this order a few minutes before German mountain troops landed at Narvik quay. As soon as he heard that foreign warships had entered the harbour he sent for Major Spjeldnaes and his company commanders; also present was a Major Omdahl and a number of staff officers. Sundlo gave orders to prepare for battle, stressing the instructions about not firing on the French and British.

Major Spjeldnaes set up his headquarters in a nearby primary school. Apart from the distant sounds of firing in the harbour he knew little of the military situation. He sent Captain Gundersen down to the waterfront to assess the situation. On arrival, Gundersen was surrounded by German soldiers who were being briefed by Herr Wussow, the Germans consul in Narvik. Wussow pretended to believe that Gundersen was an emissary sent by Colonel Sundlo and forced him into a car with General Dietl. They drove into Narvik to find the garrison commander.

Meanwhile Major Spjeldnaes ordered his companies to take up defensive positions, with No. 1 Company under Captain Stromstad detailed to go to the harbour area and repulse any enemy attempt to land. As Stromstad moved off he was halted by a strong contingent of German soldiers, who sealed off the school. The German lieutenant in charge of the troops went into the school, where Sundlo had just arrived.

The enemy officer produced a document which claimed that the Germans had come in peace with the agreement of the Norwegian government. Sundlo asked for a thirty-minute truce to assess the situation. The German, knowing that resistance at the harbour had ceased, agreed. Sundlo conferred by telephone with the District Commander at Harstad, who delegated full responsibility to him. General Dietl now arrived at the school. He saluted Sundlo and addressed him as a 'friend of the Germans', knowing that he was an active supporter of Quisling.

Instead of being completely submissive, Sundlo complained about the heavy Norwegian casualties at the harbour. At this Dietl changed his stance and told Sundlo that Narvik was firmly in the hands of the German forces. Unless Sundlo ordered all Norwegian troops to lay down their arms at once, the German warships in the harbour would reduce Narvik to ruins. Faced with this ultimatum Sundlo surrendered the town. The time was 6.15 a.m., 9 April 1940.

While this was going on Major Spjeldnaes had contacted the Norwegian commander of the 6th Division (General Fleischer) by telephone. Fleischer gave clear orders that the Germans should be resisted: 'Go into action and throw the enemy into the sea.' Fleischer then spoke to Sundlo, and, when informed that Narvik garrison had capitulated, the General told Sundlo to consider himself under arrest.

At this time Major Omdahl entered the room. Although holding the same rank as Spjeldnaes he was senior in length of service and thus assumed command. He conferred on the telephone with General Fleischer who told him to arrest Sundlo and to get as many Norwegian troops as possible out of Narvik. As Sundlo had already been arrested by the Germans, the two Majors decided to ignore the capitulation and assembled some two hundred fully armed soldiers. As they were leaving a German officer ordered them to halt. Speldnaes brushed past him, answering in German, 'We are marching'.

Within minutes the Norwegians came against a road block where a German officer told him that he had orders to prevent the movement of Norwegian soldiers. Again Spjeldnaes replied, 'We are marching', in such an authoritative manner that the German reluctantly stood aside and the Norwegians marched towards the railway station. This was strongly held by the enemy and Major Omdahl decided to by-pass it and follow the railway track out of the town. At the mouth of the first tunnel they were overtaken by two Norwegian ski-runners bearing a written message from Colonel Sundlo ordering them to lay down their arms and return to the town. Omdahl convinced them that he was doing the right thing and the two ski soldiers joined the rest of the Norwegian troops as they marched towards the mountains.

By 8 a.m. Dietl was able to wireless General Falkenhorst at Hamburg and tell him that Narvik and the Norwegian military base at Elvegaardsmoen were in German hands. Admiral Raeder's biggest gamble had come off but the German position was precarious to say the least. Dietl retained about twelve hundred mountain troops to defend Narvik, the remainder had fanned out to the north and east to search for the soldiers of the Norwegian 6th Division who were now mobilized under the determined and aggressive General Fleischer.

In Narvik harbour Commodore Bonte, the German naval commander, faced an imminent attack from the British warships now concentrated outside Ofotfiord. Apart from the *Jan Willem*, only one of the expected tankers had arrived. The German destroyers were almost out of fuel and Bonte had orders to return to base as soon as possible. Under the circumstances it would be dangerous to split the small force. Bonte decided to hang on until 10 April. This decision played into the hands of the British Second Destroyer Flotilla who were preparing their plans to force their way into Ofotfiord.

Admiral Raeder, concerned mainly with extricating his capital ships from the growing Allied naval threat, was unaware that the British Second Destroyer Flotilla was about to attack Narvik harbour. He had good reason to be complacent. By 9 April 1940 the Germans had secured the five major ports and occupied the main commercial centres of Norway. The most important airfields were in their hands and the exit port for their Swedish iron ore seemed now to be in their grasp. The complete surprise they aimed for had eluded them. But by speed and sheer effrontery they had achieved their goals, though not without serious setbacks. Hitler hoped to win over the Norwegian people and in the early stages of the invasion the Germans observed, in general, the terms of the Geneva Convention, unless forced to act otherwise. After their initial shock, however, the Norwegians were more than merely resentful. As always when mass killing occurs, the victims of aggression meet violence with counter-violence.

As the Norwegian piecemeal mobilization got under way the government, acting on the plenary powers granted them at Elverum, accepted Hitler's challenge and began the daunting task of communicating with their widely dispersed armed forces. Their aim was to resist until help arrived from outside.

Vidkum Quisling tested his newly assumed authority on the evening of 9 April. He had declared himself Prime Minister and, using the captured Oslo radio station, announced to the nation that mobilization had been cancelled.

Quisling's orders were that the people should stay in their homes and await further instructions. This added to the general confusion but it did not stop the young men taking to the mountains. Quisling's next step was to attempt to form a government which would meet the demands of his German masters. The members of the Labour Government and some officials had left with King Haakon, and Quisling's followers were in such ill repute with all the regular political parties that Quisling was almost isolated. The newly proclaimed 'Prime Minister' was forced to assume the portfolios for Defence, Foreign Affairs and Justice himself.

His next move was to assemble the top Civil Servants at their respective Ministries so that they could take the oath of allegiance. None of them turned up. They refused to give up their keys and Quisling fell back on German help to force his way into the departmental buildings.

Quisling then cabled all Norwegian Legations overseas, demanding their adherence to the new régime. With one exception they failed even to reply. By this time the Germans were convinced that a puppet government under Quisling was not going to work. The German Minister, Dr Braüer, attempting to negotiate a 'cease fire' at Elverum, was told by King Haakon that he would rather abdicate than accept a Quisling government. On the morning of 10 April it was clearly stated that the Norwegians were going to resist 'come what may'. The Storting dispersed and the Norwegian Crown Princess and her children were persuaded to cross the border into Sweden.

On the diplomatic front the Germans met defeat in two key areas. King Haakon refused, under coercion, to dissolve the legitimate government.

And Vidkum Quisling, despite his bravado, failed to form a puppet administration. Hitler had imposed Quisling upon Dr Bräuer, hoping that an acceptable measure of collaboration could be forced on the Norwegian people. It must be said that Bräuer wanted to avoid a harsh régime if possible. He was an able diplomat with a good understanding of the Norwegians.

When Quisling failed, Bräuer proposed the formation of an administrative council to run the country under German guidance. But Hitler was enraged at 'the stubbornness and stupidity of this ridiculously small country and its petty King'.* He now insisted on a drastic policy change: if the Norwegians chose to refuse his offer of friendship then he would discipline them as he had disciplined other recalcitrant nations. Existing orders that the Norwegian King and his government were to be hunted down and 'eliminated' were now given high priority.

Before leaving Elverum for comparative safety farther north, the Norwegian government had appointed a new Commander-in-Chief. He was Colonel Otto Ruge, the elderly Inspector-General of Infantry who had earlier planned the successful defence of Elverum against the German parachutists. He was promoted General and with dour determination set about organizing resistance to the enemy.

It was obvious that the earlier attempt to a general mobilization had been ineffective. Many of the military depots and divisional headquarters were in German hands. The official mobilization lists had been captured. But General Ruge estimated that a third of the eligible servicemen had succeeded in reporting to a military unit of some kind. His immediate task was to establish communication with these in an attempt to build an effective defence force.

By 10 April the Germans were in control of Oslo radio station and the main communication centres in the south. But, fortunately for the Norwegian defenders, they were not able to monitor the extensive telephone network. Later these channels became a virtual life-line to resistance groups and to some Allied units. The Norwegians were denied the resources of the arsenals and supply depots in the south. Five of the six divisional headquarters were in German hands (the 6th Norwegian Division was in the north based on Harstad, in the Lofotens).

Every officer was forced to act on his own initiative, guided by the local conditions. General Ruge knew nothing about the situation in Telemark, Stavanger and Trondheim. His staff, collating random reports coming into his mobile headquarters, discovered that elements of the 1st Division were

*Riste, p. 57.

at Mysen, the 3rd at the mouth of Setesdal, north of Kristiansand, and the 5th around Stören and Steinkjer.

The news from Narvik was more encouraging. The German 3rd Mountain Division was reported to be cut off from supplies, while the naval force was penned in the fiords by the British Second Destroyer Florilla. The Norwegian 6th Division was intact under the command of General Fleischer, holding the ground between the port of Narvik and the Swedish frontier. Ruge resolved to hold on until the Allies came to his aid.

Already, without waiting for orders, small isolated groups of Norwegians were actively opposing the enemy, using whatever weapons they could find. An example of this sort of spontaneous resistance is transcribed from a tape made for the Imperial War Museum by Mr H. Meltzer (Tape No. 9159/2), then a young Norwegian student.

The German invasion came as a complete surprise to Meltzer, who just heard of it on 8 April by reading the evening paper. Some time after midnight he heard a 'distant thunderstorm' which turned out to be the sound of gunfire from Oslofiord.

The next day he went to work as usual and, when volunteers were called for, became a stretcher-bearer at the local hospital. Meltzer's father had been away on business and returned a few days later. When he saw his son he said, 'If I were you I wouldn't be sitting here now.' After dinner that day Meltzer packed a rucksack and took a train up into the mountains. He intended to join a group of volunteers formed under an Army lieutenant who had refused to give up when the local regiment surrendered.

Meltzer found the volunteers in the early morning and was given a military jacket to wear over his civilian clothes. He had no experience of firearms but was handed a rifle and given rudimentary instruction in its use. The group was mainly civilians with a sprinkling of soldiers on the run from the Germans:

> We could do exactly what we wanted to do. We had no military discipline at that time. There were all types, people had come in from all over Norway to join in the fight. We had found a dozen machine guns and we also found a lot of food so we had plenty of rations. We also got some trucks which we manned.

Meltzer became one of a heavy machine-gun section, operating in deep snow, high up in the mountains. Their agreed aim was 'to keep the passes open for British troops coming to western Norway'. It is clear that the group expected and welcomed the imminent arrival of the British. When asked if they thought that the British would come to turn the Germans out Meltzer replies:

> Yes, because we hadn't been to war since 1814 and we were not war-minded one bit and our threat was the Germans. We thought 'What are they doing here? Haven't they any better occupation than to make war . . . just you wait until the British come and hunt you down'. Because during the First World War we existed because we were protected by the British navy. I don't think you realize that in Britain. The importance of our prosperity in Norway is entirely to do with the British keeping the sea lanes open, whatever came, and we were very pro-British all the time, because during the First World War our merchant navy was sailing for the British and we had heavy losses.

Meltzer goes on to say that the group knew exactly where the Germans were and could plot their movements. This was because of the 'openness' of the telephone network, which was still manned by Norwegians. They soon had their first skirmish with the enemy. The look-out spotted a German convoy approaching a stone bridge:

> We lay behind the bridge there, and there were lots of us. There was no real command. Suddenly one fellow said, 'Now I can see them coming'. I was behind a stone there and very close to the bridge. Then they came across the bridge and they stopped there and we fired and they had some losses there. We took about fifty prisoners.
>
> They were Austrian soldiers and to begin with we didn't know what to do with them. We had shot a few of them. We had very few casualties. We had some wounded ourselves but nobody was killed, but the Germans had five or six killed and some of these soldiers were so shocked that they jumped across the bridge and down into the river and just were taken by the water and disappeared. We took their gloves away and their braces so they couldn't escape.

Meltzer's group operated in the mountains for some weeks, carrying out ambushes in different localities. They were bombed by German planes on occasions but kept well inside the snow line. Then a courier came to tell them that the enemy had threatened to bomb all the farms in the area in which they operated unless the ambushes stopped. They hid their arms in caches near remote chalets in the hills.

By now the group had grown to between seventy and ninety men. When they dispersed some of them went to their homes, others reformed into smaller bands to fight on in other localities. A group of about ten decided to surrender to the Germans. Meltzer, with three others, decided to make for their home locality. They had skis but couldn't use them because of the condition of the rapidly melting deep snow. They wore improvised snowshoes and late at night arrived at an isolated farm. Meltzer knocked at the door and asked for accommodation:

> The farmer there was a very religious man, and he asked me, 'Have you killed any soldiers? If you have done that you will go to hell'.
>
> At that time, when you had had weeks of fighting, and very tired and exhausted, you felt very low . . . in the first fight with the Germans I was behind

a stone. I heard something like bees going past me, and I thought that was very funny until I discovered there was a German behind a tree firing at me. But I shot him before he had a fine shot at me.

I hadn't tried to fire at anything alive before and because I had killed some Germans, when this was all over I felt like a murderer. That is what I've felt ever since. I've felt guilty because I've done this of my own free will, not under orders. Not forced to do it, and therefore you feel very, very guilty ever after.

At this point the interviewer asked Meltzer:

'Even though at that time you must have felt a sense of patriotic duty?'

Yes. But at the same time, because we went and saw these soldiers we had killed, I spoke to one of them before he died and he was the same age as I and he came from Grasse in Austria. He was just a young boy and you had a lot of sympathy for him, who was dragged into this. I feel it was against his will too.

Interviewer: 'Did he say he was just there against his will?' No, but he was just . . . to hear them crying out 'Mamma!' or 'Mutter! Mutter!'. They were crying all the time and they were just young boys like we were. I felt awful, and having caused this death to him, or he was severely wounded, it was a shock.

There was an hotel in their operational area where a doctor lived. The group took the wounded to him, their own and the Germans. It was the best they could do. After leaving the farm Meltzer and his companions headed for his home town. Being a small group they covered up to fifty kilometres a day, using the brief dusk and wooded areas to avoid the ever-present German aircraft.

Meltzer resumed his studies as soon as possible after getting to his home. He was depressed by the general air of uncertainty and, in some quarters, defeatism. After meeting up with like-minded comrades he began collecting small arms and stockpiling them in safe houses against the time when a resistance movement could be organized. There was a small number of local Norwegians actively collaborating with the Germans and one of these became suspicious and warned Meltzer: 'Ah! Remember that we've got a close eye on you.'

On family advice Meltzer left for Sweden, where he was interned. After a while he escaped and joined a Norwegian boat trying to sail to Scotland but was forced back into Swedish waters by bad weather. When asked if he had learned any important lessons from his 1940 experiences Meltzer said:

Yes. It really made us grow up as a nation. Until then we had been part of something – we had been allied with Sweden, we had been allied with Denmark, and in the First World War we relied on the British navy to keep us out of mischief. But we learnt the lesson that we had to be prepared ourselves, we coudn't really just leave it to others to fight our wars.

So I have been ever since in the Territorial Army where I am a Major. I am very well aware of our problems. We've got a very large Home Guard and we can occupy all the essential points right away while we mobilize.

Our government is prepared that they should not be taken with their pants down any more. They realize we cannot fight anything on our own any longer and that's why we joined NATO. After the war Sweden wanted us to form an alliance with them, but it was turned down because it would not be strong enough. But we have to pay our share of any war – we couldn't just leave it to the big nations. We are all in the same boat.

While Meltzer was fighting in the mountains the Norwegian royal family and the nucleus of the government were being hunted by the Germans.

On the morning of 11 April a Norwegian emissary from Quisling tried in vain to induce the King to return to Oslo. In the early evening of the same day the Luftwaffe found the royal party in the small village of Nybergsund near the Swedish border. In the attack that followed they narrowly escaped liquidation by high explosive and incendiary bombs by taking cover promptly in the woods.

On 13 April the King made a proclamation to the people of Norway: For more than a century my people and my country have not had to live through so dark an hour of trial, and I appeal urgently to all Norwegian women and men to do the utmost that every single individual can do to save the liberty and independence of our dear country.

Norway has been the victim of a blitz-attack from a nation with which we have always had friendly relations.

The powerful opponent has not hesitated to bomb the peaceful civilian population in towns and country districts. Women and children are exposed to death and inhuman sufferings.

Our position today is such that I cannot inform you where in Norway I myself, the Crown Prince, and the Government reside. The armed German forces directed a violent attack against us when we were in a small country district undefended and without any fortifications.

High explosives, incendiary bombs, and machine guns were directed against the civilian population and ourselves in the most unscrupulous and callous way. The intention of the attack could be only one: to annihilate at once all of us who were assembled to solve the difficulties and promote the interests of Norway.

I thank all those who are at their posts with myself and the Government in this fight for the independence and liberty of Norway.

I ask all of you to commemorate those who gave their lives for our fatherland.

God save Norway!*

This emotional appeal triggered a countrywide response. Resistance to the Germans stiffened. The Norwegian Chief Justice, Paal Berg, attempting to stabilize the political situation (and thus undermine the influence of Vidkum Quisling), telephoned the Norwegian Legation in Stockholm and

*Carl J. Hambro, *I saw it happen in Norway*, pp. 50–51.

issued a formal statement. This had the authority of the Supreme Court of Justice. Its aim was to make clear to the world that the legitimate government of Norway was being prevented by the Germans from carrying out its democratic function.

Berg's statement proposed the introduction of a Council of Administration. It put forward the names of loyal, trustworthy Norwegians who were ready to serve on the Council. These men were able and highly respected, they were influential members of the professions. None of them was a Nazi sympathizer and all were opponents of Quisling.

A letter was despatched by courier to the King. It explained that the Supreme Court of Justice had made it clear to the German authorities that the Provisional Administrative Council did not replace or usurp the authority of the legitimate Norwegian Government.

The institution of the Council clearly indicated that Quisling and his followers should give up their claim to represent political authority in Norway and that Quisling himself should declare his loyalty to the Council.

The next day Quisling publicly announced his loyalty to the Council over the radio. The Administrative Council, composed of as many of the nominees as could be assembled, took up its duties forthwith. All the leading organizations, including the Council of Trade Unions, publicly declared their loyalty. One of the first official statements of the Council announced that 'the so-called Government set up by Major Quisling in Oslo at the moment when German troops occupied the town has been withdrawn'.

The same statement called upon all Norwegians to work together to free their country from occupation. Most of the people of Norway now looked to Britain to help them defeat the invaders.

The British were urgently re-thinking the plans for their expeditionary force. On 9 April, 1940 the Allied Supreme War Council met in an emergency session. The hope of being invited by the Norwegian government to land on friendly soil had gone. The 'blatant act of war' perpetrated by the Germans cut through false hopes and muddled thinking as the Council considered its main task: how to select an objective within the realistic reach of the armed forces now alerted and ready for a landing in Norway.

The bulk of these forces had been armed and equipped for the hoped-for peaceful landing. The intentions of the Norwegian Government, now on the run, were not clear. The intention of the Germans in invading Scandinavia was also unclear: was this a massive 'red herring' prior to an enemy putsch through Belgium?

In the light of the latter eventuality the withdrawal of troops from the Western Front to reinforce the Norwegian Expeditionary Forces was out of the question. The position in the Middle East was anxiously examined. The concentration of men and war material in and around Egypt could not be interrupted. And what was Russia, lurking massively to the north of Narvik, going to do?

The Chiefs of Staff had already met, straight from their beds, at 6 a.m. They decided, on the scant intelligence available to them, that the Germans had not yet firmly secured Narvik and that a British battalion should leave at once for northern Norway. The naval members thought it essential to prevent a German build-up at Trondheim and Bergen. It was resolved to discuss this with the War Cabinet when they met at 8.30 a.m.

It was put to the War Cabinet that the French Chasseurs Alpins should be diverted from the Narvik force to take part in the recapture of Trondheim and Bergen (despite the French insistence that Narvik should be the prime target). The Cabinet's conclusion at its first meeting was that no action should be taken against any of the three ports until the Admiralty had clarified the naval position. Later that morning at their second meeting the War Cabinet decided that a Narvik landing would probably be opposed by the Germans. It was confirmed that Bergen and Trondheim should be the main objectives. Orders were given that all available British battalions must be ready to move by 12 April. Precise targets were not indicated until a later meeting of the Supreme War Council.

Churchill, the First Lord of the Admiralty, backed by the Chief of the Imperial General Staff, met the Military Co-ordinating Committee at 9.30 that evening. Supported strongly by the French, he was back on his old hobby-horse of the capture of Narvik and advised against invading either Trondheim or Bergen. Other landing points were considered in addition to Narvik. Among them were Namsos, north of Trondheim, and Aandalsnes to the south. In the event these were the ports on which the Allies finally decided, but a valuable twenty-four hours had been wasted as committees and councils thrashed out their differences.*

At this stage some sort of framework emerged for the Allied invasion forces. This was still fluid as far as the actual units assigned to operational areas were concerned. That is to say, various formations were transferred at short notice from one command to another. A case in point is the 5th Demi-Brigade of the Chasseurs Alpins, consisting of three battalions. Originally destined for the Narvik area, they were diverted to Namsos while still at sea.

A combined naval and military force, code named Avonmouth, was to operate around Narvik. The original intention was to take the port in 'one

*Derry, pp. 64–65.

fell swoop', using all available forces in a combined operation. But a mixture of vile weather, rugged terrain, poor communications and plain human misunderstanding was to prevent this, despite the willing and dogged persistence of the Allied fighting men.

The naval force was commanded by Admiral of the Fleet the Earl of Cork and Orrery, who was appointed Flag Officer, Narvik. The commander of the land forces was Major-General P. J. Mackesy. The two did not see eye-to-eye and this later led to major problems.

In a separate operation an Allied contingent, codenamed Mauriceforce, was to land at Namsos, some 350 miles south of Narvik. They were to be one prong of a pincer movement to take the enemy-held port of Trondheim. This strategy was adopted when the planned naval attack on Trondheim, spearheaded by Royal Marines, was abandoned. Mauriceforce consisted of a Territorial Army brigade of three battalions, inadequately supported. It was reinforced by the 5th Demi-Brigade of the French Chasseurs Alpins, under General de Brigade Béthouart.

The overall commander of the Allied force was the famous First World War VC, Major-General Sir Adrian Carton de Wiart, whose aggressive style was hampered by the same climatic and geographic conditions that bedevilled the Narvik expedition. His British troops were inexperienced, poorly prepared and badly backed up. The contingent of ski-trained Chasseurs were practically immobile because the French had failed to supply the necessary ski equipment.

The second prong of the pincer landed at Aandalsnes. From there it intended to push north to join up with Mauriceforce in the attack on Trondheim. But the rapid German advance from south Norway forced them to turn south towards Lillehammer where they fought dourly against overwhelming odds until they were evacuated on 3 May.

This expedition started out under Brigadier H. de R. Morgan as a Territorial brigade of two battalions with one battery of light anti-aircraft guns.* These units were later reinforced by a Regular Army brigade from France whose three battalions fought with distinction until forced to withdraw. Known as Sickleforce, this contingent did not experience the extreme conditions of weather and terrain to quite the same extent as the two expeditions further north. But they were outnumbered by an enemy equipped with tanks and artillery as well as superiority in the air. Thus, in effect, the Allied Force despatched to Norway consisted of three distinct groups, whose operations will be separately recorded.

They were sustained by the vigorous naval support of the British Fleet, backed-up by submarines and other warships from Allied nations. This

*On 20 April Brigadier Morgan handed over command of Sickleforce to Major-General B. C. T. Paget.

dominating naval presence ranged from capital ships such as HMS *Warspite* to small minelayers. Their story demands (and has received) far more authoritative coverage than can be given here, although it must be recorded in outline.

In the first volume of his book on the Second World War (p. 480) Winston Churchill commented on the state of the expedition as it prepared to sail for the Arctic Circle:

> They lacked aircraft, anti-aircraft guns, anti-tank guns, tanks, transport and training. The whole of Northern Norway was covered with snow to depths which none of our soldiers had ever seen, felt or imagined. There were neither snowshoes nor skis – still less skiers. We must do our best. Thus began this ramshackle campaign.

At noon on 9 April the British 2nd Destroyer Flotilla led by Captain B. A. W. Warburton-Lee in HMS *Hardy*, with HM Ships *Hunter* (Lieutenant-Commander L. de Villiers), *Hotspur* (Commander H. F. H. Layman), *Havock* (Lieutenant-Commander R. E. Courage) and *Hostile* (Lieutenant-Commander J. P. Wright) in company, was ordered to Narvik. At this time the Admiralty had been informed that only one German warship had arrived at Narvik. But Captain Warburton-Lee was told by Norwegian pilots that six ships 'larger than his' and a submarine had been sighted off Narvik. They also reported that the approach to the harbour was mined.

Warburton-Lee's orders were to enter the fiord to prevent a German landing. When he signalled the Admiralty about the changed situation he told them that he would attack at first light on 10 April, hoping that the high tide would protect him against mines.

The German commander, Bonte, waiting for supplies of fuel for his destroyers, relied on his U-boats patrolling the entrance to Ofotfiord for protection. The tanker, *Jan Willem*, had refuelled one of the destroyers but Bonte did not want to leave harbour until 10 April. Two of his warships were anchored off Ballangen, about twelve miles to the south, and three were nearer Narvik, in Herjangsfiord. That left four German destroyers actually moored in the harbour, while one patrolled the entrance. That evening (9 April) Commodore Bonte had been told by a patrolling U-boat that the British flotilla was heading west, away from Narvik. He saw no cause for alarm.

Warburton-Lee had five destroyers against the enemy's ten. His ships were lighter (under 1,300 tons) and not so heavily gunned. But he had the important advantage of surprise and at 4.30 a.m. on 10 April he led the

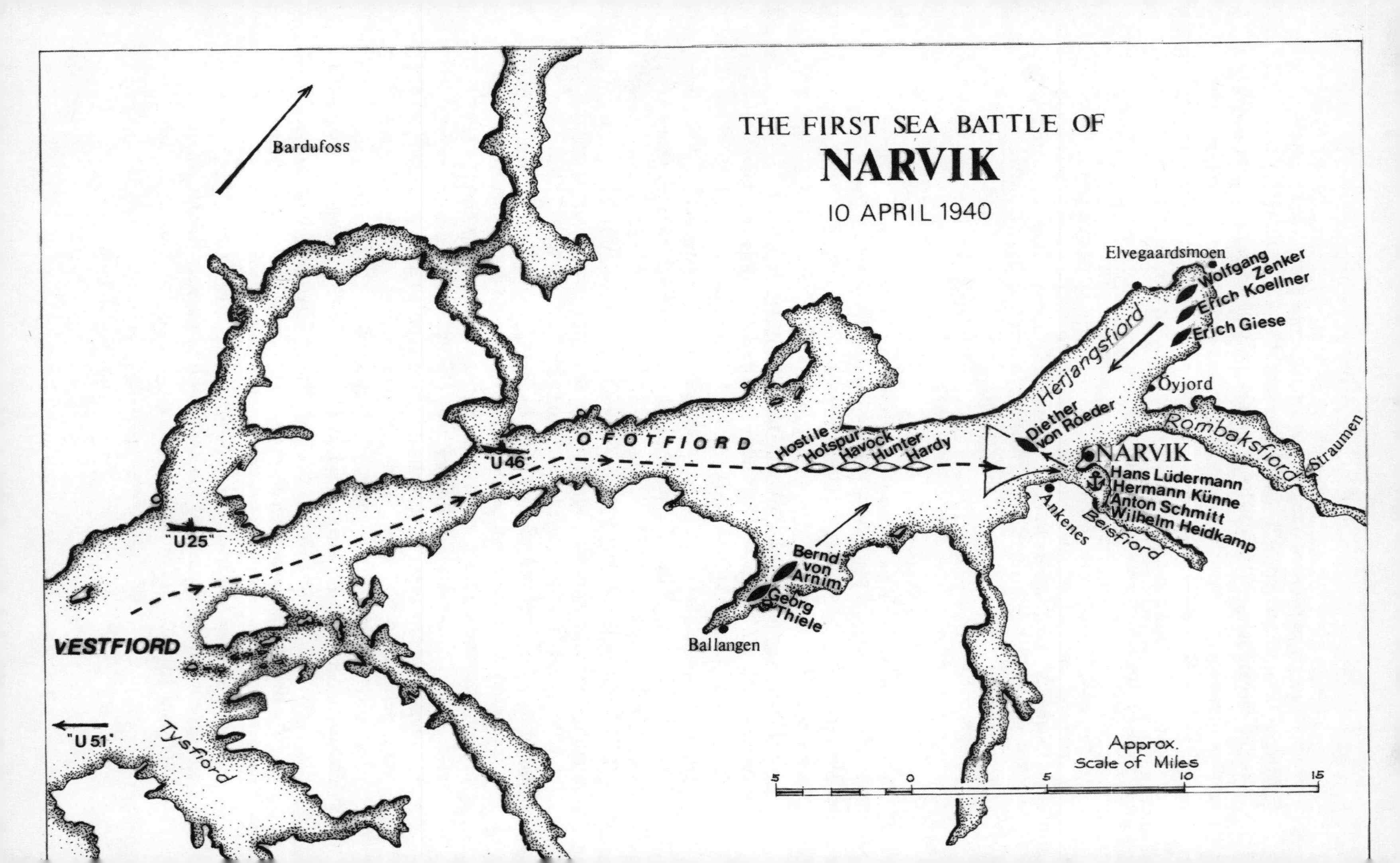

THE FIRST SEA BATTLE OF
NARVIK
10 APRIL 1940
Bardufoss
Elvegaardsmoen
Wolfgang Zenker
Erich Koellner
Erich Giese
Herjangsfiord
Öyjord
Rombaksfiord
Straumen
Diether von Roeder
NARVIK
Hans Lüdermann
Hermann Künne
Anton Schmitt
Wilhelm Heidkamp
Ankenes
Beisfiord
OFOTFIORD
Hostile
Hotspur
Havock
Hunter
Hardy
"U46"
"U25"
Bernd von Arnim
Georg Thiele
Ballangen
VESTFIORD
"U51"
Tysfiord
Approx.
Scale of Miles
5
0
5
10
15

Hunter and the *Havock* towards Narvik harbour entrance. The other two destroyers acted as his rearguard. German records show that the first indication of an attack was the explosion of the torpedoes fired by the *Hardy* as she entered the harbour. One torpedo sank the flotilla leader, the *Wilhelm Heidekamp*, killing Commodore Bonte and many others. Another enemy destroyer was sunk and three others disabled.

When *Hardy* disengaged, *Hotspur* went in and sank two merchant vessels. The German ships immediately opened fire but the British destroyers escaped damage. They attacked in turn, sinking several merchantmen later found to be carrying German supplies. Captain Warburton-Lee withdrew and regrouped the flotilla as the snow flurries stopped and visibility improved. The *Hardy* led the others into a second attack, each destroyer firing into the merchant ships through the harbour mouth. A third attack was mounted before the small force retired into Ofotfiord. And then their luck changed.

At about 6 a.m. the British ships sighted the three enemy destroyers which had been anchored in Herjangsfiord. The range was about four miles as the German ships began firing. Warburton-Lee gave the order to disengage and increased speed to shake off the enemy, knowing that ammunition was dangerously low. But as they widened the gap the German destroyers *Georg Thiele* and *Bernd von Arnim* came out of Ballangen bay into their path.

The weather was misty and the *Hardy* challenged the oncoming warships, to be met with a salvo from the enemy which hit Warburton-Lee's ship squarely on the bridge. The captain, who had just sent the signal 'Keep on engaging enemy', was badly wounded and most of the bridge complement were killed.

The Captain's secretary, Paymaster-Lieutenant Stanning, took the wheel until relieved by a seaman and then assumed command of the blazing ship. Stanning made for shallow water and beached the *Hardy* about three miles from the village of Ballangen. The crew helped the wounded through the icy water on to the foreshore, where Captain Warburton-Lee died. He was awarded the first Victoria Cross of the War.

The *Hunter* and the *Hotspur* had both been hit and in the melée they collided. While both ships were interlocked they came under heavy enemy fire and when *Hotspur*, using auxiliary steering, managed to pull clear, the *Hunter* sank. By now *Havock* and *Hostile* had engaged the enemy and covered the crippled *Hotspur* as the British ships withdrew towards the sea. The attacking German warships, low on fuel and ammunition, made no attempt to follow. As they came down Ofotfiord the British destroyers met the enemy ship *Rauenfels*, carrying ammunition. After a challenge she was fired on and blew up before sinking. The First Battle of Narvik cost the British two destroyers, with a third seriously disabled.

Of the German flotilla two of their largest destroyers had now been sunk and two put out of action. Three more had been damaged, while their fuel and ammunition supplies were critically low. Captain Bey, the senior surviving German officer, was left with the destroyers *Wolfgang Zenker* and *Erich Giese*, both seaworthy, fully fuelled and stocked with ammunition. On the night of 10 April he received orders to break out and at 8.40 p.m. left Narvik. Within two hours of sailing he sighted and identified a British cruiser and two destroyers. Captain Bey realised that to challenge would mean disaster and turned back to Narvik.

Another destroyer was made ready on 11 April but the weather had improved and visibility was too good to attempt a breakout. That night, while patrolling Ofotfiord, two of his three destroyers ran aground and were slightly damaged. On 12 and 13 April repairs and other preparations prevented an escape attempt. German intelligence reports warned that strong British naval forces were closing in on Narvik. Captain Bey raided all available stocks to arm and fuel the eight destroyers that remained. He beached a damaged warship in Ofotfiord to be used as a static battery and dispersed his destroyers in the side fiords lining the approaches to the harbour. The scene was set for the Second Battle of Narvik.

Admiral Whitworth had transferred his flag to the 30,000-ton *Warspite*. The Admiralty had accepted the risk of using the huge battleship in the narrow waters between the Lofotens and the Norwegian mainland. She had a screen of nine destroyers and, for the first time, the aircraft of HMS *Furious* became available to support action against the enemy around Narvik. In the late afternoon of 12 April a formation of eight Swordfish aircraft penetrated the low cloud over Narvik but failed to hit the German warships. Two British planes were lost.

A scouting aircraft from *Warspite* sank an enemy submarine in the mouth of the Herjangsfiord on 13 April and was able to report back to the fleet that the German destroyers had taken up battle stations. At noon that day the destroyer *Hero* led the British force into Ofotfiord. Swordfish from the *Furious* attempted to divebomb four enemy destroyers in front of the port but failed to do any damage.

Captain Bey, acknowledging the power of the *Warspite*, ordered his destroyers into Rombaksfiord but the *Herman Künne* failed to respond and was surprised and torpedoed by HMS *Eskimo* after her crew had scrambled ashore. Return fire from the German ships had failed to register, except that the *Punjabi* had her main steampipe damaged and was forced to withdraw for an hour or so.

Three British destroyers forced the entrance to the harbour and torpedoed enemy ships, including one destroyer which had been engaged by the *Warspite* under the mistaken impression that she was firing at a shore battery. During the attack the *Cossack* was hit by a shell and went aground near the harbour entrance.

The *Warspite* was far too bulky to negotiate the narrows at Straumen but four British destroyers led by the *Eskimo* pushed resolutely into Rombaksfiord to be confronted by two German warships. A torpedo from the *Hans Lüdemann* blew the forecastle off the *Eskimo*, but she managed to make her way back through the narrows stern-first so that her sister ships could get into the fiord.

When the British destroyers finally got through they found one German destroyer aground on the rocks three miles up the fiord while the other three lay against the shore at the end of the inlet. Their crews had left the ships and headed inland for the railway and comparative safety. The *Warspite* took up a watch-dog post off Narvik in the late afternoon as Admiral Whitworth sent his despatch off to London.

He was able to report destruction of all the German destroyers plus one submarine, leaving only a dozen or so merchant ships, most of them damaged, in the harbour. Narvik was quiet and Whitworth assumed that the opposition had been quelled and considered sending in a party of sailors and marines to occupy the town.* But German aircraft had been sighted further south and there was much to do in tending the wounded and replenishing ammunition and stores.

Whitworth thought the better of it and withdrew the British force into Ofotfiord. Two destroyers had been despatched to Ballangen to bring back the survivors of the *Hardy*. Considering the ferocity of the fighting, the British casualties were light: Twenty-eight dead and fifty-five wounded. The Second Battle of Narvik had established the supremacy of the British navy in the seas around northern Norway. The occupation of Narvik port was thus postponed while the troops who were soon to invest it were already en route.

The Allied force now assembled for the counter-attack against the Germans in Norway was substantially the same as that earmarked for the abortive Finnish undertaking. The Narvik expedition was spearheaded by the 24th Guards Brigade, made up of 1st Scots Guards (Lieutenant-Colonel T. B. Trappes-Lomax), 1st Irish Guards (Lieutenant-Colonel W. D. Faulkner) and 2nd South Wales Borderers (Lieutenant-Colonel P. Gottwaltz). Many of the men in this Regular brigade had recently seen service in Palestine or on the North-West Frontier of India.

*Admiral W. J. Whitworth: Despatches (Section 44). In a later despatch Whitworth recommended that Narvik 'should be occupied without delay' but this was not acted upon.

They were well trained, well led and their morale was high. They were supported by a light anti-aircraft battery, Royal Artillery, and two Field Companies of the Royal Engineers. The French contingent of Chasseurs Alpins, Foreign Legion and the Polish Brigade were moving up to their embarkation areas as elements of the main military convoy gathered near Cape Wrath, off northern Scotland.

Three of the hired transports bore a 'royal' resemblance, the *Empress of Australia*, the *Monarch of Bermuda* and the *Reina del Pacifico*. The other two troopships were Polish, the MV *Batory* and the ill-fated *Chobry*. Two companies of the Scots Guards, with part of their battalion headquarters, had sailed with General Mackesy in the cruiser *Southampton*. With them was a detachment of Royal Engineers. The rest of the battalion had embarked in the *Batory* as early as 7 April, loading and unloading stores as conflicting orders were carried out.

In the early morning of 11 April they were at Scapa Flow in company with the *Chobry*. The growing naval escort included the battleship *Warspite*, carrying the flag of Lord Cork, four cruisers, the repair ship *Vindictive*, and a large number of destroyers. The liner *Reina del Pacifico*, carrying the 2nd South Wales Borderers and elements of the Royal Signals, RASC, RAOC and RAMC, had sailed on 12 April. Although stocked with supplies for a luxury cruise her sleeping accommodation was grossly overcrowded, with men sleeping in the corridors and even in the ornate First-class dining saloon.

The Irish Guards had sailed on the same date as the Scots in the *Monarch of Bermuda*, buoyed up with false rumours of the recapture of Bergen and Trondheim and lurid newspaper accounts of 'the shores of Norway awash with the bodies of dead Germans'.* The CO (Lieutenant-Colonel W.D. Faulkner) assembled his officers to issue the secret orders he had carried from London. The 24th Guards Brigade were to land at Narvik and occupy the peninsula. Maps should then have been issued but unfortunately they were in another ship. In any case the ship's wireless had received a German radio report that Austrian mountain troops had already occupied Narvik. A Sunderland flying boat was droning overhead as the Irish Guards awaited their next batch of operational orders.

Two of the three territorial battalions of 146 Brigade, 1/4 King's Own Yorkshire Light Infantry (KOYLI) and 1/4 Lincolnshires, were in the *Empress of Australia* with 55 Field Company of the Royal Engineers. The other TA unit, the Hallamshire battalion of the York and Lancaster Regiment, had earlier embarked on the County Class cruiser HMS *York*, bound for Bergen. They had been detailed for garrison duties in a 'peaceful'

*In fact the shores of Oslofiord on 9 April could be said to be 'awash' with the German dead from the sunken *Blücher*.

port and their scale of arms, ammunition and general supplies was based on that premise.

But when German warships were reported at large in the North Sea, the *York* was ordered to sail at once to join the Home Fleet. The Hallams were disembarked at a moment's notice. Their equipment and stores were bundled over the side willy-nilly, leaving essential items in the warship. The Hallams moved to Glasgow and embarked on MV *Chobry*, which then sailed to rendezvous with the main convoy. In worsening weather, ill-prepared but in good heart, the Allied Expeditionary Force for Northern Norway headed slowly towards the Arctic Circle.

THE AREA OF
NARVIK
14 APRIL - 8 JUNE 1940
Scale of Miles
5
0
10
Sjövegan
Harstad
Borkenes
Lavangen
Bardufoss 25 miles
Fossbakken
Gratangen
Lapphaug
Elvenes
Labergdal
Vaagsfiord
Skaanland
HINNÖYI
Tjeldsund
Bjerkvik
Hartvigvatn
Kuborg Plateau
Elvegaard
Kobberfjell
Kuberget
Bogen
Lenvik
German Wks
Herjangsfiord
Seynes
Öyjord
Jernvatnene
Liland
Rombaksfiord
Straumen
Rundfjell
Björn fjell
NARVIK
Straumsnes
Haugfjell
Ofotfiord
Wk. of "Hunter"
Beisfiord
Wks
Mt. Fagernes (4166 ft)
Skjom
Wks
Sildvik
Hundalen
German Wk.
Wk. of "Hardy"
Ankenes
Emmenes Pt.
Haakvik
Skjomnes
(4751 ft)
Storvatn

PART THREE

The Allies land in Norway. Operations in the Narvik area.
The move to Bodö. Operations around Mo and Mosjöen
14 April to 31 May 1940

The Allied base was at Harstad on the island of Hinnöy in the Lofotens. It was not the ideal site. Although barely thirty-five miles from Narvik in a direct line, the distance was much greater in sea-miles. To reach Ofotfiord the narrow passage of the Tjeldsund had to be negotiated. Although this was surveyed by the British navy and marked with buoys, navigation was tricky in the treacherous April weather.

The expedition's military commander, Major-General P. J. Mackesy, had embarked with his staff at Scapa Flow on 12 April. With him in HMS *Southampton* were two rifle companies of the Scots Guards and a few staff officers. On the same day, Admiral of the Fleet the Earl of Cork and Orrery (called by the sailors 'Ginger Boyle'), sailed from Rosyth in the *Aurora*. Each had been separately briefed. This was in breach of the principles of joint command and was to lead to a clash of personalities which provokes controversy to this day. Churchill's principal staff officer, General Ismay, had written:

> The Chief of the Naval Staff and the Chief of the Imperial General Staff acted with sturdy independence. They appointed their respective commanders without consultation with each other; and, worse still, they gave directives to those commanders without harmonizing them. Thereafter they continued to issue separate orders to them. Thus was confusion worse confounded.

On 14 April, as HMS *Southampton* nosed through the Vaagsfiord towards Harstad, General Mackesy had no doubts about his mission. He was to land his force at Harstad, reassemble his equipment and ammunition and make a plan to eject the Germans from Narvik. There was no reliable information available to him about a German presence on Hinnöy so he ordered his soldiers below decks as he entered Harstad harbour. He despatched two of his staff officers to contact the local authorities. They returned with several Norwegian army officers who confirmed that Hinnöy was clear of Germans.

The Norwegians stressed the importance of boosting the flagging morale of the soldiers of the Norwegian 6th Division who were defending the approaches to Bardufoss airfield. Consequently Mackesy decided to sail in the *Southampton* for Sjövegan, about thirty-five miles north-east of Narvik. On arrival the Scots Guards, under the command of Major H. L. Graham, disembarked to reinforce General Fleischer's men.

On 14 April as the *Aurora* approached the Norwegian coast, Lord Cork received a signal sent by Admiral Whitworth, the commander of the Battle Cruiser Squadron. Whitworth had received reports from Norwegian pilots and fishermen on the condition of the German forces in Narvik following the two naval battles. He estimated the enemy strength as between fifteen hundred and two thousand. (Other sources, some of undoubted enemy origin, gave various estimates up to seven thousand.)

Whitworth reported that the occupying troops were disorganized, shellshocked and demoralized. The clear implication was that the time was ripe to land an assault force to take the port of Narvik by storm. Cork resolved to do this, using the 350 Scots Guards in HMS *Southampton*, reinforced by some two hundred sailors and marines. Accordingly he signalled the *Southampton*, asking General Mackesy to meet him in Skjelfiord in the Lofoten Islands that evening (14 April).

Radio reception was poor, as the mountains 'screened off' the fiords, and Lord Cork's signal failed to get through until Mackesy was actually disembarking the troops at Sjövegan. The General decided to carry out his original plan. He signalled Lord Cork, questioning the feasibility of an immediate attack. He made it clear that he preferred to wait until the main convoy arrived on 15 April before contemplating any move.

In the meantime Cork had received a message from the Admiralty: 'We think it imperative that you and the General should act together and that *no* attack should be made except in concert'. This displeased Lord Cork, who knew Churchill's views on the quick capture of Narvik. The two men, just weeks earlier, had spent 'many intimate hours strolling in the garden' as the First Lord briefed the Admiral: 'Do not hesitate to run risks, strike hard to seize Narvik'.*

These 'instructions' were not committed to paper: '... we left him exceptional discretion and did not give him any written orders. He knew exactly what we wanted.'

Cork himself states in a later despatch:

> My impression on leaving London was quite clear that it was desired by His Majesty's Government to turn the enemy out of Narvik at the earliest possible moment, and that I was to act with all promptitude in order to attain this result. (*London Gazette* (Sup.) dated 8 July, 1947, page 3168)

* Churchill (Vol 1, p. 483).

There was no rapport between Churchill and Mackesy. The General received conventional written orders signed by General Sir Edmund Ironside, Chief of the Imperial General Staff, on 10 April 1940.* These orders indicated that a base at Harstad should be set up before any operation was undertaken: 'Your initial task will be to establish your force at Harstad, ensure the co-operation of Norwegian forces that may be there and obtain the information necessary to enable you to plan your further operations.'

The instructions went on to say that General Mackesy was not intended to land troops in the face of opposition and stressed: 'A landing must be carried out when you have sufficient troops'. General Ironside sent a personal letter with Mackesy's orders. It contained details of reinforcements and told Mackesy not to worry about paying for locally-obtained supplies, but 'Don't allow any haggling over prices'. Ironside went on to estimate that there were 3000 Germans in Narvik – 'they must have been knocked about by naval action'. In contrast to the written orders instructing Mackesy, in effect, to organize a secure base before undertaking further operations, Ironside wrote this sentence: 'You may have a chance of taking advantage of naval action and you should do so if you can'. Then he added, 'Boldness is required'. The letter ended 'Good luck to you. We know your responsibility and trust you'. Mackesy needed all the luck he could get.

On 15 April HMS *Aurora* arrived at Harstad and Lord Cork and General Mackesy met for the first time. In the *Journal of the Royal United Services Institution* of December 1970 (pages 28–33), Piers Mackesy, the General's son, comments on this confrontation in a spirited defence of his father's decision on 14 April not to attack Narvik:

> What was required at Narvik was not only to be right, but to persuade his naval colleague and make the position clear to Whitehall. Mackesy was not a conciliatory man, and he did not gladly accommodate himself to those in high places with whom he disagreed. He had sailed for Narvik already convinced that the plan was inept and the expedition badly mounted.
>
> And at Harstad he was confronted by a total stranger sent by the statesman whom he knew to be chiefly responsible for the Scandinavian adventure and its disastrous organization. Many witnesses of that first encounter in the *Aurora* were to recall the instant antagonism of the two commanders. Mackesy's intellectual intolerance confronted the impetuous judgement and masterful temper of an Admiral of the Fleet of immense and anomalous seniority who outranked the Commander-in-Chief of the Home Fleet.
>
> This extraordinary encounter, devised by Churchill in defiance of all the principles of combined operations, was worsened by the fact that neither commander had chosen, or was in full sympathy with, his Chief of Staff. For this none of the parties was to blame.

* Derry, Appendix, A, pp. 247–9.

Lord Cork later confirmed that he was indeed unaware of General Mackesy's operational orders. In the *London Gazette* Supplement already quoted, the Admiral stated:

> I was astonished to hear that not only was his (Mackesy's) force embarked as for a peaceful landing, and in consequence was unready for immediate operations but that orders he had received, and given to him just prior to sailing, ruled out any idea of attempting an opposed landing. *Thus the General and myself left the UK with diametrically opposite views.* (Author's italics)

In a similar report* General Mackesy explains his reasons for opposing Lord Cork's plan to attack Narvik on 15 April.

> Blizzards, heavy snow storms, bitter winds and very low night temperatures were normal. Indeed until the middle of May even those magnificent soldiers, the French Chasseurs Alpins, suffered severely from frostbite and snow blindness.
>
> Troops who were not equipped with and skilled in the use of skis or snowshoes were absolutely incapable of operating tactically at all. I had no such troops at my disposal when I first landed. Shelter from the weather was of vital importance.
>
> It soon became certain that the enemy held Narvik in considerable strength. All the existing defences had been handed over intact by the Norwegian garrison. A personal reconnaissance convinced me that the topography favoured the defence and that an opposed landing was quite out of the question so long as the deep snow and existing weather conditions persisted and so long as my force lacked landing craft, tanks, adequate anti-aircraft defence and air co-operation.
>
> The problem was, of course, not merely one of landing but one of carrying out a subsequent advance of several miles. Yet, owing to the configuration of the ground, not even during the first mile could support be given by ships' guns.

After a lapse of almost fifty years, to hazard a guess about the chances of success if the attack had been launched becomes mere conjecture and value-judgement. The Historian of the Scots Guards has written:

> In the light of what is now known of the demoralized state of the German troops and sailors after the *Warspite*'s victory, it is hard to resist the conclusion that a swift, bold landing on the 14th or 15th would have had a good chance of achieving a decisive success. (*Norway – The 1st Battalion*, footnote, p 29.)

There is no doubt that the enemy was demoralized. Contemporary accounts such as those of the Mayor of Narvik (Theodor Broch) and the Norwegian writer, John Waage, are unanimous on this point. How long would this demoralized state endure? Broch comments on 'a complete collapse on 13 April and a quick recovery next day'. The history of the German soldier

* *London Gazette* Supplement, 10 July 1947, p. 3179.

shows how dour and resilient he is in defence.

The German military commander, General Dietl, an able and resolute commander, knew that Hitler would not easily forgive a defeat at Narvik. The enemy garrison inside the town was comparatively small. Of Dietl's well-trained 3rd Mountain Division, the 1st and 3rd Battalions of the 139th Regiment were driving north against the Norwegians at Lapphaug. The 2nd Battalion held the bay, and the railway to the east above the shore of Rombaksfiord. There were other uncommitted soldiers repairing the railway. All of these, relatively unaffected by the British naval bombardment, could be recalled to Narvik in a matter of hours.

The sailors from the sunken or beached German destroyers had not given up. Their commanders quickly formed them into *ad hoc* units. Professor Hubatsch records that more than two thousand sailors were formed into Naval Battalions. The 'Erdmenger' Battalions were said to be particularly aggressive. There can be little doubt that these naval reinforcements, armed, equipped and clothed from the captured Norwegian Army base at Elvegaard, would have rallied to Dietl in defence of Narvik.*

In the view of the present writer (who 'stood-by' with his battalion, the 2nd South Wales Borderers, for an impending assault on Narvik), there was a strong possibility of a successful landing on 15 April.

> Quite naturally the enemy troops in the vicinity of the harbour, and those who could be seen over the open sights of naval guns, had withdrawn to higher, safer ground. During the two naval battles they had sustained many casualties and the unaccustomed sight of their comrades' bodies floating in the harbour was unnerving for them.
>
> Their expected supply ships had not arrived. Food was getting scarce. Many Norwegians, encouraged by their own civic leaders, had evacuated the town. Those left refused to accept the German occupation currency and were generally 'awkward'. There was an air of despondency, a feeling of being 'cut off'. Many of the fighting troops had left to find and disarm the Norwegian soldiers who had refused to capitulate. Consequently the reduced number of German officers left in the town failed to maintain a high standard of discipline and a trickle of deserters headed for the Swedish border.
>
> General Dietl had withdrawn his headquarters to the high ground along the railway to the north-east. He knew that several hundred tons of provisions were on their way to him through southern Sweden and he wanted to ensure a clear passage for the much-needed supplies.
>
> Meanwhile mail for the German sailors, and small amounts of essential stores, were being dropped daily by aircraft operating from the Trondheim area. For Dietl it was a matter of holding his force together and hanging on until reinforcements arrived, piecemeal through Sweden or by air when a suitable landing ground could be completed by Norwegian forced labour.

* The author, when at Narvik in May 1987, was told by eye-witnesses that the survivors of the sunken German destroyers, armed with Norwegian weapons, were eager to avenge the loss of their ships if the British attempted to land at Narvik.

A few German parachute troops had already landed. Yes, I think Lord Cork's plan might have succeeded. The assault force, given a little luck, could have gained a foothold in the harbour area of Narvik. I wont attempt to guess at casualties. But how long could they hold on? The Germans had complete air superiority. They could have reduced Narvik to ruins, as indeed they did to the business quarter of the town in early June. On 15 April the Germans still held the heights around Narvik. The harbour area could be enfiladed from the railway area to the north-east, from the slopes of the Ankenes peninsula to the south, and from Fagernes mountain behind the town.

This is all conjecture, of course. But had we succeeded in taking Narvik on 15 April the signal telling London of our triumph may well have been quickly followed by a message of disaster. No one will ever know.*

Harstad was a small wooden town of some four thousand inhabitants. The phlegmatic fisherfolk found themselves outnumbered by a concentration of urgent, jabbering, foreign soldiers, all seeking shelter from the biting wind. In addition to the front-line troops there were some three thousand 'base details', field bakeries, mobile bath units, even a railway construction company of the Royal Engineers; in short, the essential equipment and stores necessary to sustain an army in the field. The troops were disembarked on 15 and 16 April. The quay were cleared of stores by the 18th and it was then that the confusion really started.

In the rush to get the convoy under way little attention was paid to the tactical loading of the ships. Items for Namsos had arrived at Harstad and vice versa. Guns had been separated from ammunition, in some cases never to be reunited. Specialized equipment had been poorly packed and arrived unserviceable. Each individual soldier had some thirty pieces of equipment in three kitbags. Half of this was a special 'winter issue', much of it originally intended for the Finland expedition.

To relieve the congestion every available building was commandeered. The CO of the Irish Guards moved his men as far out of the town as possible. The South Wales Borderers occupied a large, ramshackle fishmeal factory standing on stilts above the snow level. The pungent smell of fish permeated everything; fish hanging on long lines to dry, fish in various stages of preparation, fish-heads among the debris floating along the edge of the fiord. The British soldiers, mostly not too fond of fish, found this overpowering stench unpleasant, to say the least.

The Royal Engineer Field Companies found it almost impossible to accommodate their large and complex store of equipment. Priority was given to demolition stores and to delicate instruments; Sappers came last. The Royal Army Service Corps unit commander was fortunate in contacting the British Consul, Mr Per Sanvig. This Norwegian businessman represented the Anglo-American Oil Company and was able to locate

* Author, in an interview with Dr Conrad Wood, for the Imperial War Museum, October 1985.

sites for petrol depots. He organized civilian vehicles for the RASC, whose own essential transport had not yet arrived at the base.

Lack of transport was a major drawback for the Allies throughout every phase of the campaign. Lorries, trucks, load carriers of any kind were never available in sufficient numbers to move men, stores and equipment around the difficult and often primitive road system. Taxis and private cars were pressed into use. In many cases willing drivers offered their services free.

At Harstad, and throughout the entire campaign, this dearth of suitable vehicles was partly rectified by the universal use of the *sköyter*. This small Norwegian fishing boat, called the 'puffer' by the British and the 'pic-pic' by the Poles, literally saved the day. So important did they become that they later merited an article in *The Army Quarterly*.* Hundreds of lives were saved by the use of this bustling little craft.

At sea the Fleet exercised extreme vigilance. An enemy submarine, *U49*, was sunk as the convoy eased its way into Harstad on 15 April. HMS *Fearless*, which sank the U-boat, rescued most of the crew and retrieved a document showing the disposition of the enemy submarines in the Lofoten area. The next day Dorniers and Junker 88's of the Luftwaffe bombed the town quay, killing a British Military Policeman. The concentrated anti-aircraft fire of the Allied ships was the only defence available. The heavy and light anti-aircraft guns of the Royal Artillery were in the second echelon of the supply convoy and had not yet arrived. The high-level bombing continued, but very little damage was caused to shore installations, as most of the bombs fell in the fiord.

General Mackesy was anxious to get his troops established on the mainland, as near to Narvik as possible. Two peninsulas, Öyjord to the north and Ankenes to the south of Narvik, were the obvious choice. Enemy activity was observed on both but detailed information of German defences was not available. Mackesy decided to move the Irish Guards to the area of Bogen, north of Öyjord and the South Wales Borderers to Ballangen, south-west of Ankenes.

Narvik lies on a tongue of land jutting into the Ofotfiord. Behind it is the huge mass of Fagernes mountain (Pt 1270). The two peninsulas already mentioned rise several hundred feet on either side, covered in scrubby trees, mainly silver birch. The town was effectively protected from the fire of the flat-trajectoried naval guns unless the British warships could get close into the harbour entrance. Mackesy wanted to get his field artillery onto these promontories. And to do so he had to take and hold them with the infantry of 24th Guards Brigade.†

The hazards Mackesy now faced were precisely those that had caused

* Peter Dalzel: 'The "Puffers" at Narvik', *The Army Quarterly* (April and July 1965).
† 1st Scots Guards, 1st Irish Guards and 2nd South Wales Borderers.

him to disagree with Lord Cork's plan of attack. The General's son highlighted them in his *JRUSI* article:

> Judged therefore as a normal landing operation Narvik was a serious proposition; and this was not a normal landing. None of the conditions which were to be regarded later in the war as necessary for an assault landing were present. There was no landing craft; the troops would have to tranship from warships to open boats and fishing craft and make their run in to the beach in full view of the enemy. Nor could the concentration or run-in be covered by darkness, for the Arctic summer was approaching and already the night had been reduced to a short interval of twilight.
>
> The only fire-support must be provided by naval guns, for the troops had no artillery to support them from across the fiords, and the special support craft which were evolved in later years were as yet unborn. Though the navy had enormous confidence in its power to smother the shore defences, it was a confidence not securely founded. At this stage of the war naval officers knew little about observing fire on land, and as experience at Bjerkvik and Narvik was later to prove, even machine guns under direct observation from the sea could keep on firing till they were actually mopped up by troops. Nor was much H.E. ammunition available.

What enemy opposition was the infantry of 24th Guards Brigade likely to meet? The second battalion of 139th (Carinthian) Mountain Regiment held the high ground around Narvik. They had ten heavy machine guns, twenty-seven light machine guns, six heavy and eighteen light mortars, and two mountain guns. With supporting arms. the battalion could muster about 750 fighting troops, some of whom had fought against a redoubtable enemy in Poland. As recently as 13 April they had been reinforced by two 75 mm guns. If hard-pressed, they could call upon their sister regiment, the 1st/139th, a half-day's march away to the north of Rombaksfiord.

Hitler had been informed of the Allied naval victories and of the critical situation at Narvik. He began to have second thoughts about his orders to hold on to the port at all costs. Hitler suggested to his staff that General Dietl should give up Narvik and break out to the south where he could link up with the German force at Trondheim. General Jodl, one of the top Wehrmacht officers, explained to the Führer that it was impossible even for mountain troops to get through the rugged, snow-covered mountains to the south. Jodl also ruled out airlifting Dietl's men from Bardufoss. He pointed out the disastrous loss to men and morale that this would entail: 'One should not give up a thing for lost until it has been lost,' he told Hitler.*

However, after a visit by a staff officer from Berlin, Dietl did seriously discuss evacuating Narvik on 6 May. He decided to fight on.

* Moulton (p. 163), quoting Professor Hubatsch.

Winston Churchill reacted angrily to Lord Cork's message that the frontal attack on Narvik was off. Mackesy's proposal to move to positions presumably unoccupied on the approaches to Narvik did not harmonize with the First Lord's plans. He produced a draft telegram to the Military Coordination Committee for onward transference to Cork and Mackesy on 17 April:

> Your proposals involve damaging deadlock at Narvik and the neutralization of one of our best brigades [24th Guards Brigade]. We cannot send you the Chasseurs Alpins. The *Warspite* will be needed elsewhere in two or three days. Full consideration should therefore be given by you to an assault on Narvik, covered by *Warspite* and the destroyers, which might also operate at Rombaksfiord. The capture of the port and town would be an important success. We should like to receive from you the reasons why this is not possible, and your estimate of the degree of resistance to be expected on the waterfront. Matter most urgent.*

Lord Cork put pressure on Mackesy for an immediate attack on Narvik. The General stuck to his guns. He had given Brigadier Fraser his orders and the deployment of 24th Guards Brigade went ahead as planned. The two companies of Scots Guards landed from HMS *Southampton* had moved inland towards Bardufoss airfield, acting as a defensive screen for the Norwegians. General Fleischer intended to attack the Germans at Lapphaug and moved three of his battalions, supported by 75-mm guns and a mountain battery, into position.

On 18 April the Irish Guards embarked at Harstad for Bogen in HMS *Vindictive*. High-level German bombing held up movement for five hours but there were no casualties. They were ferried ashore by puffers to the west of the Öyjord promontory at a small village called Liland before occupying Bogen and Lenvik. The rudimentary road, now covered in deep slush, ran east and north across the Öyjord peninsula to Bjerkvik and on to Elvenes and Gratangen, all occupied by units of the German 139th Mountain Regiment and the Naval Battalion Kothe.

Lieutenant-Colonel Faulkner, CO 1st Irish Guards, attempted to contact the Norwegian outpost halfway between Lenvik and Bjerkvik. Communications were difficult. The use of runners, slow and tedious, was widespread. Each company had at least one; officers used their batmen. If a message was vital or complicated an officer was sent, usually the Intelligence Officer or one not otherwise occupied.

The battalion Signals Officer, Lieutenant J. Gilliat, laid line to the detached companies. On the odd occasion he managed to get through by heliograph when the sun was high. Communication to the warships was by lamp, sometimes frustrated because the naval operators were much

* Churchill, *The Gathering Storm*, p. 486.

faster and more accurate. There was one wireless set only. This was the 'rear-link' to brigade headquarters, worked by highly professional Royal Signals operators. Patrols were confined to the roads because of the deep, wet snow. Attempts to train suitable officers and guardsmen as skiers were not very successful and Norwegian volunteers were used where possible.

On 22 April orders were received for an assault on the port of Narvik. This was to be mounted on 24 April (which several officers remembered as the anniversary of Gallipoli). The attack would be preceded by a bombardment by *Warspite** and as many other warships as could be mustered. Lord Cork had stressed the importance of this heavy bombardment, which was designed to break the morale of the 'already demoralized' enemy garrison. General Mackesy was not over-impressed by this and when the two leaders met on 18 April he emphasized that no attack would be made if the bombardment was not completely effective.

On 19 April Mackesy went on a reconnaissance of the approaches to Narvik aboard the *Aurora*. He took with him the commanders of the assault troops and found the area 'quiet and without movement'. On return he signalled General Ironside, the CIGS, repeating his belief that a naval bombardment could not be militarily effective. He defined a successful bombardment as 'one which induced the enemy to surrender before the troops landed', and expressed unease about the safety of Norwegian civilians in Narvik.†

Meanwhile Colonel Faulkner had issued his own orders. The plan was to take the town from the north, where there was a small harbour called Vasvik. The only maps available were rather poor reproductions of a Norwegian survey of 1906. The hatching was blurred and indistinct, and many low-lying areas had since been built upon. On 23 April the CO and his unit commanders made a close-in reconnaissance of the landing area from the destroyer *Beduin*. They got a perfect view of their line of approach and felt much happier as they returned to Liland. They disembarked in heavy snow which developed into a full-scale blizzard. The assault was called off.

The Irish Guards were literally snowed-in as the blizzard added to the already thick snow. On 24 April HMS *Warspite*, with three cruisers and eight destroyers, bombarded for three hours anything looking remotely like a military target. The Mayor of Narvik, Theodor Broch, later reported that a German sentry post near Vasvik had been destroyed and that the enemy corpses lay unburied for several days.

* The author, crouching in the snow on the mainland, vividly remembers the rushing sound of the huge shells from the *Warspite* passing over his head like the noise of an express train going through a tunnel.

† On this day, 19 April, the War Office changed the codename of Mackesy's command from Avonforce to Rupertforce.

But the results of the bombardment disappointed Lord Cork, who had assumed overall command of the expedition on 21 April by order of the War Council. The Admiral reported that the 'tempestuous weather' and low visibility prevented any realistic estimate of damage to the enemy. A landing in the immediate future was out of the question. There was nothing to indicate any intention of a German surrender although Norwegian observers claimed that enemy casualties had been high.

The 27th Demi-Brigade of the Chasseurs Alpins (6th, 12th and 14th Battalions) had been held in reserve for the force at Namsos. They were now commanded by Lieutenant-Colonel Valentini, who had taken over from General Béthouart, and arrived at Narvik on 28 April. The 12th Bn was sent down to Bogen to take over from the Irish Guards. This French battalion was to advance against the Germans at Bjerkvik, while the 6th Battalion was taken by puffer to Gratangen prior to attacking the enemy at Labergdal. The 14th Battalion, for the moment, remained in reserve.

An officer of the rear party of the Irish Guards at Bogen recalls the arrival of the 12th Bn Chasseurs Alpins:

> A large Seine barge, very low in the water, came slowly to the shore. A short, fat man, wearing a huge beret, jumped ashore. He explained that he was the Quartermaster of the Chasseurs, and had brought the advance party and essential stores. The Frenchmen than began to roll ashore many barrels of wine.

Apart from patrolling the road from Liland towards Bjerkvik the Irish Guards used puffers to probe areas further afield. The Intelligence Officer (Captain Gordon-Watson) took a party across the widest part of Ofotfiord to Ballangen where HMS *Hardy* was beached. In a small hospital they found some of the *Hardy*'s sailors who were being cared for by the local people. There was no sign of the enemy. Gordon-Watson took the sailors back to Liland from where they were evacuated to the base at Harstad.

The advance headquarters of 24th Guards Brigade moved from Skaanland to Bogen as No 2 Company of the Irish Guards prepared to move out. Early in the morning a German ski patrol entered the village and an exchange of shots occurred. Despite a follow-up by the French, there were no casualties on either side. These appear to have been the first shots fired at close quarters by the Germans against the Allies in the Narvik area. For the next two weeks the Irish Guards patrolled the few roads to the north of Narvik while the Chasseurs moved eastward into the German-held area around Bjerkvik at the landward end of Herjangsfiord.

Bored by inactivity, lack of mail and the absence of beer, the Guardsmen's disappointment at not being selected to attack Bjerkvik was modified by the realization that the Chasseurs were better able to fight in snow than they were. But even the redoubtable French mountain fighters found the going in the mountains too much for them:

> On 2 May General Béthouart, in command of the French and Polish forces around Narvik, had visited Harstad to report to Mackesy that the Chasseurs Alpins could do little in the deep snow of the mountains. Recognizing the folly of pressing the attack where only the Germans and Norwegians were qualified to fight, he was more resolute than the British in facing the alternative of an opposed landing. General Fleischer (commander of the Norwegian Sixth Division), had earlier suggested a landing at Öyjord, but Mackesy hoped to reach Bjerkvik by an overland advance beside the fiord. Now at last it was agreed that the French should land at Bjerkvik from the sea.*

In the meantime command of 24th Guards Brigade had changed. Brigadier Fraser, wounded when visiting the South Wales Borderers during a German attack on the Ankenes peninsula, had been evacuated to Harstad. The new brigade commander was Lieutenant-Colonel T. B. Trappes-Lomax, CO of the Scots Guards, being the senior battalion commander in the field.

Then came the depressing news that the Allied forces at Namsos and Aandalsnes had been evacuated on the second and third of May. This left the Luftwaffe free to step up their operations in the Narvik area with some success. The Polish destroyer, *Grom*, was sunk on 4 May and most of her crew were lost. An intensive run of enemy air raids caused the Irish Guards to pay more attention to dispersion and concealment. When land targets became unprofitable the Luftwaffe concentrated on the British warships in the fiords. HMS *Aurora* was caught in the narrow neck of an inlet with no room to turn. A bomb from one of the Heinkel 111's landed squarely on a gun turret, causing casualties. *Aurora* pulled out to sea to bury her dead and patch up the damage.

Colonel Faulkner's battalion was now dispersed around the Ofotfiord. Battalion HQ, numbers 2 and 4 Companies, were at Liland, with a detached platoon at Evenes. Number 3 Company was at Lenvik while number 1 Company had been sent around to Skjomnes, near Ankenes, in reserve for the South Wales Borderers, who were pushing northwards towards Narvik. But the failure of the Allied pincer movement on Trondheim had freed the main enemy forces. News that the Germans were moving rapidly towards Mosjöen, north of Namsos, called for an urgent regrouping of Allied troops. One company of the Scots Guards was already at Bodö, guarding the airfield. Lord Cork received permission to move 24th Guards Brigade to the Bodö area. At the same time the command of the Allied Land and Air Forces changed. Lieutenant-General C. J. E. Auchinleck replaced General Mackesy at 1830 hours on 13 May.

* Moulton, p. 223.

Shortly after the Irish Guards moved to Bogen, the 2nd Bn South Wales Borderers (2/SWB) was landed on the mainland at Skaanland. This small village was situated opposite Hinnöy across one of the narrowest parts of Vaagsfiord, about twenty miles from Narvik. The battalion quickly found comfortable billets in the large barns scattered around the village. As usual, the hospitable local people helped in any way they could, willingly providing milk and fresh vegetables for sterling as well as the Norwegian currency the soldiers now received as pay.

Shortly after arrival 2/Lieutenant John Morgan-Owen was sent for by 'B' Company commander (Major Garnons-Williams) and detailed to carry out the battalion's first operational task on the mainland:

> The locals reported seeing a German plane drop a bomb on a hilltop a few miles outside the village. Apparently there was no explosion and rumour now had it that this was a 'gas bomb'. I was detailed to take my platoon, scale the mountain and bring back a sample of whatever debris we could find on the top.
>
> A requisitioned truck took us as near to the foot of the hill as possible, passing several Norwegian children who were ski-ing nearby. Being young and keen, I gave the orders for a tactical advance up the mountain: a scout in front, then the point section, followed by the main body. The rearguard must pay attention to my field signals, I said. Within a few hundred yards the thick wet snow modified my intentions. We floundered upwards, clad in our fur hats and thick, full-length tropal coats, rifles slung around our necks to leave both hands free.
>
> The young Norwegian skiers had caught us up and watched these ineffectual military antics with some amusement. Speaking English, they discovered our intentions and long before we were half-way up they had climbed the hill and skied back. They reported that there was a mound of fresh earth up there and little else.
>
> Totally exhausted, with half my platoon straggling behind me down the hill, I reached the summit. We had no information about the whereabouts of the Germans. After gathering a sample of the yellow earth in my runner's messtin I gave the orders for the descent. Each man was to keep his rifle handy and his eyes skinned as he made his individual way to the bottom. The platoon Sergeant with a section of men would form the rearguard. We came down quite quickly, dodging the scrubby trees and rocky outcrops. Some of the soldiers tucked their long coats under them and slid down on their backsides. I reported to Company HQ with my few clods of earth. We heard nothing more about the incident.*

The soldiers and their officers quickly learned the basic rules for operating in snow. The ever-present, low-flying German scout aircraft fired at any promising military target. Strict track-discipline was enforced along paths already made by the villagers. Virgin snow was left untrodden and the local pattern of movement scrupulously observed.

* Major J. G. Morgan-Owen, CB, MBE, QC, in a letter to the author, 6 June 1987.

Little could be done about managing the mound of special clothing which, while necessary in severe weather and bitterly cold nights, impeded movement through the enveloping snow. Each man had, in addition to his usual kit, 8 pairs of socks, one pair each of rubber boots and special arctic shoes, 3 pairs of gloves, 2 thick sweaters and the same number of leather jerkins. This was topped by a fur hat and the whole was covered by a full-length, lambskin-lined, tropal coat. Apart from the double kapok sleeping bag these items filled two kitbags and weighed about forty pounds. Unfortunately, the kitbags had not yet been issued.

Lieutenant-Colonel P. Gottwaltz, CO of 2/SWB, briefed his company commanders on the battalion's role in General Mackesy's plan for the assault on Narvik. If the Irish Guards succeeded in forming a bridgehead on 24 April the South Wales Borderers would 'advance through them, and mop up the town under cover of the naval bombardment'. But the blizzard swept down through Vaagsfiord and troop movement became impossible. As we have seen, the assault on Narvik was called off.*

2/SWB moved across Ofotfiord to the small sulphur-mining settlement of Ballangen. They arrived at 4 a.m. in a fleet of puffers and the CO set off at once on a sea-borne reconnaissance of the Ankenes area. The soldiers took advantage of the Sulphur Company's showers to have a much-needed bath, while Colonel Gottwaltz reported to Brigade HQ. He was ordered to move immediately to the vicinity of Haakvik, on the edge of the Ankenes peninsula.

The leading company, travelling in puffers, landed at a small jetty at Skjomnes, about four miles from Ankenes village. The rest of the battalion travelled in naval vessels and were rowed ashore in open boats by sailors on 29 April.

> Most of us got ashore dry-shod as the beach sloped gently down to the water. We staggered through the thick slush towards the small wooden houses on the landward side of the narrow road. We were weighed down with signal stores, lamps, field telephones and heavy drums of cable. Our rifles, loaded with safety catches on, were suspended by their slings across the top of the pile. My orders were that German patrols had been spotted in the hills behind Haakvik but the latest reports indicated that the place was unoccupied. We should keep a keen lookout. There were no civilians in sight.
>
> We fanned out as we approached the nearest house and I sent two men to cover the rear entrance. I went up to the front door and knocked. A young girl of about fourteen came to the door. She put her hand to her mouth and retreated into the dim room. I followed her in, smiling and chatting in English, rifle crooked across my arm with the safety catch off. An old man was dozing next to a huge stove; he didn't look up. There were two elderly women in

* Despite the deep snow the Germans flew a Nazi flag from the top of Fagernes mountain. The gunners of HMS *Aurora* removed this flag with one shell on 1 May.

the back room, looking apprehensively through the door.

I saw steam rising from an iron kettle on the stove: 'Tea?' I asked, pointing to the kettle. The girl's face brightened and, reaching for a teapot, she started to make a brew. Four of my soldiers were inside now, smiling and offering Army-issue chocolate as they babbled reassuringly away in their strong Welsh accents. 'Tiske?' I questioned the girl, 'Are there any Germans?' 'No Germans,' she said in English. 'Are you from England?' The two women came smiling into the room, bringing cups and saucers. I posted a sentry outside the house, set up a signal lamp and made contact with our destroyer out in the fiord. (Author)

The battalion's front extended some five miles along the mountains lining Ofotfiord to the south-west. The CO gave orders to picket these strategic heights, some of which overlooked the town of Narvik. The obvious difficulties of supplying the soldiers with ammunition and food were quickly put in perspective when one of the company commanders said, 'Look, if the Germans can do it, so can the Welsh'.

The Signals Officer, Lieutenant Peter Martin, realizing that there would not be enough line to link up all outposts, used every possible means of communication. The carrying parties organized to take regular supplies of hot food and stores up to platoon positions brought back with them information about enemy movements.

The 12th Battalion of the Chasseurs Alpins had arrived and were allocated to the almost impassable high ground overlooking Narvik across Beisfiord. A field telephone link was set up and a working arrangement between the two battalions. The Chasseurs' specialist ski patrols began to probe towards Lake Storvatn where the enemy had been located. Morale rose when a detachment of 203 Field Battery, Royal Artillery, arrived with two 25-pounder guns.

In the very early hours of 30 April Captain Campbell-Miles, the Adjutant of 2/SWB, was awakened by a commotion outside his billet. Shots rang out and an agitated sentry reported that a German ski patrol had come down from the hills and called a halt just outside the Adjutant's quarters. As soon as he recognized them he opened fire but they disappeared into the gloom without loss, leaving their skis.

Colonel Gottwaltz had pushed 'D' Company, under Captain Charles Cox, along the coastal track to provide cover for the left flank. The intention was to prevent the Germans from occupying the Ankenes peninsula. The enemy controlled the Narvik ferries and had easy access to the nearest southern shore of Beisfiord, known as Ankenesstranden. With this in mind the 2/SWB occupied Baatberget, about a mile and a half from Ankenes village.

Captain Cox ranged his company along a ridge just short of Emmenes Point. The seaward edge of Narvik could be seen but Ankenes itself was out of sight. The Germans had observed this landing at Haakvik and brought forward mortars and an 'unidentified' gun* to shell 'D' Company's platoon positions. Brigadier Fraser came forward on a reconnaisance and was caught in the open by the mortar barrage. He was hit in the throat by a splinter of shrapnel.

> When the enemy mortars opened up I was told to get a line to 'D' Company from battalion HQ as quickly as possible. I took four of my best men and started down the coastal track as fast as the slush would allow. We had no time to take cover and the little fountains of snow thrown up as the mortar bombs exploded made us quicken our pace.
>
> As we approached a small cluster of buildings I saw three men in uniform on the edge of the fiord. One had the red tabs of a brigadier. He was sitting on the ground and his chest was covered in blood. There was a field dressing around his throat and it was quite obvious what had happened. I stopped to help, sending three men ahead with the drums of cable and keeping the other man, with a signal lamp, with me.
>
> We signalled to a destroyer out in the fiord and within a short time a boat rowed towards us. We balanced the Brigadier on a large piece of driftwood, an old door, I think, and floated him to the boat. The sailors lifted him aboard and the other two men followed. As they rowed away I was left up to my knees in the Arctic sea. I could do nothing about my sodden clothes and as I ran along the track toward 'D' Company the water squelched out of my oversized boots.
>
> It was some time before we could get back to battalion HQ. We took with us one of the German prisoners captured by 'D' Company. He was the first enemy we had seen, a big country lad from Austria. His initial shock had subsided and everyone was quite matey, handing him cigarettes and trying to get him to understand English. The Luftwaffe had arrived by now and when we were forced to take cover in a culvert the prisoner pointed proudly upwards and said, 'Heinkel! Heinkel!' But there was no ill-feeling, we were all young soldiers and not yet used to modern war. (Author)

At about 1500 hours on 30 April, when the enemy fire intensified, 18 platoon, which was forward of the ridge in open ground, suffered casualties. The platoon commander, 2nd Lieutenant R. C. Holt, the platoon sergeant and another soldier were wounded. PSM R.F. Richards calmly led the platoon back to cover then returned under heavy fire to the wounded men. He dressed their wounds and carried them one by one back to safety. (PSM Richards was later awarded the Distinguished Conduct Medal for this action.)

Further research in Norway† indicates that the attack on the forward positions of 2/SWB was organized by Major Hausells, the 'Town Major'

*This gun was probably one of the half-battery of mountain guns operating with Group Hausells in the mountains above the Ankenesstranden (See Appendix A).

† Taken from German 'Day books' (War diaries) translated by the Director of the Narvik War Museum (Nils Ryeng) for the author, 30 May 1987.

(Ortskommandant) of Narvik, using Number Seven Company of 139th Mountain Regiment. Hausells knew of the Allied probe towards Ankenes and may have mistakenly believed that the withdrawal of 18 Platoon signalled the evacuation of 'D' Company's positions.

On 1 May 2/Lieutenant R. Davies was leading a reconnaissance patrol towards Ankenes when he ran into a strong column of Germans advancing towards Baatberget. He was able to get away without loss. Two hours later a 'considerable number' of the enemy advanced down the coast road towards 'D' Company's positions.

Captain Cox opened fire with every available weapon and the German column, dropping boxes of rations and pots and pans, made for the sparse cover of the hillside, some taking shelter in a barn and other buildings. From there they fired down on 'D' Company's positions, killing three soldiers and wounding others. At this point the Navy intervened:

> About this time, while my attention was directed to the right, our 'attached destroyer' (joined by the cruiser *Aurora*), having heard the firing, moved forward from her usual position off Emmenes and signalled 'Have all your patrols returned?'
>
> Cursing the Navy for worrying me in the middle of a battle with what I thought was a routine signal, I replied in the affirmative, whereupon the destroyer proceeded to within a few yards of the shore and opened up with everything she possessed (as did the *Aurora* from further out).
>
> It was just light enough (at 0300 hours) to see the main German attack coming in on the left flank. Fortunately the left forward platoon was well equal to the situation, but had it not been for the Navy's vigilance and timely assistance, both material and morale, we might well have been hard-pressed. In the middle of the firefight which followed the destroyer signalled, 'Got your friends in the bag'. She certainly had.
>
> As it became lighter it was an amazing sight to see a ship firing 4-inch shells at single Germans from point-blank range, and at the barns in which they had taken shelter. One shell went through the front of a big barn and out at the back; at the same time the roof rose in the air and descended again, apparently in the proper place, the walls remaining upright.
>
> A significant feature of the action was that among the enemy dead, wounded and prisoners, not a single officer or NCO was found ... when collecting the enemy wounded the Hun, true to type, shelled us as the stretchers were being put into a lorry. One German, apparently lifeless on a stretcher after twenty-four hours in the snow, jumped up and ran as hard as he could for our lines.*

Later, interrogated prisoners put the strength of the attackers at about one hundred, a fairly strong company. They confirmed that there had been heavy casualties among the Germans. From the amount of stores left behind by the fleeing enemy it was apparent that they intended to set up a company base. They were armed with mortars, machine guns and the

* Captain (now Brigadier) C. F. Cox, in an article for *The Journal of the South Wales Borderers* (1941).

usual small arms, and carried wireless sets and kitchen equipment as well as substantial stocks of food.

The following day, 2 May, at about 0900 hours, a single enemy aircraft flew over battalion HQ and accurately dropped about fourteen small, high-explosive bombs. They burst among the South Wales Borderers' billets, including the officers' mess, wounding the mess cook. Three soldiers of Headquarter Company were killed and three wounded. The other casualties were the rear-link wireless operators of the Royal Corps of Signals, one of whom was killed and the other wounded, later to die in hospital. The bombs also killed an old Norwegian woman sheltering in a nearby barn. This death seemed to shock the soldiers more than the loss of their comrades.

The Chasseurs operating on the right flank of 2/SWB gradually edged their way through the rugged terrain towards Narvik, leaving the Welshmen to man outposts over an extended front which stretched endurance to the limit.

But there was a strong leavening of reservists among the young 'militiamen' in the ranks. Many of these reservists were NCOs, and most had served on the Indian Frontier or in Palestine. They passed on their campaigning expertise and provided a pool of practical knowledge which was invaluable to the young officers and less experienced soldiers in the battalion.

In early May the 1st and 2nd Battalions of 13th Demi-Brigade of the Foreign Legion and four battalions of the 1st and 2nd Demi-Brigades of the Poles arrived in the Narvik area. A few days later (6 May) the first consignment of anti-aircraft artillery arrived, eight 3.7 inch guns.

When the South Wales Borderers moved up to Haakvik a 'Reserve Company' had been left at Ballangen to hold the first-line reinforcements and the back-up stores. Rations came to them across Ofotfiord from Skaanland, where the Royal Army Service Corps, under Major Miller, had set up a Supply Depot on a snow-covered swamp. The regular puffer service distributing supplies was disrupted and the reserve company, cut off from the base, was forced to use up its emergency rations to survive. A slaughtered sheep, vegetables and milk were purchased from a local farmer. This helped them out as they sent urgent messages back to the base.

Two days later a puffer arrived with the rations and Captain John Posser, the Quartermaster, who arranged for the company to draw its supplies independently by boat. When the CQMS submitted his indent he discovered that twice the normal amount would be issued because Captain Prosser's indent had also been included. The error was reported but the RASC clerk insisted that the figures should stand.

When CQMS Tom Flower returned with the double rations everyone expected extra food to make up for the enforced fast. But this did not happen.

That day I received a message saying that one of the Independent Companies [lately transferred from the Mosjöen area] would be arriving by boat. Could I feed them and fix them up with haversack rations? They were met, fed and sent off with thick corned-beef sandwiches. It was a very friendly parting.

The double rations continued to come through and were stockpiled against a future emergency. Just before the snow began to clear a company of the Foreign Legion arrived unannounced. Their reputation as good fighters was not in doubt, but to me they looked a scruffy and ill-disciplined lot. Many of them were Spaniards but there were two Englishmen among them. These made for the kitchen pleading for tea, bacon and eggs, anything after the thin soup and bread they had subsisted on.

The French Warrant Officer (the Adjutant) was very snooty when I pointed out the latrines and asked if his men could, please, use them instead of fouling up our camp. We thought of doing a deal with them, our rations for their wine, until we tasted it; it was like vinegar.

CQMS Flower goes on to write about the arrival of the bodies of the soldiers killed during the South Wales Borderers' operations on the Ankenes peninsula:

Six of our dead arrived and some German bodies, which were buried separately. I contacted the local Pastor and he agreed to provide coffins and a suitable burial ground. I detailed fatigue parties to work in relays because the snow was very deep. We buried them in a communal grave about three feet deep in the frozen ground, which was all we could manage.

I personally laid them in their coffins because some of them were friends of mine. When I came to John Briggs I saw that his sensitive hands had been blasted where he had held the Bren gun up on its tripod to fire against the enemy plane. I must confess that I wept because he was such a talented pianist. The Pastor said the prayers and we laid them to rest. I got wooden crosses made for each one with number, rank and name, and drew a good representation of the regimental badge on them. They are still there, I believe.*

The Foreign Legion detachment accommodated by CQMS Flower came from the 1st Battalion who, with the 2nd Battalion, had arrived with 13th Demi-Brigade at Harstad on 6 May. They left Ballangen almost immediately to take part in the fighting at Bjerkvik. Their place was taken by units of the Polish Highland Brigade, commanded by Brigadier-General Z. Bohusz-Szyszko, who had landed three days later.

This brigade originated around Podhale, a mountainous region in south Poland. Not all of them were mountaineers but they were united by hatred of the Germans and a burning ambition to set their country free. They

* Ex-CQMS Tom Flower in a letter to the author, who visited the graves at Ballangen in May, 1987. The bodies had been moved to the village cemetery and the graves are well tended, each with a traditional headstone. The grave of Captain Warburton-Lee VC is nearby.

were organized in two Demi-Brigades, two battalions in each. In common with other formations in the expedition they were under-equipped, especially in heavy weapons. Due to faulty loading at Brest, they had ammunition supply problems and their thirty-eight fully laden trucks had been left behind in France.

The Polish 2nd Battalion had been sent to reinforce the French forces investing Bjerkvik. They arrived on the morning of 13 May, after a gruelling fifteen-mile march through rough country to find that the battle was already over. Bottling up their impatience and disappointment, the Poles regrouped at Bjerkvik and embarked on 15 May to relieve 2/SWB in the Ankenes area.

The South Wales Borderers had received orders to proceed to Harstad and embark in HMS *Effingham* for the 160-mile trip to Bodö. The handover went off smoothly.* The Welshmen left behind most of their food stocks and their artillery back-up before leaving by sea for the Lofotens. Their first operation had cost them six dead and seventeen wounded.

During these happenings the Norwegians had issued the two companies of Scots Guards at Sjövegan with snowshoes and white camouflage cloaks. The Scotsmen moved up to Fossbakken on the Bjerkvik–Bardufoss road as a defensive reserve for General Fleischer's forces. It was understood that they would hold a rear position during the Norwegians' attack but, because of their obvious limitations in deep snow, would not be expected to take part in the assault.

The severe blizzard which had halted the planned assault on Narvik covered the area around Gratangen with an additional two feet of snow. On 23 April the 1st/16th and 2nd/15th Norwegian battalions attacked the Germans at Lapphaug, supported by twelve 75-mm guns.

The 1st/12th, backed by a mountain battery, advanced across country down the Fjordbotneiddal to converge on Gratangen from the north. They were caught in the blizzard, became isolated and disorientated, and were overwhelmed by a strong German counter-attack. The survivors managed to withdraw to Lavangen. Out of a strength of 648 the 1st/12th lost thirty-four killed, sixty-four wounded and 180 missing. Of their company commanders, two were killed, two wounded (one of whom died), and one became snowblind.†

* One 'lubricant' of the exceptionally good relationship between the Welshmen and their Polish allies took the form of a Polish Medical Warrant Officer, who circulated with a large waterbottle filled with several pints of rum. This he distributed with great generosity, raising considerably the morale of the Borderers. John Morgan-Owen relates that after one 'medical' session the Pole confided: 'I have tried the Norwegian girls, drunk and sober, but I had no luck. This is because they have ice in their loins.'
† Moulton, quoting *Krigen i Norge – Nord-Norge* Vol. 1, p. 222.

On 25 April the Norwegians doggedly resumed the attack. Supported by one of their patrol vessels, which shelled the German positions at Gratangen, they forced the enemy to abandon the Lapphaug–Gratangen road and to withdraw towards Bjerkvik. General Fleischer had lost one of his most efficient battalions and now reorganized his division into two brigades (the 6th and 7th), before resuming the advance towards Bjerkvik on 1 May.

On the same date the two Scots Guards companies left the Norwegian 6th Division and rejoined their 1st Battalion. Their CO, Major Graham, assumed command vice Lieutenant-Colonel Trappes-Lomax, who was now the acting Brigadier of 24th Guards Brigade. After being briefed and de-briefed for a tentative plan to attack Narvik on 8 May, the battalion worked on an extension to the small airfield at Skaanland. News of the German advance toward Mosjöen changed the Allies' strategic pattern and on 11 May the 1st Scots Guards embarked in HMS *Enterprise* for Mo, some sixty miles south of Bodö. (On the same day Hitler launched his blitzkrieg against Holland and Belgium).

Sailing in the same convoy were the destroyer *Hesperus*, the sloop *Fleetwood* and a small merchantman named *Margot*. They carried a troop of four 25-pounder guns from 203 Field Battery, three Bofors guns of 55 Light Anti-Aircraft Battery and a detachment of 230 Field Company, Royal Engineers. The Scots Guards' orders stipulated that they were to hold Mo 'at all costs' in the face of General Feuerstein's fresh Mountain Division, now advancing rapidly from Grong.

'Three old river boats and a flat-bottomed barge' brought the Irish Guards back to Harstad from Liland. They embarked for Bodö on the MV *Chobry*, a well-appointd modern Polish ship, on 14 May. The Luftwaffe was active over Vaagsfiord but dropped no bombs near them as they left harbour. The officers turned in amidships and everyone prepared to get some sleep before landing on a possibly hostile shore. A laconic entry in the Irish Guards' War Diary records unemotionally the events of the night of 14/15 May:

> 0015, 15 May. HMT *Chobry* bombed and set on fire. Ship abandoned.
> 0930, arrival of *Stork* and *Wolverine* at Harstad.

Behind that bald entry lies a story of calm courage in the finest traditions of the Guards. But a hint of mystery still surrounds the identity of the aircraft which carried out the attack. *The History of the Irish Guards* (p 42) states: 'At midnight three Heinkels bombed the ship.' The official history by Dr Derry leaves things open by saying that the *Chobry* was attacked from the air as she left the seaward extremity of the Lofoten Islands. General Moulton's version says: 'she [the *Chobry*] was attacked by German aircraft.' This implies that more than one plane was present.

But several eye-witnesses have categorically stated that one plane only carried out the attack. Some of them were sure that the aeroplane carried no identification signs.

In May, 1987, the author, on a visit to northern Norway, talked to Nils Ryeng, the Director of the Narvik War Museum. Ryeng was well aware of the conflicting stories about the *Chobry*. He said that the German pilot who actually carried out the bombing had visited the War Museum. Ryeng made a note of the pilot's explanation:

> Although it was still light there was a sea mist and I came down low to fly over the ship. I went around a second time and bombed the ship. Then I flew over it a third time to verify the damage.

The pilot confirmed that there were no other aircraft in the immediate area. When Ryeng questioned him about the story of an unmarked plane, the pilot said emphatically that his aircraft carried the usual Luftwaffe markings. Perhaps layers of ice had obscured the signs, or the angle of the aircraft had deceived the sea-level observers.

The bombs fell amidship and killed the Commanding Officer and most of the senior officers. One of the survivors gives a graphic account of the impact of the bombs:

> There was an explosion, and I jumped out of my bed and went to the door of the cabin. There must have been a second explosion because I was lifted off the floor with the door in my hand. I was blown right past the bathroom, across the cabin, and hit my head on the side of the ship. There were cries and yells and smoke and fire but somehow Basil Eugster and I managed to crawl through the broken glass and debris up on to the deck . . .
>
> We launched a lifeboat, very clumsily I think, and it soon filled to capacity. We managed to get Major Gilbart-Denham, who was very badly wounded, aboard (he died in hospital later). We pulled alongside the *Stork* and got aboard.*

Meanwhile the survivors were struggling up on to the deck of the *Chobry*. RSM Stack's voice could be heard above the uproar, bellowing, 'Get on parade – face this way!' At the same time, mingling with the RSM's stentorian shout, the voice of the Irish Guards' padre could be heard clearly reciting the Rosary. It was taken up by many of the Guardsmen as they came up on deck. Two Drill Sergeants formed the Guardsmen up in orderly ranks. The roll was called. Only four men were reporting missing. Guardsman 'Mushy' Callahan of No. 3 Company suspected that they were

* Brigadier Michael Gordon-Watson, OBE MC, in an interview with the author, 20 November, 1986.

trapped by fire in the hold. He threw a rope over the ship's side and swung himself from porthole to porthole until he discovered them and hauled them one by one on to the deck. The destroyer *Wolverine*, and the sloop *Stork* came alongside and the Guards remained steady until an improvised gangway was rigged. The naval officer supervising the re-embarkation, Commander R. H. Craske RN, wrote:

> Not a man moved until I gave the order .... When they did move they did so at a deliberate walk, refusing to part with their weapons. It was naturally not possible to single out any one particularly, but I did notice the very admirable conduct of the Roman Catholic Chaplain. (Father Vincent Cavanagh, Order of St Benedict)

This superb discipline held good when the Irish Guards arrived back at Harstad. Many of the survivors were dressed in boilersuits and seamen's greatcoats given by the sailors. A few were clad in a single blanket. The wounded were taken off to hospital at once. Drill Sergeant Peilow, one of the first ashore, found a suitable area to serve as a parade ground. Markers were put out and those who could parade fell in with their weapons. Normal routine was resumed.

Captain Gordon-Watson found himself the senior officer among the survivors. He went ashore dressed in silk pyjamas, a pullover, and slippers donated by the captain of the *Stork*. He was met by General Auchinleck, who told him to assume temporary command of the battalion, and began at once to re-equip his new command and to allocate jobs to those fit to undertake them.

Casualties were remarkably light, but apart from the small arms carried off the ship by the men everything had been lost. The three tanks belonging to a troop of 3rd Hussars, the only British tanks in Norway, went down with the ship. Despite these setbacks the Irish Guards declared themselves to be ready for operations within forty-eight hours.

The 2nd South Wales Borderers left Harstad for Bodö in the cruiser *Effingham* at 0400 hours 17 May. Speed was of the essence and the warship was pushed to its limits as it navigated the Vestfiord. To avoid attack by enemy aircraft the Captain veered away from the usual route and struck an outcrop of the Faksen shoal while doing twenty-three knots.

> I think that it was about 8 p.m. I distinctly remember that Gracie Fields was singing on the ship's intercom. There was a tremendous crunch and the ship tilted to port at an alarming angle before coming back on to even keel. For a moment, except for the hissing of steam, there was almost complete silence, then naval officers began calmly issuing instructions. This cue was quickly

followed by the officers and NCOs of the South Wales Borderers and company groups soon began to form up on the decks.

The destroyer escort had reacted immediately and the destroyer *Echo** came alongside as the *Effingham* rapidly settled lower into the water. By the time ropes had been attached it was possible to step from the high deck of the cruiser on to the well-deck of the *Echo*. Bottlenecks occurred at the places where it was convenient to get on to the destroyer and queues began to form. Naval officers on the *Echo* wanted to get the troops aboard quickly so that they could cast off before the *Effingham* sank. Some obstruction was caused by Bren-gunners slinging their weapons across their shoulders. Soldiers were hanging on to rifles with one hand and attempting to clamber down ropes with the other.

I heard a naval commander shouting, 'Dump those weapons, there's no time to lose, get aboard, get aboard!' Next to me a South Wales Borderer Warrant Officer snarled, 'Hang on to those bloody rifles!' As the War Diary records, very few small arms were left behind. (Author)

The incident happened only twelve miles or so from Bodö, but it was necessary to take the troops back to Harstad base to replace lost equipment. The *Echo* transferred the South Wales Borderers to the cruiser *Coventry* and went back to the stricken *Effingham* to take off her crew. There was no panic. The soldiers formed up as if on parade. There were no casualties although one man, Private Kimberley, fell into the sea. Some accounts say that he went in twice. The author has no recollection of this but remembers that, apart from a slight cold, Kimberley was unaffected by the freezing plunge. The ribald remarks of his drier comrades can be imagined.

Within hours of boarding the *Coventry* a strong rumour spread throughout the ship that a Norwegian was at the helm when the ship struck the reef. It was alleged that he was a follower of Quisling and that the sinking of the *Effingham* was a deliberate, traitorous act. One version of the story was emphatic that the Captain of the *Effingham* executed the 'traitor' on the bridge by shooting him in the head. This rumour, like many others of its kind, seems completely without foundation.

Coming so soon after the *Chobry* disaster, this further weakened the fighting capacity of 24th Guards Brigade. Apart from what could be carried by the soldiers, everything went down with the ship. The field ambulance equipment and vehicles, ammunition and other vital stores were missing. The biggest loss of all were the ten Bren-gun carriers of 2/SWB. These had been unusable at Ankenes but were desperately needed in the Bodö area.†

On arrival at Harstad the Borderers found that the authorities had not

* Captain S. K. Spurgeon, RAN, the captain of the *Echo*, travelled from Australia to a reunion with old comrades of the South Wales Borderers at Brecon in 1980.

† Four of these carriers were later salvaged by the Navy and subsequently used against the Germans in the Mo area and also at Bodö. The *Effingham* was sunk later by the Royal Navy. (*London Gazette* Supplement, 10 July 1947, p. 3174).

recovered from the unexpected return of the Irish Guards. When the CO went ashore to enquire about breakfast for the battalion he found no arrangements for reception had been made. The Irish Guards rallied around and provided a meal for the troops. A fleet of civilian vehicles took the battalion to Borkenes, about twelve miles from Harstad, on the west coast of Hinnöy.

A frantic search for arms, ammunition, signal and mortar equipment began at once. The Quartermaster scoured the island for razors as the personal kits of the soldiers had been left below decks and lost. The Signals Sergeant persuaded a Royal Marine detachment to part with several large drums of cable. These weighed sixty pounds each, and caused communication problems later in the mountains south of Bodö. The reorganization began on the day of return (18 May) and by 1100 hours on 19 May two companies ('B' and 'C') were re-equipped and despatched to Bodö by destroyer that night. But essential stores were in short supply and it took three days to equip the remainder of the battalion, who boarded a fleet of puffers for the trip:

> It was late evening when we clambered into the hold of the puffer. The skipper had just come in from a fishing trip and the hold was awash with bilge water over a carpet of mangled fish. Because of the dangers posed by low-flying German aircraft the crew battened down the hatches and we were left in the gloom surrounded by stinking fish. Amazingly, morale was high.
>
> Haversack rations had been issued and were, as usual, soon disposed of. When beams of early sunlight penetrated the hold twelve hours later someone pounded on the hatchway and asked if there was any breakfast. A crewman shouted down that we could share their rations and this was received with some satisfaction. A shallow dish was lowered into the hold. It was full of raw fish. Suddenly no one wanted breakfast. (Author)

Prior to the forced evacuation of Namsos and Aandalsnes on 2/3 May, Lord Cork had shown little anxiety about the Bodö–Mo–Mosjöen area, but on 4 May he signalled the Admiralty, asking them to define policy and responsibility in that area:

> Request I may be informed of the general policy regarding Bodö, Mo and Mosjöen. It seems most important to hold in force the Mo road leading north. From Admiralty messages it appears the forces being sent are hardly adequate for this purpose and with such weak detachments in the air another naval commitment comes into being. These areas do not, I presume, come under Narvik. Are there any Allied forces to the south of me?*

The Admiralty replied that large forces could not be maintained in the face of overwhelming enemy air superiority. Apart from the shortage of

* *London Gazette* Supplement, 10 July 1947, p. 3173.

Allied aircraft, Bodö airfield was not suitable as an advanced fighter base. It was concluded that small parties only would be maintained at Mo and Mosjöen with the object of obstructing the enemy advance, and to prevent landing by sea and air.

It seems that no serious attempt had been made to garrison that area since the German invasion of 9 April. The Norwegian battalion at Mosjöen was sent south to Grong but was moved back in early May. However, a company of Chasseurs Alpins, one hundred strong, with two British light anti-aircraft guns was sent to Mosjöen by destroyer from the Namsos area on 30 April. They remained there until relieved by the British 4th and 5th Independent Companies on 8 May.

The Independent Companies have been called 'the forerunners of the Commandos'. The word Commando is defined as 'An elite, highly-trained, specialized force of mobile guerrilla fighters'. The Independent Companies were not of that ilk. The original ten companies were formed in April from a wide spread of Territorial units. They were specially selected volunteers but, as Dr Derry points out (p. 63), 'had had even less chance to train together and "shake down" than other units'. Only five of the companies reached Norway, where they rapidly learned from experience. Each company had up to twenty officers and about 270 other ranks.

The force was planned to operate loosely on a brigade basis and was code named Scissorsforce. Lieutenant-Colonel C. McV. (later Major-General Sir Colin) Gubbins, was promoted acting Colonel and assumed command of the force on 2 May. He was ordered to send one of his companies to the Bodö area to relieve the company of Scots Guards which had moved south from Narvik on 30 April, and to despatch two companies to the Mosjöen area as soon as possible. It was envisaged that Scissorsforce would impede the enemy by 'harassing tactics and the demolition of key points'.

Each company was issued with Arctic clothing similar to the rest of the expedition. In addition they had snowshoes and five days 'pemmican' (dried meat) rations as well as £4,000 in British and Norwegian currency to supplement the normal food issue. When occasion demanded they were expected to live off the country. It soon became evident that their role as lightly equipped guerrillas did not fit in with the heavy load of ammunition and food they were expected to carry. Fortunately for them, each company had a Norwegian interpreter.

By the time the first Independent Company landed at Mo on 4 May the enemy was making a determined and vigorous forward drive through terrain described by some Allied commanders as 'impassable'. (On 8 May the nearest Germans were thought to be one hundred miles from Mosjöen; on 11 May they were attacking the Allied defenders.)

On 7 May Lord Cork was told that Colonel Gubbins' force would now be part of his command. As already stated, the 4th and 5th Independent Companies relieved the French Chasseurs at Mosjöen on 8 May. Number 1 was at Mo, fifty air miles to the north. Numbers 2 and 3 Companies were much further north at Bodö. Colonel Gubbins left Mosjöen with Number 5 Company to link up with a Norwegian battalion, much under strength, about twenty-five miles south along the road to Fellingfors. This battalion had been driven back by the enemy and had withdrawn to Mosjöen to reorganize. Failing to get reinforcements, they had moved south again, only 400 strong, exhausted and disheartened.

The German troops of General Woytasch's 181st Infantry Division, buoyed up by their success against the Allies at Steinkjer, despite lack of transport, had taken only four days to advance from Grong, using bicycle troops as their spearhead. Realizing that they were outnumbered, Colonel Gubbins and the Norwegian commander withdrew. They took up a new defensive position covering the road and a blown bridge just south of Mosjöen.

On 10 May the German vanguard rode their bicycles into an ambush set by Number 5 Independent Company and two strong Norwegian platoons. Enemy casualties amounted to more than fifty but strong German pressure was maintained along both the road and the railway. Gubbins decided that Mosjöen town was indefensible. He sent a message back to Number 1 Company, near Mo, asking them to safeguard the line of his withdrawal, which followed the road running north to the Ranfiord. The intention was to slow down the German advance as much as possible.

But unknown to Gubbins the Germans had commandeered a Norwegian steamer, the *Nord Norge*. Manned by a company of the 138th Mountain Regiment she sailed to Hemnesberget, a town near the start of the road to Finneid, about fifteen miles southwest of Mo. Two Dornier flying boats preceded her and landed forty soldiers with mortars and machine-guns at Hemnesberget. Norwegian coastguards had reported the *Nord Norge* but Lord Cork had no ships to spare, and by the time the destroyer *Zulu* and the anti-aircraft cruiser *Calcutta** arrived to sink the *Nord Norge* the enemy troops had landed.

Just after 7 p.m. the Germans attacked a platoon of Number 1 Independent Company, who fought a bitter battle to hold the enemy at the quay. They were forced back street by street until the survivors split up to make their way back to Mo, or rejoin Number 1 Company. They were met by about 120 Norwegians who boosted their fire power considerably by bringing in four heavy machine-guns.

The next day (11 May) Number 4 Company held the ground while

* Moulton named the cruiser as *Cairo* (p. 238).

Colonel Gubbins withdrew through them with Number 5. His route north was blocked by the leapfrogging Germans, who supplied their forward troops by a small fleet of seaplanes. The enemy now had two mountain guns, landed from the *Nord Norge*

Gubbins had no alternative but to use the sea as an escape route. The Mosjöen–Elsfiord road was abandoned to the enemy and Numbers 4 and 5 Companies used Norwegian boats to embark in British destroyers. The Norwegians detoured inland to Elsfiord, leaving their heavy equipment, and ferried up to Finneid to join their comrades. Colonel Gubbins and his two companies were landed near Bodö. The convoy carrying the remainder of the 1st Scots Guards, with four 25-pounder guns of 203 Battery, RA, and the same number of light anti-aircraft guns was diverted to Mo. At 4 a.m. on 11 May the Germans entered Mosjöen.

Now that Mosjöen had fallen the Norwegians operating south of Mo were in an untenable position. With considerable courage they launched an attack against Hemnesberget but were driven back to Finneid. General Ruge, the Norwegian Commander-in-Chief, knowing that Mosjöen was just over 200 airmiles from Narvik, sent a staff officer to see Lord Cork to register his concern at the latest withdrawal. Brigadier Fraser, having persuaded his medical officer to mark him fit for duty, resumed command of the Guards Brigade. Lieutenant-Colonel Trappes-Lomax returned to the Scots Guards as CO. He asked for 'C' Company, still guarding the airfield at Bodö, to be returned to the battalion, but his request was refused. The Scots Guards established a defensive position at Stien, halfway along the road from Finneid to Mo, and waited for the expected arrival of the remainder of the Guards Brigade.

The Germans requisitioned Norwegian farm horses to pull their guns. They crossed the rugged mountain ridge from Elsfiord to Korgen, knowing that troops of General Feurstein's 2nd Mountain Division were operating north of Mosjöen. Five mountain infantry battalions with substantial artillery support had been provided, on Hitler's orders, to hasten the capture of Narvik. Feurstein was anxious to push on over the poor roads running north towards Mo before the soft snow turned into mud in the quickening thaw.

The use of warships as highly mobile artillery was denied the Allies because Ranfiord was too narrow for British cruisers and destroyers to operate with safety. A further disadvantage was that all supplies had to travel from Harstad by sea through Saltfiord to Rognan. From there they traversed a narrow road, single tracked for most of the eighty miles, through the mountains to Mo.

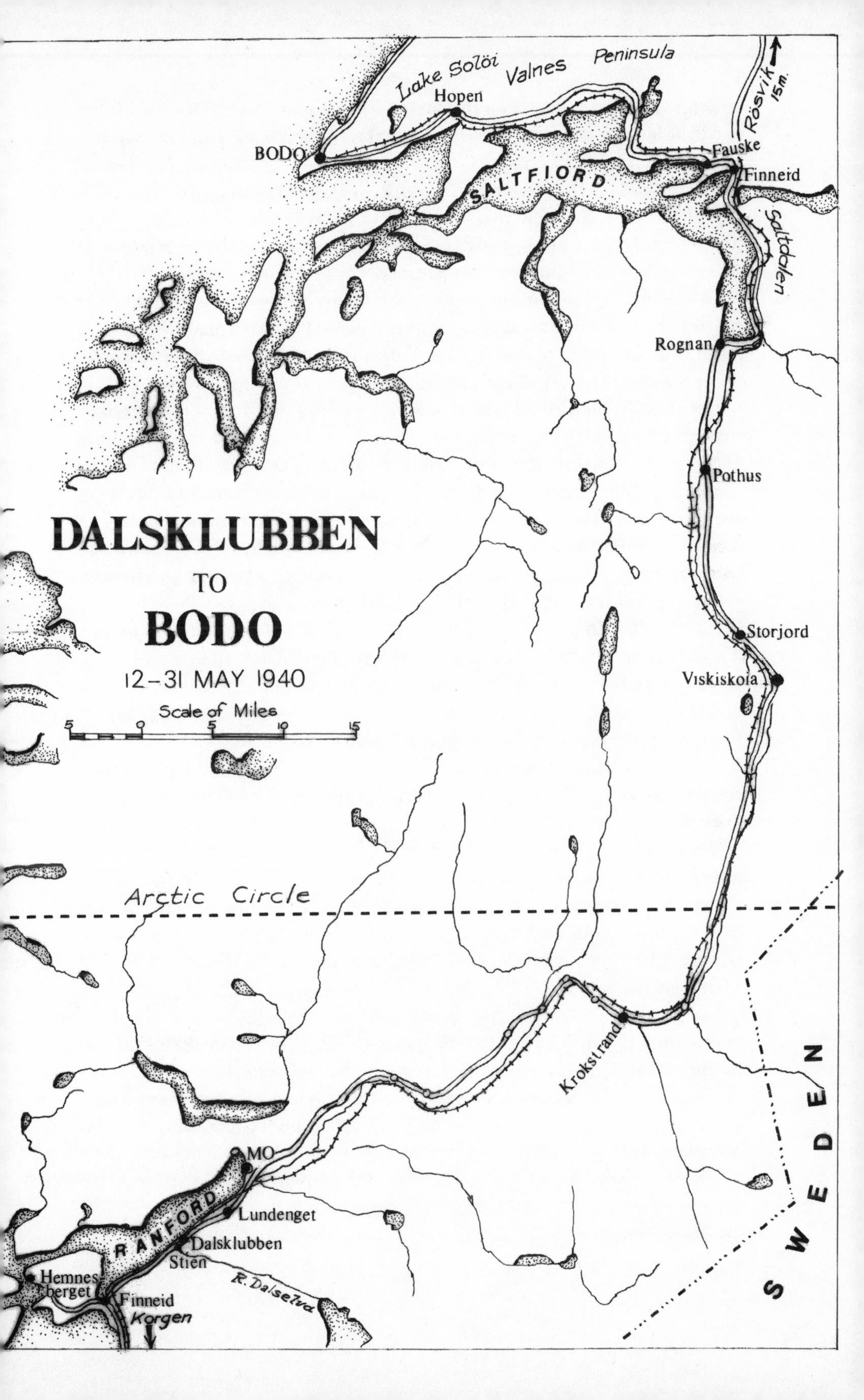
DALSKLUBBEN
TO
BODO
12–31 MAY 1940
Scale of Miles
5
0
5
10
15
Lake Solöi
Valnes
Peninsula
Hopen
BODO
SALTFIORD
Fauske
Finneid
Rösvik 15m.
Saltdalen
Rognan
Pothus
Storjord
Viskiskoia
Arctic Circle
Krokstrand
SWEDEN
MO
RANFORD
Lundenget
Dalsklubben
Stien
Hemnes
Berget
Finneid
Korgen
R. Dalselva

Brigadier Fraser had been instructed by General Auchinleck to hold on at Mo as long as possible. After a personal reconnaissance and a conference with the CO of the Scots Guards and the newly arrived Norwegian area commander (Lieutenant-Colonel R. Roscher Nielsen), the Brigadier reported that to continue to hold Mo was militarily unsound. This did not fit in with Lord Cork's plans. He was concerned about the position of Narvik and wanted the German advance stopped at Mo.

In this he was supported by Winston Churchill, who was dismayed at the loss of Mosjöen. 'It would be a disgrace if the Germans made themselves masters of the whole of this stretch of the Norwegian coast with practically no opposition from us in the course of the next few weeks or even days.'*

On 17 May the British and Norwegian position at Stien was precarious to say the least. Major Graham, once more in command, had two companies of Scots Guards near the river mouth at Stien. The Right Flank covered the main road bridge, the Left Flank defended a second bridge over the River Dalselva. Number 1 Independent Company, under Graham's command, held the road on the seaward side of Stien. 'B' Company had been withdrawn to the north of Mo as a rearguard. The four 25-pounder guns were in the rear. 'B' Echelon (administration), was sited near 11 Platoon of 'B' Company to the north of battalion HQ on the road to Mo. There was no question of tactical picketing. Apart from an acute shortage of men the snow on the hills was too deep and wet for movement.

The Germans, having mopped up the remnants of the Norwegians at Finneid, now began to move against Stien. The 2nd/137th Mountain Regiment, about 1,700 strong, launched a frontal attack at 6.30 p.m. Despite enemy artillery and machine-gun fire, the two forward companies of the Scots Guards held their positions.

Two miles to their rear the men of 'B' Echelon were attacked by what was thought to be an enemy parachute detachment dropped in the hills to the east. They were, in fact, ski-troops of the 137th Regiment. The Guards held them off until midnight, when the whole defensive position became critical. The 25-pounders were of little use as communications to them had been disrupted.

Hand-to-hand fighting had broken out on the left flank as the brief twilight fell. Number 16 platoon's commander, (Lieutenant Ramsay) was wounded, and in the mêlée Guardsman J.H. Bryson† inflicted heavy casualties on the enemy and was an inspiration to all. The Left Flank Company was now surrounded and cut off from communication with battalion HQ.

The Germans attempted to restore the blown bridge with wooden

* Derry, p. 184.

† Guardsman Bryson was awarded the Distinguished Conduct Medal for this action.

planks, but sustained heavy casualties. They then switched their main thrust down the river valley, using their expertise on the snow-bound slopes to infiltrate around the British left flank. At 0200 hours on 18 May the battalion was ordered to withdraw, having lost three killed and about seventy wounded. Most of the Left Flank Company failed to get the order to withdraw but rejoined the battalion later. It now became clear that German paratroops had in fact been dropped and had taken part in the attack on Lundenget.

Brigadier Gubbins* arrived during the night. He had been appointed acting brigade commander in place of Brigadier Fraser whose wound had worsened, causing him to be evacuated to England. Gubbins telephoned General Auchinleck and afterwards gave orders for the whole force to retire to the north of Mo. Colonel Trappes-Lomax, who had been organizing the defence of Mo, gave the withdrawal order to the Norwegians, who promptly commandeered most of the civilian transport, leaving the Guards to march back to Mo.

Lord Cork, mindful of Churchill's stricture about the need to hold on at Mo, issued, through General Auchinleck, firm orders that the Saltfiord–Bodö area must be held. Trappes-Lomax, reassuming command of the Scots Guards, was in a better position to gauge the strength of the German attacking forces. He was much against trying to fight a rearguard action across twenty miles of snow-bound country in which his troops were confined to a single narrow road. Nevertheless he was ordered to do so and between 19 and 22 May the Scots Guards stubbornly defended this ground, using three successive company positions.

On 23 May the battalion, tired and depressed after continual withdrawals under heavy enemy air attack, prepared to meet the first German assault north of the snow belt. At this point Lieutenant-Colonel Trappes-Lomax was relieved of his command for 'failing to hold the enemy further south'.

'B' Company had returned to the battalion on 20 May after many privations. With them came Captain Count Erik Lewenhaupt, a Swedish officer who had joined the battalion at Dalsklubben. Major Elwes, 'B' Company commander, paid tribute to Count Lewenhaupt for his support in getting the company to safety. Another foreign national, Captain Ellinger, a Dane commanding a company of Norwegians, provided machine-gun cover and did invaluable service at Stien and throughout the subsequent withdrawal.

Major Graham, once more in command of the battalion, drove north to reconnoitre Viskiskoia where the Scots Guards were to make their next

* The story goes that when Brigadier Gubbins arrived at the Scots Guards Battalion HQ he inadvertently 'borrowed' a civilian car used by Major Graham. In the boot of this car was the battalion's stock of precious Scotch whisky, which was never seen again. This did not enhance Gubbins' popularity.

stand. The War Diary frankly portrays a steadily worsening morale:

> The men were utterly exhausted and a certain demoralization had set in in consequence of fatigue, loss of kit, a succession of rearguard actions, and continuous menace from the air, which invariably disclosed every position to the enemy.

By now ammunition for the 2-inch mortars had been used up. The 2nd Independent Company, which had come back into the line, had acute difficulties in getting supplies up to their mountain positions and the 25-pounder guns were still not fully effective because of lack of signal stores. Orders had been received from Brigadier Gubbins that the position at Viskiskoia must be held until 27 May. The German attack began at about 1500 hours on 23 May and it was during the heat of battle that the Scots Guards heard that Lieutenant-Colonel Trappes-Lomax had been ordered back to the base at Harstad 'on the grounds that, in crossing the snow belt, he had not carried out Colonel Gubbins' orders' (on 20 May).* The impact of the news on the battalion is recorded in the War Diary:

> This crushing blow took place in the middle of an enemy attack, and it is hardly to be wondered at that the morale of both officers and men was still further shaken by the loss of a Commanding Officer for whose personality and ability everyone had the highest respect, and in whom everyone had the greatest confidence.

As the German attack developed, their Carinthian ski troops occupied the high ground on the Scots Guards' undefended right flank. The enemy were now able to enfilade the whole of the defensive position. There was no adequate anti-aircraft defence against the Luftwaffe's concentrated attacks. Brigadier Gubbins, who had arrived during the afternoon, now rescinded his order to hold the ground until 27 May and ordered a withdrawal. The battalion started to pull out at 2000 hours and by midnight were back in an equally precarious position at Storjord.

Throughout the withdrawal from Stien to Viskiskoia one section of 230th Field Company, Royal Engineers, had worked with the Scots Guards. At Stein the enemy were held off in time to prepare defensive positions, then the Sappers blew the bridge over the River Dalselva. Under Major R. K. Millar, the section relied upon their battered compressor truck to get themselves and their meagre stores from one bridge to another. In three weeks on the move, with just one day's rest at Krokstrand, they blew some thirty bridges, often under enemy fire.

Sadly their efforts did not significantly slow the German advance:

* *Scots Guards Regimental History*, (First Battalion, p. 45).

This disappointment was a tribute to the outstanding efficiency of the enemy's bridging column and reflected the weakness of our rearguard actions in covering the demolition gaps.

The Germans, with unchallenged control of air and flanks, harassed our troops with certain knowledge of every position and movement . . . but the short delays gave invaluable periods of relief to the jaded troops, without kit, exhausted and utterly unready for this tough ordeal.*

There was, inevitably, another bridge at Storjord. But before the Sappers could blow it the Scots Guards were ordered to withdraw through the Irish Guards, fourteen miles to the north, where a stand was to be made at Pothus.

At midnight on 24 May the Scotsmen passed silently through the defensive positions of the Irish Guards in the Pothus woods. The History comments: 'Normally on such occasions considerable banter of a traditional kind is exchanged between the Jocks and Micks. There was no banter that night.'

On the same day, (24 May), the Defence Committee, set up by the newly formed Churchill Cabinet, recommended that Northern Norway be evacuated.

The hastily reorganized Irish Guards reached Bodö on 20 May, travelling in destroyers and a straggling convoy of puffers. They spent the night in some discomfort on the quay amid piles of stores recovered from HMS *Effingham*. Their History claims that a 3-inch mortar was 'salvaged' from amid the pile of equipment and that the finder commented 'The South Wales Borderers would surely be pleased to lend us this'. (p 54)

The battalion moved up the Saltfiord to Hopen in a flotilla of puffers under British naval command. Near the village of Godones they met Lieutenant-Colonel H. C. Stockwell, the former CO of Number 2 Independent Company, who now commanded all British troops in the Bodö area. Known as Stockforce, they operated under the direction of Brigadier Gubbins. It was decided to make a stand in the Saltdalen valley, considered to be the only practical route from Mo northwards.

Colonel Stockwell and Captain R. McGildowny (Irish Guards), reconnoitered the line of the road as far south as Pothus. They decided that the conformation of the river, the road, the two bridges at Pothus, and the wooded terraces, formed a bottleneck which would impede the German advance up the valley. The intention was to hold the enemy while the considerable build-up of troops in the Bodö area was organized into a strong defensive force.

* Brigadier R. S. G. Stokes, *Royal Engineers History*, Part 2, 'Narvik 1940', p. 182.

Two companies of 2/SWB had landed immediately after the Irish Guards; there were four Independent Companies in the area, and General Fleischer had sent the 1st/15th Norwegian battalion from Bardufoss to Bodö.

General Auchinleck* had been informed that three more Independent Companies would be sent out from England, plus a battalion of Chasseurs Alpins. He considered this force strong enough to hold the estimated four thousand Germans, with tanks and artillery, now advancing from the Mo–Mosjöen area. He hoped to challenge the enemy air power with help from the Fleet Air Arm and with aircraft transferred from Bardufoss to the partly prepared airfield at Bodö.

It was on this optimistic premise that fifty-five men of Number 2 Independent Company moved to the hamlet of Pothus. They were quickly followed by the Irish Guards and Number 3 Independent Company. By the time the weary Scots Guards marched through on 24 May, the defensive dispositions had been completed. There was a back-up of one troop of 25-pounders, with the Norwegians providing a detachment of mortars and heavy machine-guns.

Captain McGildowny, being the senior surviving officer, now commanded the Irish Guards. He gave out his plan of defence:

> No. 1 Company are on the ridge on the far side of the river. From there they can cover the bridge and prevent the Germans getting observation down the valley. When the Scots Guards have passed through, the main girder bridge will be blown. No. 1 Company will hold their position as long as they can, and will then withdraw into reserve.
>
> There is a platoon of No. 3 Company guarding the suspension bridge. When they and No. 1 are across, the suspension bridge will be blown behind them. No. 4 Company on their plateau can command a long stretch of river and the road, and No. 3 can cover the tributary behind the ridge, so that once the bridges are blown, the Germans will have great difficulty in crossing the rivers, particularly as they will have no darkness to cover them.
>
> There are Norwegian machine-gunners on No. 4's flank who can shoot across onto the road in front of No. 1 Company.†

The battalion signallers began to lay the field telephone lines. They ran out of cable halfway through and that meant that No. 1 Company could communicate only by runner. The same method was used by Number 3 Independent Company, who were in reserve. It was a hot, sunny day, and in contrast to the bleak Narvik terrain, the fields were already green with early crops. Flanking them were closely packed fir plantations. There was no sign of the enemy.

* General Auchinleck was aware that the War Cabinet had decided to abandon Northern Norway on 25 May. The decision was ratified by the Supreme War Council on 31 May 1940.

† Desmond Fitzgerald, *History of the Irish Guards*, p. 57.

But during the night of 24/25 May it was bitterly cold. The men, well wrapped up, crouched in their slit trenches waiting for action. The German scout planes had been circling during the day, deducing, from the pattern of movement below, how best to advise their infantry. At about 8 a.m. the leading German cyclists appeared round a bend in the road to No. 1 Company's front. Before they could stop, the Norwegian machine-gunners cut them down in a tangled heap. Alerted by the firing, the leading enemy company worked their way forward under cover, following the river line. Supporting them came the mortar sections and heavy machine-gunners.

The Germans began shouting invitations for the 'Tommies' to come over to them. 'Join us,' they called, 'We are your friends.' The Irish Guards' answer was to force them back with Mills grenades and small arms fire. In common with the other battalions of the expedition the Guards were fast learning the lessons of modern war. When the mortar bombs begin to fall, when the dive bombers scream down, you deepen your slit trench and keep your head down ready to fight back when the attack finally comes.

The German mortars and machine guns were now well-established on the high ground. The assault came in from both sides as the Luftwaffe arrived in the form of five Heinkel aircraft. They flew down the western edge of the Guards position in line ahead formation, strafing the edge of the wood.

As the air strike went in the Germans again attacked Number 1 Company's position. The British 25-pounders and the Norwegian mortars caused many casualties as the enemy rushed over the ridge, hurling grenades. The bridges had been blown, one of them unsuccessfully. In the close fighting Guardsman Tierney was the first fatal casualty. Number 1 Company commander, Captain Eugster, was wounded in the shoulder. As the enemy outflanked the platoon positions, the Guards were forced back, some along a footbridge, others along the river bank.

Captain Eugster,* ignoring his wound, directed the withdrawal, moving back with the last platoon. When they came to the blown bridge the river was swollen and too fast-running to ford. The soldiers pulled the rifle slings from the weapons and clipped them into a chain. Guardsman 'Red' Murphy stripped down and jumped into the torrent, holding the end of the chain. The current forced him downstream on to a small island near the far bank. The Germans above them intensified their fire as PSM Thompson urged the men across the chain and along the bank towards battalion HQ, which had been burnt out by the Luftwaffe with incendiary bullets.

The reserve company (Number 2) and Number 2 Independent Company

* Captain B. O. P. Eugster was later awarded the Military Cross.

went forward across the river to protect the left bank. By 4.30 a.m. on 26 May the left flank was reasonably secure. During the night the enemy had built a pontoon bridge across the river. Despite sniping from the Guards and the Norwegians, they succeeded in transferring the weight of their attack to the right flank. The British positions were now being infiltrated from both flanks. At about 12 noon Brigadier Gubbins from his HQ at Rognan gave the order for a withdrawal. Colonel Stockwell struggled around the Guards' positions in an attempt to contact company commanders to plan the withdrawal. The constant air attacks and concentrated ground fire of the Germans prevented it from getting under way until 7 p.m. During the withdrawal a single Gladiator fighter suddenly appeared and gave the defenders a slight respite by strafing the enemy.

During the mêlée on Number 4 Company's front some of 17 Platoon's weapons had been left behind. Guardsman Wylie* went back under heavy fire and retrieved a much-needed Bren gun and tripod as the platoon moved down to the concentration area where requisitioned transport was waiting to take the troops back to Rognan. From Rognan those who had made it to the concentration area were ferried by puffer to Finneid. The next morning, 27 May, the Irish Guards marched around the edge of the fiord to Fauske.

Number 2 Company of the Irish Guards, with men from battalion HQ and Number 3 Independent Company had, for various reasons, failed to reach the concentration area. During the next two days they rejoined the battalion, some of them having marched long distances. Guardsman P. O'Shea had gathered a band of stragglers together and brought them safely through rough country to Fauske. At the end of the campaign O'Shea's leadership qualities had earned him the Distinguished Conduct Medal.

On 27 May Colonel Stockwell concentrated his force on the Valnes peninsula. Although Narvik still had to be taken by the Allies it was now widely known that Northern Norway was to be evacuated. There seemed no point in continuing resistance in the Saltfiord area. The Norwegian Government was informed that the British intended to withdraw from Bodö, but were not told that Norway was to be evacuated.

The 1st/15th Norwegian Infantry battalion, who found it hard to believe that the British were leaving, withdrew north towards Rösvik where they fought a successful rearguard action against the Germans before embarking in puffers to escape to the Lofoten Islands.

On 27 May the forward elements of General Feuerstein's group had reached Saltdal. This force consisted of two mountain battalions, two cyclist squadrons and a battery of mountain guns. The senior officers of

*For this action, and other acts of gallantry, Guardsman J. Wylie was awarded the Distinguished Conduct Medal.

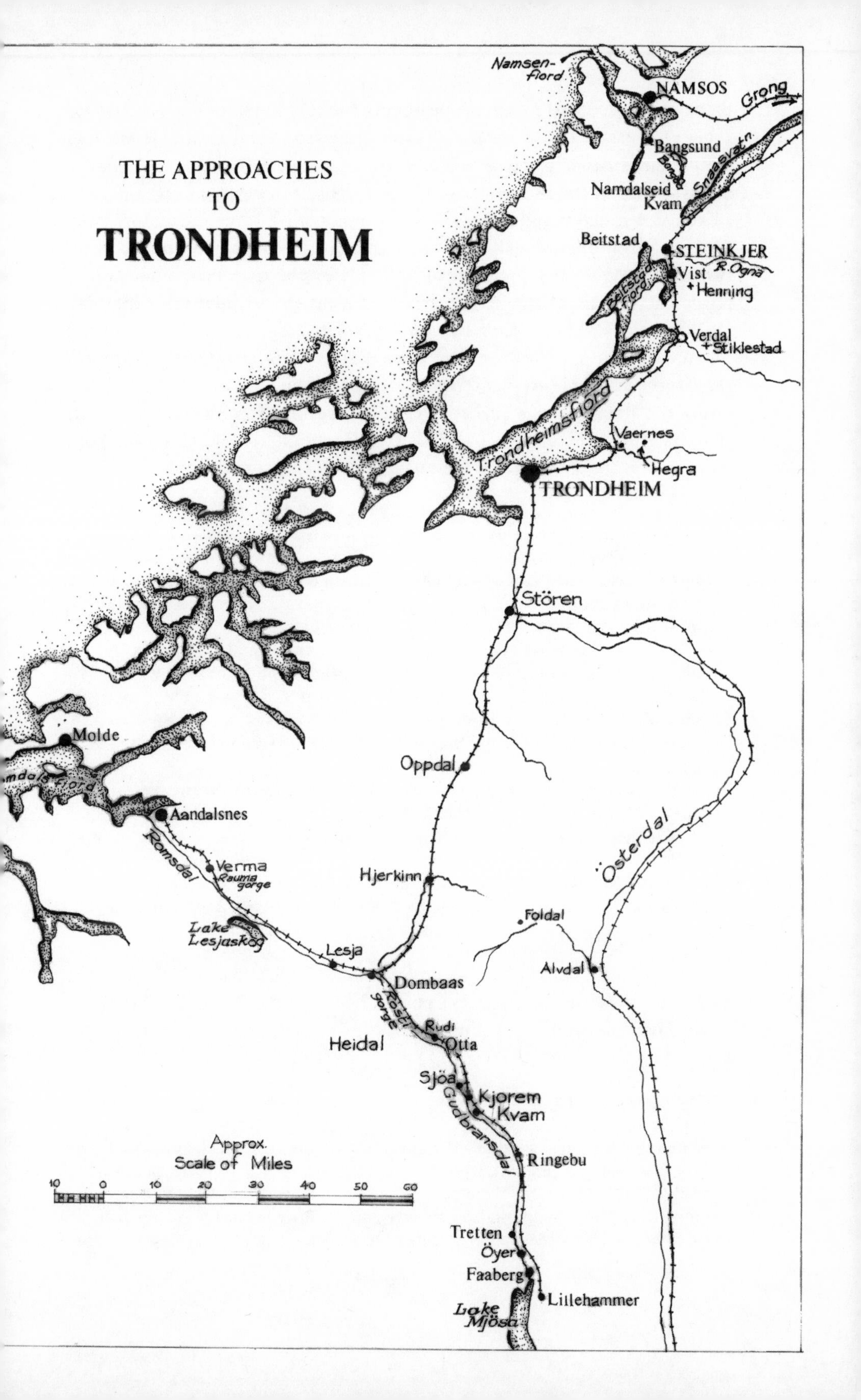
THE APPROACHES
TO
TRONDHEIM
Namsen-
fiord
NAMSOS
Grong
Bangsund
Bangsa
Snaasvatn.
Namdalseid
Kvam
Beitstad
STEINKJER
R. Ogna
Vist
+Henning
Beitstad
fiord
Verdal
+Stiklestad
Trondheimsfiord
Vaernes
Hegra
TRONDHEIM
Stören
Molde
Oppdal
Aandalsnes
Romsdal
Verma
Rauma
gorge
Hjerkinn
Österdal
Foldal
Lake
Lesjaskog
Lesja
Dombaas
Alvdal
Rosti
gorge
Rudi
Heidal
Otta
Sjöa
Kjorem
Kvam
Gudbransdal
Approx.
Scale of Miles
10
0
10
20
30
40
50
60
Ringebu
Tretten
Öyer
Faaberg
Lillehammer
Lake
Mjösa

Stockforce were well aware of the enemy build-up. There was suppressed anger and resentment at the lack of clear direction from London. Ironically, 24th Guards Brigade was now concentrated as one force on operations for the first time in the campaign.

The RAF had reappeared, albeit fleetingly, with three Gladiators from 263 Squadron operating from Bodö. One had crash-landed but the other two accounted for two German aircraft and, as we have seen, momentarily raised the morale of the British troops during the withdrawal to Saltdal. On 28 May HMS *Glorious* arrived off North Norway. On board was 46 Squadron, equipped with Hurricanes. In terms of potential air support Stockforce appeared to be better served than ever before.

For the Norwegians, who had been actively engaged against the Germans since 9 April, the news of the British intention to evacuate Northern Norway was devastating. Dr Derry comments (page 214):

> The Norwegians, who had only recently transferred a battalion (the 1st/15th) to this area from Bardufoss to reinforce the remnants withdrawn from Mo, found the decision quite inexplicable and therefore sinister. They did not, however, feel strong enough to fight at Finneid on their own, so they joined under bitter protest in the withdrawal to the Isthmus, which was divided into two sectors, the Norwegians defending the northern half.
>
> At the same time they were almost equally distressd and alarmed by the failure to bring forward reinforcements from Bodö, the more so as we had recently had Gladiators operating from there to give air cover. These local difficulties were cleared up to some extent when news of our intention to evacuate Bodö came through Norwegian Divisional Headquarters to their local commander.
>
> The reason for this evacuation was still unknown to any Norwegian, and it naturally seemed madness to them because of the resulting threat to Narvik. All that their represenatives could achieve, however, was a promise that our evacuation would not take place for three days,. This would enable them to withdraw their own troops from the northern half of the Fauske isthmus to Rösvik, which was then the terminus of the main road north, and to arrange for their evacuation in fishing boats to the Lofoten Islands.

But we know that the strategic plans of the Allies had been overtaken by momentous events in another part of Europe, that is, the breakthrough by the Germans in the Low Countries. The Norwegian historian, Professor Riste, puts this in perspective (p 51):

> (We have seen that) after three weeks of fighting, a notable feature of which was the total German superiority in the air, southern Norway had to be abandoned to the invaders. In the north, on the other hand, the Germans were kept under steady pressure from the Norwegian and Allied forces, and were gradually forced back to the area between Narvik and the Swedish frontier. German reinforcements started an energetic advance northwards after their conquest of southern Norway, but they had a long way to cover besides being

harassed by British and Norwegian troops.

What really sealed the fate of the campaign in North Norway, however, was not the tide of local events but the increasing impact of the victorious German advance in France. On 24 May the Allies decided that Norway would have to be evacuated. Notwithstanding the moral and tactical victory of the successful re-conquest of Narvik, nothing could thereafer prevent the final abandonment of the campaign in Norway.

Allied strategy in Norway was now concentrated on two main issues, the recapture of Narvik and the evacuation of the Bodö area. The land and air forces were combined under the title of the North-Western Expeditionary Force* commanded by General Auchinleck, who had direct access to the Chief of the Imperial General Staff. Lord Cork's position seemed rather ambiguous as far as overall command is concerned. He was, however, still Flag Officer, Narvik, and in 'supreme command' in that no other officer had been appointed to that position.

Although orders to evacuate Norway had been given, the drive to recapture Narvik was still very much alive. The French General Béthouart had been given command of all land forces in the Narvik area. His grasp of both mountain and winter warfare and his success in the Bjerkvik area in command of the Chasseurs and the Foreign Legion made him the obvious choice. The Norwegians had confidence in his leadership and co-operated wholeheartedly in the plans to retake Narvik.

Auchinleck's other, and perhaps more difficult, strategic problem, was how to extricate his troops from the Bodö area in the face of the quickening German advance.

As a port, Bodö provided good facilities for an evacuation. Situated at the end of a promontary, it had a wide and lengthy concrete quay, backed up by four useable wharves. The Gulf Stream kept it ice-free and also ensured that its climate (in late May) was equable enough for the large-scale use of small craft. This factor also worked for the enemy, whose airforce was increasingly active in the eighteen hours of daylight now prevailing.

General von Falkenhorst, the German Commander-in-Chief, aware of Hitler's anxiety over the position of the port of Narvik, decided to split his forces. One column made for Rösvik on the first stage of their bid to reinforce General Dietl's beleaguered soldiers at Narvik. They were to traverse 'one of the wildest mountain districts'† before they reached their

*The title of NWEF was applied to General Massy's command, (from London), over all forces outside the Narvik area and was, theoretically, in use from 21 April to 7 May.

† Derry (p. 216) quoting the Norwegian commander in the Mo–Bodö area, Colonel (later Major-General) Roscher Nielsen.

comrades on Björnfjell mountain. The other German column made for Bodö.

Auchinleck probably knew nothing about the German group branching off to the north. He estimated that there were about 4000 enemy troops, with tanks and artillery, advancing from Mo. It was decided to move the British defences behind Finneid, where the Fauske isthmus provided a ten-mile stretch of comparatively flat ground. This led directly on to the Bodö peninsula. It appears that this area was selected to secure an easier route for withdrawal to Bodö rather than a better *defensive* line.

On 26 May the Scots Guards, after withdrawing through the Irish lines, were dispersed around Hopen, eleven miles from Bodö, enjoying a well-earned rest. 'A' and 'B' Companies of the South Wales Borderers had been operating around Bodö airfield on the outskirts of the town since 21 May, subject to constant enemy air attacks. The remainder of 2/SWB arrived by puffer on 25 May. The Adjutant (Captain Campbell-Miles) records in the War Diary his concern over the 'lack of control' around the harbour area. 'Too many civilians,' he writes, remembering the stories of Germans at Narvik dressed in plain clothes. Some had used women's clothing, while many were dressed in captured Norwegian uniforms. There were constant false alarms as the South Wales Borderers patrolled up into the mountains towards Lake Solöi.

On 26 May the author was told to report to the battalion's tactical headquarters on the edge of the Saltfiord:

> Lieutenant Gillespie, the Assistant Adjutant, told me to lay a telephone line to an observation post on a high feature about a mile and a half to the west along the coast road. He explained that enemy infiltration by sea in small craft had been reported by the Norwegians. 'B' Company had been detailed to man the post and report anything suspicious to him. He told me that their patrol would be at the mountain top to meet me and warned me to keep a sharp lookout for the enemy.
>
> We tried to locate the exact position on a rough Norwegian map but, even though we were practised map-readers, the contours were too blurred and inaccurate.
>
> We walked along the road until we could see the mountain top clearly. It had a peculiar rock formation which was unmistakable. I rounded up the special team of four signallers with whom I had built up experience over the past five weeks or so and we loaded a Norwegian open truck with our kit. The only cable I had left was the sixty-pound drums that I had scrounged from the Marines at Harstad. The Norwegian driver seemed unusually surly and failed to help us load the truck.
>
> We laid the first mile of cable from the truck at a pretty fast pace until we came to the foot of the mountain. When we unloaded the gear the driver jumped into his cab and started to drive towards Bodö. I quickly stopped him and told him he would have to wait to take us back as I knew that Tac HQ

was on the move. The driver spoke no English but indicated that he was hungry and wanted food. He refused a packet of army biscuits but accepted half of my haversack ration. We left our heavy clothing in the truck and started to climb in jerkins and white sweaters.

As we reached the snow line we found it impossible to manage the big drums of cable because of their size and weight. We carried a six-foot length of piping as an improvised pivot on which to rotate the drums and we wedged this between two scrubby silver birch trees. I left one signaller with the drum and a spare cable while we started to plough through the snow, pulling the cable after us.

My right-hand man, Lance-Corporal Bryn Gould, as usual proved a tower of strength. Two of us hauled the cable while the other trod a path ahead. When Gould was not pulling the pace slowed considerably. At the end of the first drum I left a signaller there while Gould and I went down the mountain to bring up the other drum. It took us four hours to get to the top.

We rested just below the crest, near the rock formation. Then Gould and I unslung our rifles and cautiously went on to the summit, expecting to find the 'B' Company patrol. There was no one there. We brought the last drum forward to a sheltered spot and, after hammering the earth pin into the frozen ground, we connected the field telephone.

Much to my relief we got through first time. The operator brought Lieutenant Gillespie to the phone and I explained the situation to him. He said he'd send a runner at once to 'B' Company asking them to man the lookout. I described the view from the top. I could see the coastline down to Bodö and the Hjertoya islands beyond. There was no sign of small craft in our sector of Saltfiord but I could see a warship, probably a destroyer, near the horizon.

Lieutenant Gillespie advised me to return as soon as possible because the Germans were closing in and Tac Headquarters were moving to a new location. He gave me the map reference and I reminded him that the line we were speaking on would have to be extended to their new position. We came down the mountain like a party of schoolboys, slipping and sliding, laughing a lot. When we reached the bottom the truck was missing.

In a nearby building they found an abandoned motor cycle. It was full of petrol and in perfect working condition. The author ferried his companions one by one down the badly rutted track to find his unit. They had no difficulty in locating the new headquarters and, having safely stored the motor cycle, went in search of food.

I found my small detachment installed in a barn near the roadside. As I entered the broken door I saw a mutilated carcass to which was loosely attached a cow's head, complete with horns. One half of the barn door was laid across bales of straw and on it was a large chunk of raw meat. One of my signallers, stripped to a long-sleeved vest, covered in blood, was belabouring the meat with a pickhelve.

'What's going on' I said, 'Where did you get that meat?'

'Found it' he said. 'It was lying by the side of the road,'

'Been hit by a bomb, or something,' said one of the others. 'It's quite fresh,' he added defensively.

'Why are you bashing it like that?' I asked.

'To make it tender, Sergeant. I don't know how old the cow is, do I?'

Later, when we were all satiated with the half-raw meat, the truth came out. That morning rumours of German patrols in the vicinity caused them to be extra cautious. When the move was completed they saw the barn and went in to investigate its suitability as a billet. The pickhelve wielder heard a noise inside and challenged whoever was in there to come out. When there was no answer he threw a Mills grenade under the door. When they burst in they found the dead cow and decided it would be a pity to waste the meat.

The next day (27 May) at about 1830 hours, Private (later RSM) Leslie Morgan of 8 Platoon, 'B' Company, was on duty at the observation post on the mountain top. He rang Tac HQ and asked to speak to Lieutenant Gillespie. Morgan reported that Bodö was being heavily bombed. He gave the officer a running commentary as the town burned to the ground.

In the regimental histories of the units caught in the bombing of Bodö there are slightly different versions of what happened on 27 May. However, most of them agree that in the early evening a substantial force of German bombers laid the town in ashes. Bodö hospital lies on high ground between the town and the airfield. It was clearly marked with red crosses. Captured enemy maps are annotated to show that its exact position was known to the Germans. It was ruthlessly bombed.

(On 31 May, 1987, when in Norway, the author met Captain Störe of the Royal Norwegian Air Force. Captain Störe attended a reunion of K100, the Luftwaffe Group which bombed Bodö on 27 May 1940. One of the pilots who took part, Horst Gotz, was a *Wienerbarn* child, evacuated to Norway after the First World War. He was looked after by a Norwegian family in Bodö and went to school there. Herr Gotz told Captain Störe that when flying over Bodö he and other pilots dropped their bombs either in the sea or in the mountains rather than help destroy the town which had shown them such kindness.)

The Danish officer, Captain Ellinger, whose Norwegian machine-gunners had courageously supported the Guards on 14 May, was at the hospital:

> Some of my Scots Guards friends had arrived and gave splendid help at the hospital. It was amazing that among all that misery and suffering around me I do not remember having heard a single cry. Everybody did his very best; discipline and morale were perfect. The Norwegian nurses were, as always, splendid. We soldiers owe them a big debt of gratitude.*

* *Scots Guards History*, p. 47.

The Irish Guards also had several wounded in the hospital. Brigadier Gordon-Watson relates how Captain Eugster, and Captain Clowes, the Adjutant of the Scots Guards, tied their sheets together to form a rope and let themselves down from a window of the burning hospital. Fortunately the building was strongly constructed and stood up well to the bombing. The number of casualties was remarkably small, most of them being trapped under falling masonry.

Earlier that morning, at about 8 a.m., there had been a surprise attack on the airfield by German fighters. Their superior numbers overwhelmed the two surviving Gladiators and both were shot down. On this occasion the runway was not badly damaged but in the later bombing it was completely wrecked. The few remaining Bofors guns were put out of action and four-fifths of the houses in the little town were destroyed.

Meanwhile orders had been given for the whole of Stockforce to withdraw. Many of its units went into the newly-formed Bodoforce, commanded by Brigadier Gubbins. Number 3 Independent Company covered the withdrawal into the Mjones area. Numbers 1 and 4 Companies, with a troop of gunners and a Field Section of Royal Engineers, moved through Hopen to come under command of Bodoforce on 29 May.

These units, with the RAMC, the wounded and some administrative detachments were evacuated in two destroyers on 29 May. The next night the Irish Guards, Numbers 2, 3 and 5 Independent Companies, and the Military Police detachments, were taken off in the destroyers *Firedrake* and *Fame*. The Irish Guards embarked 750 men in under ten minutes. The Bodoforce Operation Order (No. 7) covering the evacuation was signed by Captain Sir Walter Barttelot, the senior Staff Officer, (who had been with Brigadier Fraser when he was wounded at Ankenes).

Two battalions now remained on the Bodö perimeter: 1st Scots Guards and 2nd South Wales Borderers. They were ordered to defend positions along the general line Myren – Myrneset – Steinmoen – Esneset. The Scots Guards held the right and the Borderers the left of the line, which ran just south of Lake Solöi. Ironically, this final stand has been described by the Scots Guards as 'the first really good defensive position which the battalion has occupied and on which the Germans could have been held'. (*Scots Guards History*, p. 47.)

'B' Company of the Scots Guards under Captain Godman held an outpost on high ground immediately west of Hopen bridge. At 1830 hours on 30 May the enemy closed in on 'B' Company. The Royal Engineers of 230 Field Company blew the bridge as heavy mortar and machine-gun fire was brought to bear by the enemy. The Germans suffered considerable casualties from our 25-pounder guns, but at 0200 hours on 31 May 'B' Company were forced to withdraw through the South Wales Borderers, who successfully held the enemy with the help of one of the few carriers left in action.

At 1915 hours the Scots Guards, led by Left Flank Company, started their planned withdrawal on time, having first destroyed all non-essential equipment.

The War Diary of 2nd South Wales Borderers described 31 May as 'probably the longest day most of us have experienced'. As the battalion gradually withdrew, the rearguard was taken up by 'C' Company, 2/SWB. They were commanded by Major I. T. Evans, a much decorated veteran of the First World War, who also had under command a company of Scots Guards and the troop of 25-pounder guns. Together they held off the enemy vanguard until all British troops were clear. The last detachment to engage the enemy was the carrier crew of PSM 'Jarvie' Johnson of the South Wales Borderers, who held off the leading German cyclists while under machine-gun fire. PSM Johnson had earlier evacuated the RE demolition squad. For these two actions he was later awarded the Distinguished Conduct Medal.

Meanwhile the sad but inevitable destruction of Allied arms, equipment and stores went on. To prevent the Germans benefiting from the accumulated stockpiles, the forward units had disposed of all non-essential equipment before finally withdrawing to Bodö quay. Much of it was dumped in Lake Solöi.

The troop of 203 Field Battery, RA, having supported the infantry to the bitter end, carried out the task dreaded by all Gunners – they spiked their guns. The Sappers of 230 Field Company, RE, hung on to their faithful and much-used compressor-truck until the very last moment. Near Bodö quay they destroyed the one piece of machinery that had sustained them all the way from Mosjöen: 'As solemn an occasion as the putting-down of a faithful old war horse'.

Lieutenant Bacon, RASC, having ensured that two days' supplies of food for the soldiers was ready for loading on to the destroyers, dumped the remainder of the field rations. Some of the transport eventually went back to the Norwegian owners from whom it had been requisitioned. Army vehicles were destroyed, mainly by burning. The Sea Transport Officer, Lieutenant-Commander Nicholas, hung on to as many of his pool of puffers as possible. Almost all embarkation was from the main quay, but in the event of disruption by enemy bombing Nicholas was responsible for providing an alternative embarkation area at Skiviken, which also provided a ferry service when required.

By midnight on 31 May the Scots Guards had passed through the smoking ruins of Bodö and embarked in the destroyers *Echo* and *Delight*. Apart from personal arms, the only stores taken aboard were six thousand rounds of ammunition. The battalion had suffered ninety-seven casualties, of whom thirteen were killed and thirty-six taken prisoner.

Surprisingly, the main quay had not been bombed or strafed. Thronged with soldiers, in almost perpetual daylight, it offered a tempting target to the Luftwaffe. The South Wales Borderers abandoned the last British defence post at 2345 hours on 31 May. They were grateful for the lack of enemy air activity as they filed on to the quay.

They embarked, with Brigade Headquarters, 200 Scots Guards, the remaining RA and RE troops, and the RAMC Advance Dressing Station in the last three destroyers, one of which was the *Arrow*. By 0100 hours on 1 June the destroyers had pulled out to sea to transfer their passengers to SS *Franconia*, which took them to the Harstad base in the Lofoten Islands. There they dispersed to various localities to await the final evacuation.

Dr Derry records the departure of the last ship (p. 216):

> The last vessel to leave Bodö was a small Norwegian passenger steamer, SS *Ranen*, alias *Raven*; this had been taken into use as a British decoy ship, manned by a mixed party of naval ratings, Irish Guardsmen and South Wales Borderers, and sent in search of information and chances of surprise attack as far south as Sandnessjöen.
>
> She returned to the Rösvik area on 3 June, when her concealed armament of one Bofors, one Oerlikon and numerous machine guns held up part of the German advance northwards across the fiord. The *Raven* was again employed north of Tysfiord to cut the telephone cables by which the Germans were believed to report progress to General Dietl.

The Norwegian Government were much disturbed by the news of the Bodö evacuation. Some reports say that there was talk of a separate armistice with the Germans. Lord Cork had visited the Government in the Tromsö area on 23 May and found that the Norwegian Generals, still highly critical about the Allied withdrawal from Namsos and Aandalsnes, saw British strategic interests running contrary to their own. They were sure that Norwegian military commanders could have done better than the British in certain critical areas. General Ruge had pressed hard for Lieutenant-Colonel Roscher Nielsen to take overall command in the area of Mo, but his request was refused.

We must now travel further south and record the landings at Namsos and the subsequent movements of Mauriceforce, commanded by that redoubtable warrior, Major-General Sir Adrian Carton de Wiart, VC.

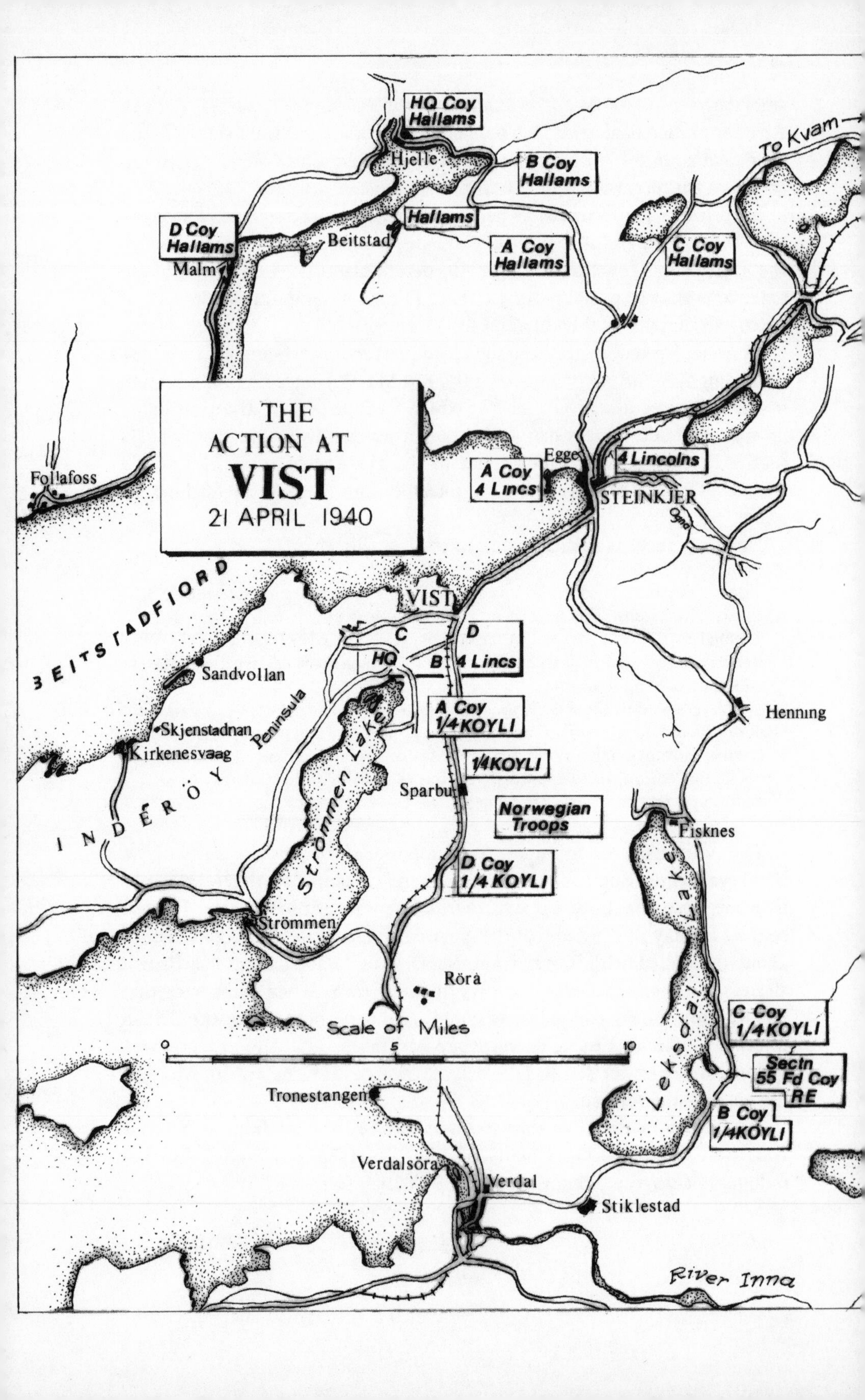
THE
ACTION AT
VIST
21 APRIL 1940
HQ Coy
Hallams
Hjelle
B Coy
Hallams
Hallams
Beitstad
A Coy
Hallams
C Coy
Hallams
D Coy
Hallams
Malm
To Kvam
Follafoss
A Coy
4 Lincs
Egge
4 Lincolns
STEINKJER
BEITSTADFIORD
VIST
C
D
HQ
B
4 Lincs
Sandvollan
A Coy
1/4 KOYLI
Skjenstadnan
Kirkenesvaag
Peninsula
1/4 KOYLI
Henning
INDERÖY
Strömmen Lake
Sparbu
Norwegian
Troops
Fisknes
D Coy
1/4 KOYLI
Strömmen
Röra
Leksdal Lake
Scale of Miles
0
5
10
C Coy
1/4 KOYLI
Sectn
55 Fd Coy
RE
Tronestangen
B Coy
1/4 KOYLI
Verdalsöra
Verdal
Stiklestad
River Inna

PART FOUR

Operations based on Namsos
14 April to 3 May 1940

It is ironic that a landing at Namsos might not have been attempted by the Allies had General von Falkenhorst, the German Commander-in-Chief, been allowed to occupy the port on 9 April, 1940. As already mentioned, he was debarred from landing at either Namsos or Aandalsnes, presumably because German naval and military resources were already thinly spread.

The Allied policy was 'not to land in defended localities'. It follows that some other port might have been selected had Namsos been occupied by the enemy. It is doubtful if the eventual outcome would have been substantially affected.

The port of Namsos was a quiet backwater. Its population, just short of 4000, worked mainly in the timber trade, with the usual Norwegian fishing and mercantile activities adding to its modest prosperity. The railway, carrying mainly freight, ran down to a substantial stone quay flanked by two wooden wharves. It is about 130 miles north of Trondheim by road. The railway branches towards Grong, in the east, adding another forty miles to the journey.

As we have seen, the original plan for the landing at Namsos was intended as a diversion to the movement against Trondheim (vide Plan R4). Prior to that Namsos had been considered as a subsidiary base for the Allied brigades earmarked for the Finnish front. When R4 was revised in the light of the German invasion on 9 April the direct descent on Trondheim was dropped in favour of a pincer movement, with Allied forces converging on Trondheim from Aandalsnes in the south and Namsos to the north.

The British battalions operating out of Namsos, codenamed Mauriceforce, were classed as second-line troops. The force was equipped to man a base and its lines of communication. The Navy would make the initial landing, followed by two Territorial brigades equipped with 'the bare minimum of stores and medical supplies'. The provisional date set for the landing of 146 Brigade under Brigadier C. G. Phillips was 15 April. The overall commander, Major-General Carton de Wiart, was appointed on 13 April; his first brief instructed him to 'provide encouragement for the Norwegian Government'. The next day his orders were extended. He was to form a rallying point for the Norwegians and secure a base for any subsequent operations in Scandinavia. But he was not to land in the face of opposition.

Accordingly, on 14 April the cruisers *Glasgow* and *Sheffield*, under Captain F.H. Pegram, organized a preliminary landing. In what was known as Operation Henry, 350 seamen and Royal Marines, led by Captain W.F. Edds, RM, were landed from destroyers and took up positions east and south of Namsos. There was no sign of the Germans. In point of fact enemy Intelligence had deduced from an intercepted naval signal that Namsos was being considered as a landing site. In consequence the Luftwaffe began to reconnoitre the area daily.

A report from Operation Henry to London, after Norwegian officers had been consulted, mentioned the regular enemy air activity and emphasized that concealment would be difficult for any sizeable force. The air aspect was highlighted by a Luftwaffe attack on the destroyer *Somali* on 15 April when she was supporting the landings at Namsos.

The report also mentioned the deep snow, which would prevent deployment and confine movement to narrow ice-bound roads.

Meanwhile, as already noted, on the afternoon of 14 April the ships carrying 146 Brigade were diverted from the Narvik convoy and turned south for Namsos. The 5th Demi-Brigade of the Chasseurs Alpins (13th, 53rd and 67th Battalions), with detachments of French anti-aircraft and anti-tank guns and a section of Engineers, under General Audet, were preparing to leave the Clyde to reinforce Carton de Wiart. This offset the loss of 148 Brigade, originally intended to be part of Mauriceforce but now diverted to Aandalsnes, south of Trondheim.*

General Carton de Wiart set out by flying boat on 15 April but was delayed by an air raid in the Namsenfiord, in which his staff officer was wounded. In view of the Operation Henry report, the Admiralty now had serious doubts about risking the large troop transports and their escorting warships in a landing at Namsos without air cover. It was therefore decided to divert the soldiers to Lillesjona, about 100 miles farther north, to avoid the attention of the Luftwaffe.

Carton de Wiart agreed to this move and started at once for Lillesjona, having discovered that 146 Brigade commander, Brigadier Phillips, had been mistakenly taken on to Narvik. On the morning of 16 April the

*See Part One, p. 2.

Empress of Australia and the *Chobry* anchored at Lillesjona. The Luftwaffe was soon on the scene, but, despite persistent bombing, there were no casualties.

The Hallamshires in the *Chobry* were transferred to three Tribal class destroyers. 'C' and 'D' companies under Major C. C. Strong, the second-in-command, were taken to Bangsund, where they were briefed by the Royal Marines who had landed earlier. The remainder of the battalion disembarked at Namsos. The 1/4th KOYLI were trans-shipped from the *Empress of Australia* to the *Chobry* by destroyer. In the process there was, once more, a disastrous mix-up or an outright loss of ammunition, weapons and equipment, some of which was left in the holds of the troopships. About half of the remaining battalion (the 1/4th Lincolnshires) had embarked in two destroyers, which left hurriedly for Namsos at the height of the air raid, leaving the rest of the battalion to follow on in the *Chobry*.

By the evening of 17 April the whole of 146 Brigade was ashore, but in some difficulties. Their inability to operate in deep snow, since they had neither skis nor snowshoes, meant that they were confined to narrow roads, thick with slush during the day. They were hampered by three kit-bags per man, two filled with Arctic clothing that could only be used occasionally. Among the 170 tons of equipment and stores which had gone astray were the 3-inch mortars which, in the absence of artillery of any kind, were the heaviest weapons embarked with them.

General Carton de Wiart had no Headquarters Staff and was dependent on an overworked Brigade HQ. Brigadier Phillips had arrived from Narvik on 17 April and was finding difficulty in communicating with his scattered battalions as there was no Army transport available. Using requisitioned civilian trucks, and the narrow gauge railway, the brigade started to move south. By 19 April they were disposed as follows:

Brigade HQ was at Steinkjer, with the Lincolns, who had 'D' Company at Vist, five miles to the south. 'A' Company was at Egge, a few miles to the north, while 'B' and 'C' remained at Steinkjer. For once their heavy clothing was welcome as the temperature dropped alarmingly at night. The ice on Beitstadfiord (at the head of Trondheimfiord) was breaking up and it was suspected that the Germans would make a sea landing somewhere in the area.

The KOYLI went south down the railway, dropping off 'A' Company at Strömmen, with a detachment overlooking the Skansund. 'D' Company got off at Röra, while 'B' Company went furthest south to Stiklestad, hoping to link up with a Norwegian machine-gun detachment holding the road bridge at Verdal. Battalion HQ was at Sparbu with 'C' Company, which was in reserve.

The Hallamshires used a convoy of civilian trucks to make a sixty-mile move to the south. 'D' Company finished up at Steinkjer and 'B' Company was spread along the north side of Beitstadfiord. Battalion HQ, with the other companies, were located around the village of Beitstad. There were thus fifty-five miles between the most forward and rearward troops of 146 Brigade.

Communications were primitive, with one or two wireless sets per battalion at the most. Tactically they were very vulnerable, as almost all the right flank of this line was open to an enemy using the inland waterways of the fiords. The British were confined by the snow to roads and tracks, while the German troops, using snowshoes, could move almost anywhere at will.

The battalion commanders complained bitterly to the Brigadier about lack of information, artillery, and air cover, then exhorted their company officers to do the best they could in the circumstances they found themselves in.

Carton de Wiart has been criticized for pushing south so soon after the poorly organized landings around Namsos. His original instructions gave him two infantry brigades plus some 4000 Chasseurs Alpins. He was informed that a naval attack on Trondheim would be timed to divert German forces from his line of advance. On the face of it his rapid move towards Trondheim seems justified.

It was in this redoubtable warrior's nature to attack, and it must have been a bitter blow to find that the promised naval diversion* had been called off and that the eagerly awaited French ski troops could not use their skis. He was not elated by the War Office signal telling him that he had been promoted to Acting Lieutenant-General: 'I felt it in my bones that this campaign was unlikely to be either long or successful.'†

The convoy carrying the Chasseurs, escorted by French and British warships, arrived at Namsos on the night of 19/20 April. On the way up Trondheimsfiord they were attacked by the Luftwaffe and some of the Allied ships were damaged. In consequence the landing was speeded up and was inadequately supervised. Carton de Wiart met General Audet on the quay and personally ordered the French soldiers to be dispersed in the woods outside the town as enemy air attacks increased. He was soon to learn that the Chasseurs' ski equipment had been left behind in Scotland, with the French vehicles, to follow on the next convoy.

At daylight the Chasseurs' hastily piled stores could be clearly seen on the wharves. The Chasseurs directed attention to their positions by firing

*The direct naval attack on Trondheim (Operation Hammer), was requested by the Norwegians, for whom the city had great cultural and political importance. The British abandoned Hammer from fear of losing capital ships. The plan was later revived as Hammer 2, but was finally rejected as impracticable on 26 April.

†Major-General Sir Adrian Carton de Wiart VC, *Happy Odyssey*, p. 167.

ineffectually at high-flying German reconnaissance aircraft. Carton de Wiart's high hopes rapidly subsided:

> These French soldiers came with a good soldierly reputation but they lacked one or two essentials that made them completely useless to me . . . they would have been invaluable to us if I could have used them. (p. 169)

Without their mules, their snowshoes or their skis, the Chasseurs were no more effective than the untrained British Territorials, who had no training for snow conditions.

The escalating Luftwaffe sorties reached a peak at about 10 a.m. on 20 April. More than sixty enemy bombers literally flattened Namsos. The air attacks lasted until the late afternoon, destroying the railhead, the rolling stock and the wooden wharves along the quay. Fortunately the local people had vacated the town, but they had taken with them most of the available transport and this further handicapped the Allies. During the raid much of the French ammunition and equipment went up in flames. General Carton de Wiart urged that no more ships should be allowed to berth at Namsos because the port facilities no longer existed.

Brigadier Phillips had met the Norwegian commander, Colonel Getz, at Grong on 18 April. The Norwegian officer explained that he had withdrawn his troops north of Steinkjer as the annual thaw had started, allowing enemy ships to sail up Trondheimsfiord towards Beitstadfiord. This danger became apparent to the Lincolns whose War Diary records on 19 April: 'The fiord is beginning to thaw and danger of enemy destroyers approaching is imminent.'*

At about 0600 hours on 21 April a German force of about 400 men landed at Kirkenesvaag and began to advance on Sandvollen and Strömmen. Other enemy detachments, supported by German destroyers, were put ashore at Hylla and Tronestangen. The flank and rear of 146 Brigade was now seriously threatened. At the same time the Luftwaffe mounted air attacks on Steinkjer and the roads to Verdal and Stiklestad.

On that Sunday morning (21 April, a day which the Lincolns' Historian notes as being Adolf Hitler's birthday) reports were received at the Lincolns' battalion HQ that the Germans had landed at Kirknesvaag. This was about twenty miles to the south-west of Steinkjer by road. The enemy was later reported to be moving north-east along the road to Vist. To meet this threat 'B' Company was sent to reinforce 'D' Company. Major K. R. M. Black, the Lincolns' second-in-command, went with them. He sent 'B' Company along the road running west from Vist railway station. About two miles down the road their leading scouts came under enemy fire and the company took cover in farm buildings along the roadside.

*Derry, p. 91.

'B' Company was joined by a rifle section from 'D' Company. They were pinned down by heavy mortar and machine-gun fire and, apart from firing at fleeting enemy targets, could do no more than hold on, hoping for reinforcements to arrive. At about 6 p.m. enemy incendiary bullets set fire to a hay loft and the entire group of wooden buildings went up in flames. 'B' Company commander, Captain H. R. Tweed, ordered a withdrawal into the woods behind the farm. Two of his sections failed to get the order and were forced to surrender, together with several wounded who could not be moved. Tweed estimated that the Germans were using at least a battalion* against Vist and withdrew, with great difficulty, into the hills east of the railway station at Vist.

It seemed that the Germans were intent on securing the neck of the peninsula around Vist. They had landed guns and mortars but were handicapped by lack of transport. Their motorcyclists quickly located carts and sledges in the scattered farm buildings and went on to search for horses. The Luftwaffe was in close support of the enemy infantry, knowing that the British were roadbound because of the snow.

A second enemy battalion had been landed, and their troops, using snowshoes, began to move towards the KOYLI at Strommen. Lieutenant-Colonel Hibbert, CO of KOYLI, ordered 'A' Company under Captain Carey to move from Strommen to meet the Germans advancing from the north-east. 'C' Company moved down from Sparbu in two ramshackle buses to support 'A', leaving one platoon to march because of lack of space. Company HQ and the spare ammunition and stores were left behind. The thick snow had prevented 'A' Company from moving beyond the outskirts of Strommen and 'C' Company in their two buses were turned around and re-directed towards Stiklestad, where 'B' Company were pinned down. Meanwhile a German Henschel float plane (nicknamed 'George' by the KOYLI) was dropping messages to the enemy infantry, plotting the exact route of the British troops.

The road to Stiklestad joins the coastal road at Verdalsöra, which was defended by a detachment of Norwegian Dragoons armed with heavy machine-guns. A section of 55 Field Company, RE, was in support of the Norwegians.

At 6 a.m. on 21 April the Norwegian positions at Verdalsöra were attacked by the Germans advancing along the road from Trondheim. Another enemy landing to the rear of Verdalsöra forced the Norwegian machine-gunners, about 80 strong, to prepare to withdraw inland to Stiklestad. The Royal Engineers had been ordered at the last moment not to destroy the Verdalsöra bridge. With the Norwegians they defended the bridge against several German attacks before withdrawing eastward.

*German warships landed a mountain battalion with guns and mortars at Kirknesvaag. Moulton, p. 170.

The vanguard of the enemy force attacking Verdal came from the 1/130th Regiment, veterans of the campaign in Poland, who had been airlifted into Vaernes. Their orders were to seize and hold the bridge.

The German force who had landed at Skjenstadnan very early on 21 April now occupied the north coast of the Inderöy peninsula. By 6.30 that evening they had forced the Lincolns out of Vist.

The enemy force which had landed at nearby Kirknesvaag attacked the KOYLI, whose two companies withdrew from Röra. Their comrades near Stiklestad retreated along the eastern shore of the Leksdalsvatn to Fisknes.

Enemy air attacks on Steinkjer had virtually burnt out the small town. There was no water, the road bridge was destroyed and the railway immobilized. Steinkjer was the main British communication centre in the area. Both Brigade Headquarters and battalion HQ of the Lincolns were forced to evacuate the town:

> Accordingly, Brigadier Phillips reported to the General (Carton de Wiart) that no position was tenable in the neighbourhood of the fiord and proposed a withdrawal along the north bank of the Snaasavatn towards Grong. Carton de Wiart, who came into the forward area next morning with the knowledge that the French were not yet ready to move, approved the proposed withdrawal but changed its direction towards the north, so as not to interfere with Norwegian troop movements along Snaasavatn.*

As soon as flying conditions became practicable on 22 April the Luftwaffe resumed their air offensive. German warships operated along the fiord bombarding the British right flank.

The KOYLI detached companies rejoined the battalion as they started to withdraw. They held their position until the late evening of 22 April and abandoned their heavier equipment, such as Bren-gun tripods, as they withdrew towards Steinkjer. Enemy surveillance from the air was now so close that some soldiers abandoned their steel helmets to avoid recognition. In single file, with linked hands, they trudged through the snow towards the dull red glow which marked the burning town.

It took them four hours to cover one and a half miles and at 3 a.m. they managed to snatch some rest in a barn. To add to their problems the few maps available were almost indecipherable and hopelessly out of date. Colonel Hibbert decided to find a way through the mountains to the north, cross the River Ogna somewhere to the east of Steinkjer and trust to luck to link up with the rest of 146 Brigade before starvation forced them to give up.

Hibbert had spent fishing holidays as a boy in this part of Norway and

*Derry, p. 93.

knew that the River Ogna would be flooded with water from the melting snow. None of the maps showed a bridge over the Ogna east of Steinkjer, but the Colonel remembered that there was a flimsy bridge across the river. At this point a Norwegian soldier called Private Mathieson comes into the story.

When Trondheim fell to the Germans Mathieson skied north to find his scattered regiment. He failed to do so and attached himself to 1/4th KOYLI. His home was in Oslo, where he owned a small fleet of oil tankers. He spoke excellent English and was in the habit of going to Scotland each year to shoot grouse. Throughout the operations he remained close to Colonel Hibbert, becoming his personal interpreter and adviser on local problems.

Mathieson had an eye for country and unerringly advised the CO on the best route through difficult terrain. Hibbert asked Mathieson to guide them through the mountains to the bridge.

At Henning Mathieson quizzed the villagers, who had heard rumours that the Norwegians had destroyed the bridge. The road to it from Henning followed a nine-mile track over the mountains. The snow was deep and the men of the KOYLI were exhausted, but Hibbert knew that he was dealing with fellow-Yorkshiremen. He was determined to get the battalion out intact. He took a risk and abandoned all the remaining stores and equipment, retaining only small arms and a few essential items. The wounded were warmly wrapped up and strapped to requisitioned sledges. At dusk the battalion, led by Mathieson, moved off in single file. En route two men of the Lincolns joined them and they learned that the Germans had entered Steinkjer. This spurred them on because the bridge they were heading for was no more than six miles east of Steinkjer. The only other escape route lay towards the Swedish border and Hibbert knew that they would never manage that distance.

The column covered barely a mile in an hour over the difficult ground. They reached a ridge and a bridge could be seen in the valley below. It spanned a deep gorge through which rushed a torrent of thaw water. The trees concealed the approaches to the bridge and a fighitng patrol was sent ahead to reconnoitre. The all-clear signal was given and the column crossed safely. 'The rest of the retreat is a tale of endurance,'* which matched that of the Lincolns. The KOYLI during the short campaign lost four men killed and one seriously wounded; forty-four of their soldiers were missing.

The Lincolns, who had borne the brunt of the fighting, had reached a

*Lieutenant-Colonel Walter Hingston, *The History of the King's Own Yorkshire Light Infantry*, pp. 69–76.

point just south of Bangsund by first light on 24 April. Colonel Newton failed to contact 'C' Company and part of Headquarter Company who had not received the order to withdraw. The two companies, about 200 strong, joined forces under Major Stokes. During a lull in the air attacks they headed north, often forced to crawl through the thick snow. They kept close personal contact during the brief hours of darkness, heading in the direction of Henning. When they got to the village they found that the KOYLI had passed through the previous evening. At Henning a windfall of stored food found in a barn was supplemented by chocolate, biscuits and much appreciated cigarettes from the village store.

Near Kvam they contacted a Norwegian outpost and found that their battalion had taken the westerly road to Namdalseid, and not to Grong as they had expected. On 24 April they encountered a Norwegian missionary who guided them without mishap to Mejer from where they were able to contact the Hallams.

Transport was provided for them to rejoin the Lincolns, where arrangements were made for the sick and wounded to be treated in the hospital at Namdalseid. The two companies had covered forty-five miles in two days over rough snow-covered country. The temperature at night bordered on freezing point, and their Arctic clothing had been lost during the fighting. All their personal weapons, rifles and Brens, had been carried to the end and no one had fallen out.

Although the Lincolns' Army vehicles had docked at Namsos on 25 April no mail had arrived for the soldiers since landing in Norway. They had had one pay parade on Norwegian soil. But they were comparatively well fed and morale was high despite their setbacks. The Luftwaffe continued to harass them as they moved north to Namsos to prepare for embarkation.

They passed through road blocks manned by the Norwegians and hurriedly skirted the burnt-out town on their way to the quay to wait for the expected destroyers. 'A' Company was detailed to collect the cherished rifles they had carried so far across the mountains and to stack them for their Norwegian comrades. The Lincolns learned much later that many of these rifles had been hidden and used for training Milorg, the Norwegian resistance movement, in the later war years.

On 2 May HMS *Afridi* came alongside the damaged quay and took the battalion aboard. They had lost two men killed and eighteen wounded, with fifty-two missing. The destroyer ferried the Lincolns out to the French auxiliary cruiser *Kantara*, where they found Brigade HQ and 700 Chasseurs Alpins. There they waited for the main convoy to form.

On 23 April Lieutenant-Colonel Robbins received orders to withdraw and the Hallams headed north through fresh snow towards Beitstad. They were unaware that the Germans were not in hot pursuit. The enemy, having achieved General Woytasch's immediate aim of securing his northern flank, were digging in around Steinkjer and consolidating their gains. The heavy snow storms that had grounded the Luftwaffe had also disrupted the German supply columns.

This lull benefited the Hallams and the other two battalions as they struggled towards Namsos. They were further helped, indirectly, by the arrival of the aircraft carriers *Ark Royal* and *Glorious*, with a strong escort, off the coast of central Norway. British aircraft attacked Vaernes airfield in strength on 25 and 28 April, causing considerable destruction. The Germans reacted quickly and drafted in 800 Norwegian civilians to repair the damage. The Luftwaffe repeatedly attacked Admiral Wells' force, which withdrew westwards to a safer area, having destroyed twenty German aircraft for the loss of fifteen of their own.

Having been in reserve, the Hallams had had no direct contact with the enemy. Their first clash came on 26 April about two miles south of Beitstad, when a German cyclist patrol blundered into a platoon position commanded by 2/Lieutenant L. M. Lonsdale-Cooper. There was a brief skirmish during which the platoon Sergeant, with the unlikely name of Innocent, killed their first German. The platoon took one prisoner before the enemy withdrew.

Two days later a helpful Norwegian civilian used the open telephone network to tell the Hallams that a patrol of Germans about twenty strong had occupied buildings on the outskirts of Beitstad. Two platoons of 'B' Company under Captain R. O. S. Dimmock moved cautiously down the single track road. The fresh snow prevented them from surrounding the buildings but Dimmock led an assault from the road and was slightly wounded in the attack. CSM Howden, in the forefront, was also hit. Ignoring his wound, Howden led the Hallams into the building where they killed two Germans and took one prisoner. CMS Howden was later awarded the Military Medal for his gallantry.

On 28 April the Hallams reached the Elden-Namdalseid area near the crest of the watershed between the two fiords. There they met the 13th Battalion Chasseurs Alpins who relieved them. The French ski troops were now fully mobile. They began to patrol the valley of the Bongaa and the surrounding heights. The 67th Battalion Chasseurs were back in reserve with 1/4th KOYLI, and the remaining French battalion, the 53rd, had re-embarked in the first stage of the evacuation of Namsos.

Following the handover to the French, the Hallams moved into reserve at Bangsund, about fifteen miles south of Namsos. From 1 May on, they acted as rearguard to the Lincolns and the KOYLI as they moved up towards the embarkation point. Thick fog prevented the destroyers moving in to Namsos harbour and the evacuation was delayed for twenty-four hours.

On 2 May the Hallams moved up to Namsos quay for embarkation. Colonel Robins and about fifty others remained on shore, searching for stragglers. The CO and his detachment eventually boarded the destroyer *Afridi* at 0230 hours 3 May, just two hours after the Sappers of 230 Field Company blew the bridge at Bangsund. As the *Afridi* pulled out from the harbour her gunners shelled the rows of largely unused Allied transport lined up on the quay, leaving them in flames.

On 27 April General Carton de Wiart received the expected message that the War Cabinet had decided in principle to evacuate Central Norway. We know that he (Carton de Wiart) had, on 23 April, suggested to the CIGS that evacuation should be considered, and it is reasonable to assume that the General had discussed with his staff the problem of getting his troops safely away through the port of Namsos.

On the same day he met Admiral Vivian, the Flag Officer of 20 Cruiser Squadron, the French Commander, General Audet, and Brigadier Phillips. They decided to plan for evacuation on two successive nights, 1/2 May and 2/3 May. Carton de Wiart agreed that the French contingent should re-embark before the British but that the French would leave a party of ski troops to operate with the British rearguard.* An empty ship was available and one French battalion, 53rd Chasseurs Alpins, was embarked at dusk on 28 April.

In his book *Happy Odyssey* (p. 172) Carton de Wiart relates that, before the meeting referred to above, General Audet 'begged' him not to leave the French troops to the last. Wiart wrote, 'He seemed much moved and I assured him that not a single British soldier would be embarked until every Frenchman was on board ship.' It must have been an emotional moment. As far as he could, de Wiart kept his word and, apart from a few specialized ski detachments, the French were got away first.

Supplies were still coming in from Britain, and on the night of 28/29 April a battery of much-needed Bofors anti-aircraft guns was landed at Namsos. Unfortunately these guns were without predictors, which meant that they could not be accurately aimed.

On 29 April Carton de Wiart received a message instructing him to send a detachment to Mosjöen by sea, and to post a rearguard at Grong. This would delay the enemy for as long as possible. The Allied force would then withdraw northwards overland to Mosjöen.

*Despatches, Supplement to the *London Gazette* of 28 May 1946, p. 260.

Carton de Wiart had doubts about the strength of the proposed rearguard at Grong. He signalled Massy's HQ, asking if the rearguard was intended to comprise his whole force. The reply made it clear that the strength of the rearguard to remain at Grong was a matter entirely for his (Wiart's) discretion.

There followed an exchange of telegrams in which Carton de Wiart strongly opposed the plan for a rearguard. He gave the following reasons: first, there was insufficient transport or petrol to sustain the force; second, and more importantly, the state of the road, which was, in Wiart's view, impassable. The thaw had started and the operation would be likely to end in disaster.

In further messages Carton de Wiart would not give way. He declared that '. . . even the passage of a small party of French Chasseurs by the land route is impossible. This operation is not to take place.' Finally, Massy wired that if, in the opinion of General Audet, the retirement of a small party of French Chasseurs by the land route was impossible, the operation was not to take place. (Massy: Despatches, Part One.)

In the event, no withdrawal by land from Grong to Mosjöen did take place. However, as we have seen earlier (see p. 71), the route to the north *was* open. Prior to the German advance, a Norwegian battalion had moved from Mosjöen to Grong. They returned along the same route in the first week in May, this time using the railway.

After them came the German soldiers of General Feuerstein's 138th Mountain Regiment. They covered the 125 miles from Grong to Mosjöen in five days, much to the consternation of the Scots Guards. Had the Norwegian commander in the area (Colonel Getz) been consulted, the real state of the road could have been ascertained. Dr Derry cites the Allied failure to comply with the order to withdraw overland to Mosjöen as 'a practical result of the lack of co-operation [with the Norwegians].'*

However, as we know, Carton de Wiart did accede to General Massy's request to send a detachment by sea to Mosjöen. On 30 April a party of 100 Chasseurs Alpins and a British detachment of two Bofors anti-aircraft guns went by destroyer to Mosjöen. A week later they were replaced by two of the British Independent Companies. During the move the Luftwaffe was very active and HMS *Bittern* and two trawlers were sunk.

By 1 May arrangements to evacuate the French contingent were complete, and at 9 p.m. they were ready on the quayside. But no troop transports or destroyers arrived owing to thick fog in Namsenfiord. The evacuation was postponed for twenty-four hours. Massy signalled Carton de Wiart, asking him to carry out the evacuation in one night instead of

*Letter to the author, 10 October 1987.

two (for obvious reasons the Admiralty was anxious to complete the task with all speed).

Admiral Vivian readily agreed and arrangements were made to get all the troops away on the night of 2/3 May. Stores and equipment were to be abandoned. By 1 a.m. on 3 May all troops, except a small rear party, were re-embarked.

Shortly after 2 a.m. the destroyer *Afridi*, with the rear party aboard, left the harbour. In the half-light there was no enemy air activity and the destroyer made all speed to catch up with the convoy.

The usual German scout plane was a little late arriving over Namsos that morning, but the scattered ships of the Allied convoy quickly caught the pilot's eye. His urgent signal soon brought a Luftwaffe bombing force from Vaernes airfield. At 8.45 a.m. they attacked the two large French transports, the first of a series of sorties which lasted until 3.30 p.m.

In the third attack dive-bombers hit and set on fire the French destroyer *Bison*. She was sunk by British destroyers as soon as her crew was taken off. The *Afridi* took some of the French survivors aboard. As she returned to the main convoy she was hit by two bombs forward of the bridge, killing ninety-three men. Among them were thirteen soldiers of the Hallams, who had been invited by the sailors to eat at a mess deck below the spot where the bombs landed.

The surviving soldiers and crewmen were taken aboard the destroyers *Imperial* and *Griffin* as the convoy formed into single line for mutual protection. The concentrated fire from the warships and the French troop-ships brought down at least three aircraft from the fifty or so attackers.

The enemy aircraft returned to base just before the British air cover appeared to escort the convoy into port. They arrived at Scapa Flow on the evening of 4 May.

As the battalions of 146 Brigade were retreating northwards the Norwegian forces were carrying out their own withdrawal. There was one vital difference in the attitude of the two forces. Whereas the British (and French) were single-minded in defending themselves as they made for the embarkation point at Namsos, the Norwegians were attempting to stop the German advance. This was part of an intermittent process which had started at Oslo on 9 April.

Since then the Norwegian 5th Division, based on Trondheim, had been out of touch with General Ruge's forces in South Norway. They were in communication with the Norwegian 6th Division further north and were heartened by General Fleischer's firm stand against the enemy north of Narvik.

The heroic defence of Hegra fort has been briefly mentioned. It deserves to be more fully recorded. The fort was built in 1907 on a hilltop eight miles inland from Vaernes. It formed part of the defences along the Swedish frontier and its guns pointed towards Sweden. On 10 April 1940, Major Holtermann, the second-in-command of the Norwegian 3rd Artillery Regiment, was looking for a rallying point after the German landing at Trondheim had scattered his regiment.

Holtermann moved into Hegra, taking with him about fifty partly-trained men with a few rifles and machine-guns. He was able to salvage and use weapons stored at the fort together with uniforms and some equipment. Volunteers swelled his ranks to 260, including one nursing sister, Ann Margrethe Bang. He organized ski patrols and scoured the surrounding hills for signs of the advancing Germans. Holtermann established a line of communication to his District Headquarters, using his more expert skiers.

There were four old 10·5 cm artillery pieces and two 7·5 cm guns, mounted on pedestals, left in the fort. Like all old-established Norwegian defences they pointed to the east and could not be used against the enemy-held Vaernes airfield.

Major Holtermann and his garrison held out against repeated German attacks and Hegra became a symbol of successful Norwegian defiance. Holtermann's stand at Hegra is an example of what the Norwegians could achieve. It seems to the author that they were an asset largely wasted by the Allies, particularly in the attempt to recapture Trondheim. Fighting patrols from Hegra inflicted serious casualties among the enemy and provided a much-needed boost to the morale of the Norwegians country-wide. The defence of the fort helped the British by pinning down German troops which might have been used against 146 Brigade. Hegra held out for a few days after the Allied evacuation but the Germans cut off food supplies and at 5.15 a.m. on 5 May Holtermann capitulated.

The local commander, Colonal Getz, had conferred with Brigadier Phillips on 18 April and explained to him that his (Getz's) troops were 'inexperienced, poorly armed militia' mobilized by the two local regiments.

Nevertheless they gave a good account of themselves as they fought dourly against the advancing Germans. Their mortars and heavy machine-guns gave valuable support to the British, as at Verdalsöra and Steinkjer. Almost to a man they were good skiers and readily took up this role to fill the disturbing gap in the British defences.

It is obvious that the senior commanders and their planning staffs in London lacked detailed knowledge of the local difficulties and special needs of the often isolated Norwegian forces. When General Massy was appointed commander of the North Western Expeditionary Force* on 19 April, his command excluded the forces in the Narvik-Bodö-Mo area but included the troops operating out of Namsos and Aandalsnes. There was some ambiguity about the chain of command in the field as far as the Norwegian forces were concerned, but it was generally accepted that the orders given by Allied senior commanders would be observed by all officers, including the Norwegians, according to prevailing circumstances.

But the Norwegians were not directly affected by the fast-moving events happening elsewhere in Europe. Their concern was with getting the Germans out of Norway and they relied upon the Allies to keep them fully informed of their strategic plans.

The Allies saw this in a different light. In their view a degree of absolute secrecy was necessary at every level on a 'need to know only' basis, and when the virtually unchallenged supremacy of the enemy in the air put our ports in Central Norway in jeopardy they did not rush to tell the Norwegians of the possibility of evacuation.

As early as 23 April Carton de Wiart had signalled London of his conviction that the evacuation of Mauriceforce should now be considered. The sequence of events which followed is covered by General Massy's Despatches, which have already been discussed.

The Norwegian commanders, including Colonel Getz, knew nothing of Carton de Wiart's forebodings. Getz was fully aware of the need to stop enemy reinforcements reaching Narvik and when on 23 April Generals Béthouart and Audet asked him to support the Chasseurs in an attack on the German left flank he agreed. Whether Getz knew of the parlous state of the retreating British troops is uncertain. But he knew that 4000 Chasseurs Alpins when fully mobile were a formidable force. The immediate objective of the combined contingent was to dominate the isthmus east of Hjelle and push on as far as possible towards Steinkjer. These plans had the consent of the Force Commander,† who agreed to make the KOYLI available as a reserve.

There was a lull in enemy air activity and the French Generals, whose troops had seen no action and sustained no losses, were prepared for an attack on the advancing Germans. The Norwegians, too, were over-optimistic and had grossly under-estimated the number of Germans in and around Steinkjer. At Grong, on 26 April, the French Generals again conferred with Colonel Getz with a view to developing a counter-offensive against the Germans but this came to nothing when, two days later, Carton

*The NWEF title was transferred to Auchinleck's command on 5 May.
†Derry (p. 95), who, on 10 October 1987, wrote to the author that 'the history of the joint operation with Audet and disingenuous behaviour over the evacuation suggests an almost contemptuous disregard for the Norwegians'.

de Wiart warned the French that an evacuation was imminent.

This information was kept from Getz until the evening of 2 May. The disillusioned Colonel, who had been urged to use his Norwegian soldiers in an attacking role, now found himself abandoned. General Moulton comments:

> Flowery wording could not redeem the shortness of this notice, due presumably to a misguided belief in the vital importance of secrecy. The Norwegians had welcomed and helped the British and French, and this was scurvy treatment. Far better to have faced the issue frankly and personally earlier. (p. 212)

On 3 May, as the Allied convoy sailed south, Colonel Getz was forced to capitulate to the Germans.

Considering that the strength of Mauriceforce exceeded 6000 men, the total British casualties were light compared with those of Sickleforce at Aandalsnes (where British casualties totalled 1402 all ranks). At Namsos nineteen were killed, forty-two wounded and ninety-six posted as missing.

As one would expect, there is no lack of post-mortem pronouncements on the failure of the Namsos expedition. In preference to well-meaning armchair critics I choose the summing-up of Lieutenant-Colonel Walter Hingston, who fought throughout the short campaign with the King's Own Yorkshire Light Infantry:

> The retreat of 146 Infantry Brigade to Namdalseidet is not a bright story in the history of the British Army. Indeed it is doubtful whether British troops have ever been forced to retire with so little effort on the part of the enemy. On the other hand it is also doubtful if a British force have ever before been asked to do so much with so little.
>
> By reason of training, equipment, lack of supporting arms and poor tactical dispositions, the brigade was bound to fail. There was no scope for initiative and no reason for the last man and the last round.
>
> Swapping punches can at times be a stupid act which, though brave, may lead to utter defeat. The criterion of success, therefore, resolved itself into a reckoning of souls saved to fight another day under more favourable conditions.*

*Hingston, p. 78.

PART FIVE

Operations based on Aandalsnes
17 April to 3 May 1940

The Regimental History of the 1/5th Battalion of the Royal Leicestershire Regiment records that its exploits in Central Norway tell of 'a battalion of partially-trained, ill-equipped men who, through sheer determination and pride in their county regiment, were able to achieve all that was asked of them'.

These words also apply to the 8th Battalion of the Sherwood Foresters, the old Nottinghamshire and Derbyshire Regiment, who served with the Leicesters in 148 (T A) Infantry Brigade under Brigadier H. de R. Morgan.

Both battalions were formed to meet the need to call to the colours as many men as possible in the shortest possible time. The aim was to get Britain on a war footing for a conflict for which she was not prepared. As we have seen, the hasty dilution of old-established Territorial regiments in 1938–39 to provide additional (but poorly prepared), battalions was to add to the many problems faced in Norway.

In early April, 1940, the 1/5th Leicesters, commanded by Lieutenant-Colonel G. T. German, were training on the Yorkshire moors. On 7 April they were ordered to proceed to Rosyth and embarked in H M S *Devonshire*. The next day, without leaving port, they were trans-shipped to the liner *Orion*, now in use as a troopship. Once more they were ordered off, and dispersed to wait until 16 April, when they finally sailed for Norway in Royal Navy vessels.

The unfortunate consequence was that their ammunition, equipment and stores, which initially had been carefully and tactically loaded, were distributed over a wide area, much of it now irretrievably lost to them.

The Leicesters finally left for Norway in two halves. Colonel German and two of his companies ('A' and 'D') were embarked with HQ 148 Brigade and its few supporting units in the anti-aircraft cruisers *Curacoa* and *Carlisle*. The convoy formed up, ready to sail, late on 16 April.

The other two rifle companies of the Leicesters ('B' and 'C'), under Major A. H. Atkins, moved from Rosyth to Aberdeen. Two days later they sailed in the *Magnus*. In the same convoy was the cargo ship *Cedarbank*, carrying the battalion's transport. She was sunk by a U-boat before reaching Norway. This forty-eight-hour separation of the two halves of the battalion significantly reduced the effectiveness of Colonel German's force. Within five days he was facing a strong enemy attack north of Lake Mjösa with his battalion at half-strength.

The 8th Foresters, under their commanding officer Lieutenant-Colonel T. A. Ford, followed the same chaotic embarkation pattern. Like their comrades the Leicesters, they embarked at Rosyth on 7 April only to be promptly off-loaded and taken to a camp at Dumfermline until 14 April. The battalion was then split. 'S' and 'C' Companies were put into the cruisers *Arethusa* and *Galatea*, while the remainder of the battalion embarked in the troopship *Orion*. But on 16 April, in the dark and during a howling gale, the soldiers in the *Orion* were trans-shipped to the *Arethusa* and the *Galatea*. In the confusion many stores were left behind, including part of the Foresters' stock of mortar ammunition.

Up to this point the destination of 148 Brigade was Namsos, to serve under General Carton de Wiart. Brigadier Morgan's orders were altered just after the convoy sailed at 7 a.m. on 17 April. This meant that the meticulous planning for operations around Namsos had been in vain.

The new instructions sent the brigade to Aandalsnes, with orders to secure Dombaas and then to operate northwards and take offensive action against the Germans in the Trondheim area. This indicated that the small force of two battalions would have to face two ways, south to Dombaas, north to Trondheim. However, one sentence in the instructions may have reassured Morgan. 'About 600 sailors landing Aandalsnes night 17/18. Their role after landing will be communicated to you later.'*

In fact the 'sailors' were originally meant to land at Aalesund, a large port south of Aandalsnes with good access to the Leads. The force of forty-five officers and 680 partly-trained seamen and Royal Marines (Operation Primrose) sailed for Norway in four sloops. While en route their destination was changed at the request of the Norwegians and they landed safely at Aandalsnes on the evening of 17 April.

Their commander, Lieutenant-Colonel H. W. Simpson RM, posted his men in platoon groups along the railway running parallel with the old road linking the mouth of the Romsdal with the small town of Dombaas. Simpson sited his Royal Marine light anti-aircraft battery near the harbour, backed up by eight naval 2-pounders. He retained two 3.7-inch howitzers but sent his two 4-inch naval guns on to Aalesund with a detachment of Marines.

*Derry, p. 251, quoting a War Office Signal of 16 April 1940.

According to Buckley (p. 43) Colonel Simpson's group were the first Allied troops to make contact with the enemy in Central Norway.* They encountered a sabotage party of about forty-five German paratroops along the railway line in the area of Dombaas. These had landed with a string of others going north from Dombaas, following the railway. Some of them had sustained injuries through being dropped from an insufficient height, their parachutes had opened partially or not at all. Those who survived, unused to the harsh conditions and bitter night temperatures, were so shaken or injured that they quickly surrendered to Simpson's men.

Meanwhile in London the Military Co-ordination Committee was having difficulties in finding a commander for the land forces earmarked to take part in the proposed combined operation to attack Trondheim from the sea. Codenamed Operation Boots (later changed to Hammer) the assault was due to go in on 22 April. Major-General P. E. Hotblack was selected to command this force and received his orders from the War Office on 17 April. But before he could take up his post he had a stroke on the Duke of York's Steps, after leaving his London club, and died.

The next day (18 April) Brigadier H. P. M. Berney-Ficklin, the commander of 15 Brigade in France, was appointed in his place. On the same day the date of the proposed landing at Trondheim was put back to 24 April. Berney-Ficklin flew to Scapa Flow on 19 April and, on landing, the aircraft crashed. He, and most of his staff, were injured and on 22 April Major-General B. C. T. Paget was appointed in his place. But the attack on Trondheim had finally been called off, and Paget's orders (from Lieutenant-General Massy),† designated him as the commander of Sickleforce, now at Aandalsnes under the command of Brigadier H. de R. Morgan.

Paget's command did not extend to the forces at Namsos or Narvik. He was instructed to co-operate with the Norwegian Army in preventing the northward advance of the German army based on Southern Norway. He was warned of the necessity to safeguard his left and rear against attack by enemy forces from Trondheim, and from parachute-landed detachments on his lines of communication. His orders made it clear that he was *not* under the command of the Commander-in-Chief, Norwegian Army, (General Ruge).

Paget's area of operations was confined mainly to the Gudbrandsdal valley, which stretched from the end of the Romsdal south to the vicinity

*The threat from enemy parachutists had begun on 14 April when landings occurred in the mountains around Dombaas. The local Norwegian battalion captured or killed many of these.

†As already recorded, Lieutenant-General H. R. S. Massy, the Commander of 5 Army Corps, had just been appointed GOC of all Allied troops operating in Central Norway. The forces operating around Narvik were excluded.

of Lillehammer, near Lake Mjösa, a distance of about 140 miles.

General Ruge had moved the headquarters of the Norwegian Army to Lillehammer, intending to defend the Gudbrandsdal and Osterdal valleys against the advancing Germans. Shortly after the partly-effective mobilization of 9/10 April the Norwegian plans were revised to give General Hvinden Haug command of the 2nd Field Brigade Group as a front-line force. This was backed up by second-line and garrison troops, the whole amounting to perhaps 10,000 men in all.

The name of this force was later changed to the 2nd Division, organized in four groups, known either by the names of their commanders or by the districts in which they fought. General Hvinden Haug commanded the Division and all eastern Norway north of the capital, but communications were difficult and orders were sometimes issued to groups direct from Army headquarters. As the situation changed, so did group formations: Group Dahl absorbed Group Mork, only to separate when Colonel Dahl moved his force to the west side of Lake Mjösa.

As the Germans, now equipped with tanks and artillery, pushed them north, the Norwegian formations fluctuated in strength as the younger men left the towns to find a fighting unit. An example is the II/IR5, an infantry battalion which had been mobilized on 9 April at Lillehammer for the neutrality watch. On 18 April it transferred from Hvinden Haug's group to Group Hiorth in the Osterdal, leaving Hvinden Haug with a mixed force which consisted of the 2nd Dragoons, a company of the King's Guard, the Torkildsen battalion and a 4-gun battery of artillery.*

None of the groups approached the strength of a British brigade. At best they mustered two battalions with a few guns and some engineers. This was the force with which General Ruge was determined to delay the German thrust along the vital axis northwards towards Trondheim. His repeated instructions to his field commanders were: 'Do not become heavily engaged with the Germans. We cannot afford to lose men and valuable equipment in a stand-up fight'. Ruge wanted to gain time, hoping that he could rely upon assurances of prompt and powerful Allied support. He was to be sadly disappointed.

Apart from one half-hearted attack, the convoy carrying Sickleforce had no trouble from the Luftwaffe. They arrived off the Norwegian coast on the evening of 18 April. To lessen the danger from air attack the force was split. One-third landed at Molde, across the Romsdalfiord to the north,

*Moulton (p. 137) quoting *Krigen i Norge* and other Norwegian sources.

1. King Haakon VII and the Crown Prince,
now King Olav V of Norway, April 1940.

2. 'The mountains rise sheer out of the fiord'; a photograph taken of Rombaksfiord, north of Narvik, by the author in April 1940.

3. The second sea battle of Narvik, 13 April 1940. The German destroyer *Georg Thiele* beached by her crew at the head of Rombaksfiord.

4. Soldiers of the 24th (Guards) Brigade landing at Harstad, Lofoten, 15 April 1940.

5. Royal Engineers and Norwegian civilians constructing Skaanland airfield, which never became fully operational.

6. Soldiers of 146th Brigade (TA) manning a checkpoint on the Namsos-Steinkjer road.

7. British stretcherbearers searching the ruins of Namsos for casualties.

8. A gun of 260th Anti-Aircraft Battery, Royal Artillery, towed by the horses of a Norwegian farmer.

9. The Vanguard of the 2nd Bn of the Polish Highland Brigade force-marching from Lenvik to Bjerkvik, Northern Norway, 13 May 1940.

10. A fighting patrol from the Norwegian 6th Division reconnoitring German defensive positions north of Narvik, 27 May 1940.

11. Soldiers of the Foreign Legion with French tanks on the Oyjord peninsula prior to the attack on Narvik, 28 May 1940.

12. German aircraft abandoned on a partly thawed lake north of Narvik, June 1940.

13. Norwegian civilians trying to retrieve belongings from their homes in Narvik, bombed by the *Luftwaffe* in June 1940.

14. Soldiers of the 2nd Bn, the South Wales Borderers, carrying personal arms and ammunition, disembarking from *S.S. Franconia* at Greenock on 10 June after the final evacuation from Northern Norway.

while the remainder landed at Aandalsnes. We know that the Marines had already landed, and Brigadier Morgan, (in Derry's words), faced: 'the rather absurd situation, not uncharacteristic of the atmosphere of improvisation in which the campaign began, that the main military force, half-expecting to find the Germans in occupation or at least the Norwegian population in need of some persuasion, was greeted at the quay by a British Consul in company with a Lieutenant-Colonel of Marines'. (p. 98)

Things now began to move very fast for Brigadier Morgan. Just after midday on 19 April he received a telephone call from Lieutenant-Colonel E. J. King-Salter, an officer of the Rifle Brigade, who, as British Military Attaché, was now working with General Ruge's headquarters in the Gudbrandsdal. King-Salter, conscious of the openness of the telephone system, described to Brigadier Morgan the parlous position of Ruge's forces. Four columns of German troops, equipped with tanks and artillery, were pushing rapidly north, constantly outflanking the inexperienced Norwegians.

By 18 April the enemy had advanced along the Glomma valley and taken Elverum, near the Swedish border. Another column took Hamar, midway along the east shore of Lake Mjösa, on the same day. Across the lake, below Gjövik, the enemy threatened the only intact Norwegian munitions factory at Raufoss. To the west they were rapidly advancing along the east bank of the Randsfiord, which put them in the position of outflanking the whole defensive network around Mjösa. Ruge was forced to commit his last reserve and now relied on Brigadier Morgan's force to relieve his desperately tired troops.*

Brigadier Morgan's orders had instructed him to secure Dombaas as early as possible. Soon after arrival at Aandalsnes he had despatched 'D' Company of the Sherwood Foresters by train to Dombaas, where they arrived about 4 a.m. on 19 April. Almost at once 'D' Company were asked to reinforce a Norwegian battalion, which had surrounded some sixty German parachutists five miles to the south. Before the Foresters could move off a signal arrived to say that the paratroops, survivors of the force dropped on 14 April, had surrendered to the Norwegians.

When Morgan got to Dombaas Colonel King-Salter, together with the French Attaché, Bertrand Vigne, arrived from General Ruge's HQ. They impressed on the Brigadier the urgent need to move his force south to the Lillehammer area. When Morgan pointed out the weakness of his force, and the fact that he was also committed to operate north towards Trondheim, he was told that if he did not reinforce Ruge then Norwegian resistance would cease and with it any hope of the Allies taking Trondheim.

*Massy, in his despatch of 29 May, 1946 (p. 2602) writes 'Lieutenant-Colonel King-Salter represented that the Norwegians were in urgent need of assistance, and stated that unless this was forthcoming immediately, the Norwegian Army would abandon all further resistance.'

King-Salter told Morgan that General Ruge had received a War Office telegram stating that 148 Brigade should at once support the Norwegian forces. General Massy's despatch is quite clear on this point:

> He [King-Salter] further stated to Brigadier Morgan that the War Office had sanctioned the 148 Infantry Brigade coming under the command of the Commander-in-Chief, Norwegian Army. Owing to the urgency of the situation Morgan decided to comply with the Norwegian request for assistance, at the same time sending a signal to the War Office asking for further instructions.

Morgan ordered his 1,000-strong force to prepare to move in support of the Norwegians. He went with Colonel King-Salter to meet General Ruge at Öyer, a few miles north of Lillehammer, reaching Ruge's HQ at about midnight on 19 April. The Norwegian Commander-in-Chief was greatly disappointed at the smallness of the British force. He had asked for at least three British battalions with full support of tanks, field artillery and anti-aircraft cover. He was bitter at not being fully informed of Allied plans, and was angry about rumours that the British were to blow up the Gudbrandsdal railway, which would have cut off his retreat.

He heard Brigadier Morgan's story about turning north to Trondheim in silence, then said firmly that as he, Ruge, was in command by order of the Norwegian Government, any move towards Trondheim must be postponed.

Brigadier Morgan was a resourceful commander; he agreed to Ruge's request. His small force was split between the two Norwegian groups astride Lake Mjösa. Morgan saw that Ruge's force were close to disintegration and hoped to boost their morale. He also realized that his own brigade was dependent upon the Norwegians for transport, communications,* rations and artillery support. The British troops had no maps, while the Norwegians knew their own territory. By dawn on 20 April, 148 Brigade was clear of Dombaas and, much to Morgan's dismay, were scattered along both banks of the Mjösa in improvised, often isolated, defensive positions.

Brigadier Morgan moved his headquarters to Lillehammer but had no real operational control over his troops. 'A' and 'D' Companies of the Sherwood Foresters (with half of HQ Company), under command of Major Roberts, arrived at Faaberg at 6.45 p.m. They left shortly afterwards in Norwegian lorries for Biri, on the west side of Lake Mjösa. The weather was bitterly

*The Germans, as mentioned earlier, had never succeeded in controlling the Norwegian public telephone network. General Ruge's Headquarters used a Lillehammer telephone number at this time. This number never varied, no matter where the HQ was subsequently located. Dudley Clarke: *Seven Assignments*, p. 109.

cold and the lake was frozen deeply enough in parts to bear tracked or wheeled vehicles.

Major Roberts reported to the headquarters of Colonel Dahl, whose group consisted on a brigade of three infantry battalions, a battery of field artillery, some engineers and an improvised supply column. Colonel Dahl told Roberts that the Norwegian left flank, running along the bank of the frozen lake, was reasonably secure. He ordered the Foresters to move to Nykirke, about eleven miles along a valley running north-west from the lake. Roberts' task was to protect Dahl's right, and because of the deep snow, he was promised a company of Norwegian ski troops to operate along his now unprotected flanks.

The Norwegian 4th Brigade, further west in the Ransfiord region, was under attack by the enemy – Group Fisher, now reinforced by Group Laendle. This was a threat to Dahl's right flank, but a more dangerous situation developed as German columns converged in a drive along the west bank of the lake. Dahl moved Roberts' small force back to the lakeside just north of Gjövik. The Foresters took up exposed positions in the open ground to the rear of the Norwegians defending the bridge at Braastad.

In the meantime Colonel Ford, with the other two and a half companies of the Foresters, arrived at Lillehammer in the early hours of the morning of 20 April. They were met on the platform by Brigadier Morgan and Colonel Dudley Clarke, a War Office staff officer attached to 148 Brigade. With them was General Ruge, who had taken time off from his arduous duties to meet the British troops.

Colonel Ford was told that part of the Norwegian 2nd Division under General Hvinden Haug was holding Lundehögda ridge, just south of Ring, on the east bank of the Mjösa. Hvinden Haug had a battalion and a half of infantry, a battalion of specialist ski troops and one battery of artillery. Supporting them was a regiment of unmounted dragoons about 1,000 strong, commanded by a Colonel Jensen.

At 10 a.m. on 20 April Ford reported to General Hvinden Haug at his HQ at Ring. He was asked if the Foresters could supply support weapons for the Norwegians. Ford provided a 3-inch mortar section and two anti-tank rifle sections, sending Lieutenant H. B. Dolphin along with them as a Liaison Officer. The two Forester Companies then took up their positions at Bröttum, on the east side of the lake, about eight miles south of Lillehammer. They remained there in reserve for the Norwegian battalion defending the Lundehögda ridge until 2 p.m. on 21 April, when General Hvinden Haug called them forward to relieve the front line troops.

Colonel German, with two rifle companies of the Leicesters under command, had detrained at Tretten on 20 April. They were taken by lorry to Lillehammer where they were told to move to Aasmarka, north-east of

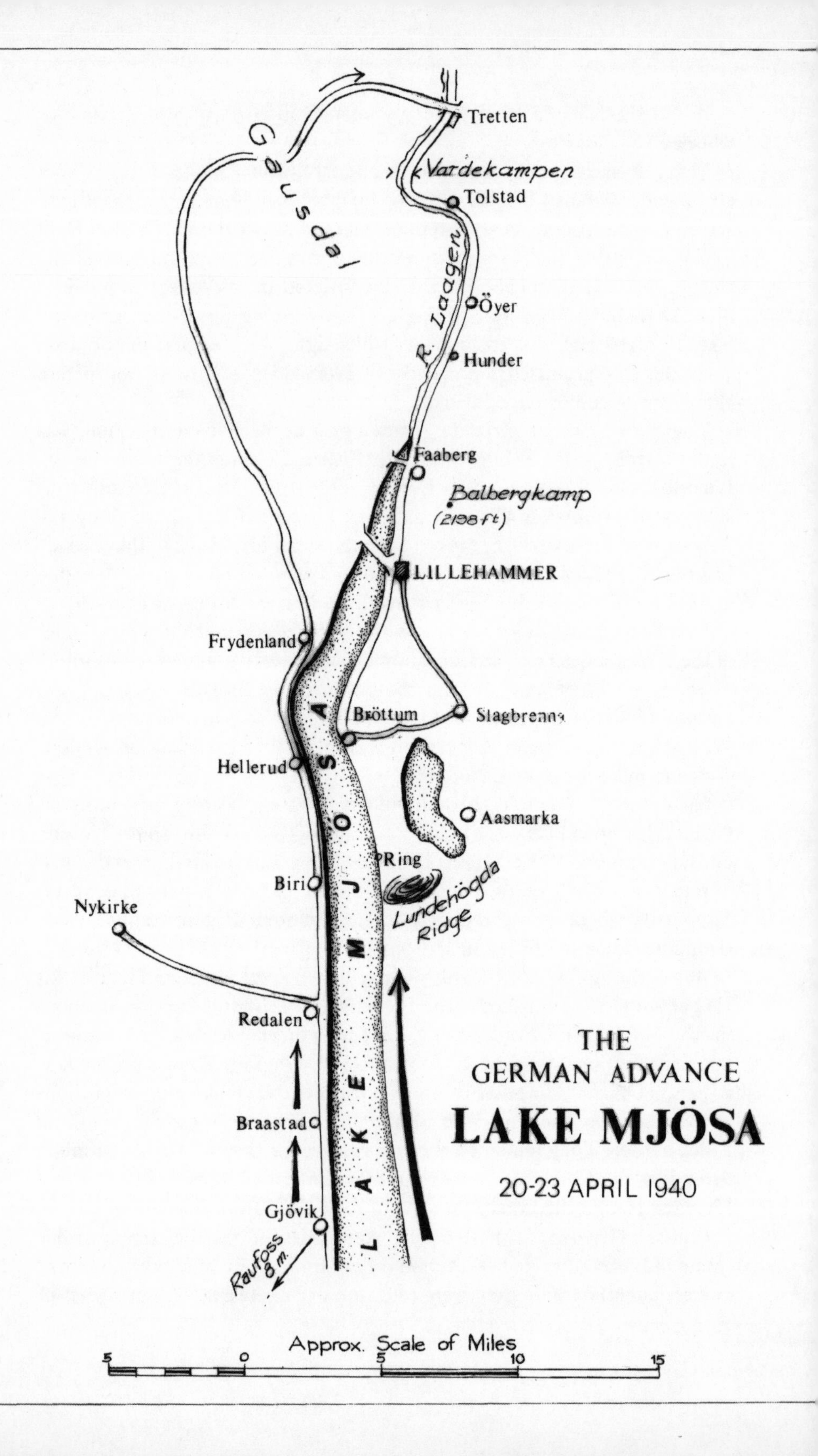
Tretten
Gausdal
Vardekampen
Tolstad
R. Laagen
Öyer
Hunder
Faaberg
Balbergkamp
(2198 ft)
LILLEHAMMER
Frydenland
Bröttum
Slagbrenna
Hellerud
Aasmarka
Ring
Lundehögda Ridge
Biri
Nykirke
LAKE MJÖSA
Redalen
Braastad
Gjövik
Raufoss 8 m.
THE
GERMAN ADVANCE
LAKE MJÖSA
20-23 APRIL 1940
Approx. Scale of Miles
5
0
5
10
15

the ridge at Lundehögda, to support the Norwegian Dragoons.

Brigadier Morgan's troops were now spread across the Mjösa front. To add to his problems they were interspersed with Norwegian units. The only complete battalion, the Foresters, were split between the two Norwegian groups, separated by the lake.

Morgan now realized how dangerous his forced dependence on the Norwegians had become. The detached companies had no requisitioned transport of their own. The brave civilian drivers of the Norwegian lorries often spoke no English and sometimes delivered badly needed stores to the wrong location. With no maps, the British had to operate in unfamiliar mountainous country, confined to the primitive roads by two feet of wet snow. The Luftwaffe had complete mastery of the air.

On the morning of 21 April the enemy began a determined assault along both banks of the Mjösa. The German General Pellengahr now had two infantry battalions, a mechanized machine-gun regiment and supporting artillery (about 4,000 men in all).

The Foresters' 3-inch mortar section came into action on the Dragoons' right flank but were quickly silenced by enemy artillery fire. Colonel Ford's men were ordered east to the rear of Aasmarka when it became clear that the Norwegians were going to withdraw from the Lundehögda–Aasmarka positions.

The British commanders worked out the order of withdrawal with General Hvinden Haug's Chief-of-Staff. The Norwegians withdrew first, followed by the two companies of the Leicesters, who had been harassed by the Luftwaffe but had incurred no casualties. They had not been very successful in relieving the Dragoons on the freezing hillside some 1,200 feet above sea level. The Norwegians, impatient and frustrated by the British soldiers' inability to move off the roads, remained in their positions around Arneberg until the Leicesters settled themselves behind Aasmarka.

The Dragoons came under heavy pressure from the enemy and, after drawing in his flank defences, Colonel Jensen was forced to withdraw through the British lines. Using the only available transport, the exhausted survivors of the Dragoons drove to a rest area about twelve miles beyond Lillehammer.

The lorries failed to return for the Leicesters, who were forced to march fourteen miles through the freezing night to Lillehammer. At the outskirts of the town the two companies were met by a small Norwegian convoy which picked up most of the party and took them to Balbergkamp, two miles to the north of the town. The small group of Leicesters who failed to get on the lorries were overtaken and captured by the Germans.

The eastern group of Foresters covered the early stages of the withdrawal from the positions at Slagbrenna. Derry (p. 107) reports a comment by the

Norwegian Colonel Jensen which, he writes, fairly sums up the whole episode: 'A difficult job; in a strange land, in frost and snow, with dark, thick woods in all directions. It might be difficult enough for us – for them [the British] it was infinitely worse.' Both companies of the Foresters got back to Balbergkamp with difficulty. The fighting troops available to Morgan on the evening of Sunday 21 April amounted to three weak rifle companies, plus the remains of a fourth.

Meanwhile on the west side of Lake Mjösa the Germans were consolidating their position before launching an attack on Colonel Dahl's defences. On the afternoon of 21 April, Brigadier Morgan and Colonel Dudley Clarke visited 'A' and 'D' Companies of the Foresters. There was considerable enemy air activity as a stream of JU 52's flew low up the lake carrying supplies and reinforcements to the German garrison at Trondheim. Brigadier Morgan warned Major Roberts of an impending withdrawal, made inevitable by the forced retreat of the east bank defenders.

This bad news was confirmed by Colonel Dahl, who had lost contact with the Norwegian 4th Division, further to the west. Dahl's own troops were exhausted after ten days of fighting. He detailed Major Roberts to cover his retreat. Roberts attended a briefing with General Ruge and King-Salter and, when the Norwegians had passed through, the two Forester companies withdrew northwards in the early hours of 22 April.

After the Norwegian engineers had blown the bridge at Stokeroen the Foresters, blocking the road near Hellerud, continued their withdrawal through Lillehammer. En route the small convoy carrying their meagre stores was cut off by the Germans and lost.

Shortly after leaving the companies west of Mjösa, Brigadier Morgan, who had been commanding the British troops in person, met the Norwegian Commander-in-Chief. General Ruge ordered Morgan to resume operational command of the scattered detachments of the Foresters and Leicesters and to form a defensive line around the bridge at Faaberg. The intention was to cover the withdrawal of General Hvinden Haug's group north into the Gudbrandsdal. When Morgan pointed out the inadequacy of his small force, General Ruge, while sympathizing, said that there was no alternative. It was then agreed that Colonel Dudley Clarke should return to London with a personal message from Ruge to the CIGS, General Ironside, urging the despatch of a strong British force to Norway. (Dudley Clarke, p. 120).

On the morning of 22 April the total strength of 148 Infantry Brigade amounted to 650 officers and men, including signallers, clerks and other administrative staff. The four rifle companies of the Foresters had sustained relatively few casualties, but 'A' and 'D' Companies of the Leicesters had lost six officers and about thirty men during the withdrawal. The two battalions now set up a single headquarters, with weak rifle companies that were much intermixed. To add to their problems the early shortage of equipment caused by the erratic loading at Rosyth and the loss of the *Cedarbank* was now worsened by losses sustained during the retreat north.

Despite the appalling conditions, morale continued to be reasonably high.* The British troops dug in around Faaberg, where Norwegian civilians had been employed to prepare basic defences. There was no time for an effective reconnaissance but Norwegian officers pointed out the main features of the defensive line. This ran from the bank of the River Laagen along a narrow lane to cross the main road and run up the steep side of the Balbergkamp, where the left flank rested.

The scattered British troops had been coming in to this position under cover of darkness and a group of farm buildings astride the main road was manned as a strong point. By the evening of 22 April the enemy had worked their way around the British flanks. Their ski troops, possibly detached sections of the 3rd Mountain Division, penetrated several miles behind the lines. Using the high ground above Hunder railway station, where Brigade HQ was situated, they caused some confusion and forced the Brigadier to change his location quickly.

On 23 April a boost was given to morale by the arrival of 'B' and 'C' Companies of the Leicesters, commanded by Major Atkins. As we know, they had embarked two days later than the main body of the battalion. They arrived, full of confidence, after an uneventful ride from Aandalsnes, where they had landed on 21 April. The tired and jaded defenders looked up from their slit trenches to see the slogan 'Joy Tours in Beautiful Norway' written across the side of the buses. The enthusiasm of the newcomers soon evaporated when the parlous position of the battalion was forcibly brought home to them.

By this time a composite force of Foresters and Leicesters about two companies strong had moved under cover of darkness to a prepared position selected by Colonel King-Salter. They were joined by one of the newly arrived companies of the Leicesters about three miles south of Tretten at Vardekampen, a high wooded hill feature where the river and the road ran through a defile.

They built stone sangars with a limited field of fire, assisted by Norwegian civilians who constructed rudimentary machine-gun posts on both sides of the River Laagen. The other fresh company of the Leicesters still held a covering position at Tolstad. In retrospect the situation was pretty hopeless. Derry (p. 110) makes this clear.

**History of the Royal Leicestershire Regiment*, p. 23.

It is possible to say that the ensuing engagement on 23 April was lost before it began, since the British Territorial troops retreating up the valley had now for the most part been without both food and sleep for more than thirty-six hours and had had no real rest for a week; they had lost much of their equipment, and were in any case without supporting arms.

The troops from the west bank of Lake Mjösa, who had just rejoined them, were in scarcely better plight after eleven hours freezing travel in open trucks, the majority of them without greatcoats. Two fresh companies of the Leicesters had also come in, as already noted, but the arrival of the second flight of the expedition at Aandalsnes on 21 April had been accompanied by a further setback.

For the motor transport of the Brigade, half the anti-aircraft guns, a quantity of urgently needed ammunition, demolition stores, and seventy-five tons of rations had been torpedoed off Aalesund in the transport *Cedarbank* – the only success obtained by German submarines against transports or storeships in the whole course of the April operation, but an important one. The three useable anti-aircraft guns were, however, ordered forward from Aandalsnes; but the troop was halted at Otta at 9.30 p.m. when the issue had already been decided lower down the valley.

Further south two companies of the Foresters were covering the withdrawal of Group Dahl. After defending a position south of Lillehammer they reached Östre Gausdal church at 2 a.m. on 23 April. They were ordered on to Tretten and arrived as the sun was rising. Cold and exhausted, they hardly had time to doss down before Colonel King-Salter asked for them to reinforce Vardekampen ridge and Major Roberts, reluctantly, agreed to send them south. The other company remained to guard the Tretten bridge, west of the river.

Brigadier Morgan had asked General Ruge for Norwegian troops to protect the hills on his left flank following the enemy ski-troop attack mentioned earlier. Three very weak squadrons of the 2nd Dragoons arrived and were positioned along the Vardekamp feature to the left of the British.

At 8.30 a.m. on 23 April the Germans attacked the Leicesters' outpost company at Tolstad, forcing them to withdraw. As the assault developed, the company commander was killed and the soldiers scattered. Very few of the company got back to the battalion.

Shortly after midday the enemy reached the narrow defile at Vardekamp. The Leicesters and the Norwegians had anticipated an assault on their positions on the hillside, but the Germans attacked the main road defences head on with three tanks. The heavy log road-block was smashed aside and the Boyes anti-tank rifle used by the British failed to penetrate the enemy armour.

A fire-fight followed, and the two Forester companies were reinforced by a third. The German infantry was held off for a while but the main road defences were not deep enough and the enemy broke through. During the fighting a small party of officers, including the Military Attaché, was surprised by German tanks. Some of them escaped by taking cover among the trees on the hillside.

The mixed Leicester and Forester companies, together with the Dragoons, were forced up into the wooded hillside and the Germans were now able to occupy Vardekampen, from where they could use their artillery against Tretten and the bridge. Colonel German's troops dourly defended Tretten throughout the afternoon, when hand-to-hand fighting developed. The Germans, using 5.9-cm close-support guns, were concentrating on Tretten and the environs of the bridge. As the casualties mounted Brigadier Morgan ordered a withdrawal. An improvised rearguard held off the enemy until about 9.30 p.m., by which time the west bank defenders, now almost out of ammunition, were able to withdraw towards the Heidal, forty-five miles to the rear.

To avoid the enemy, the men split into small groups and made their way towards Ringebu, unaware that it was already occupied by the Germans. Some of the British groups were captured, including that joined by Colonel King-Salter, who was seriously wounded. This group, led by Lieutenant-Colonel German, evaded the first enemy they encountered but were eventually taken prisoner.*

The Norwegian 2nd Dragoons, up on the saddle of the hill, had not been under serious attack. They, and a number of British troops, were able to get away safely. The Norwegian engineers detailed to blow the Tretten bridge were forced to withdraw with the British, leaving the bridge to fall into enemy hands.

The Leicesters company on Vardekampen could still be heard firing as the withdrawal got under way. Shortly afterwards they were overrun and the survivors taken prisoner. Colonel Dahl, having failed to get through to Tretten before the British retired, led his group to safety in western Gausdal.

The survivors of 148 Brigade, reduced to nine officers and about 300 men, withdrew through the Norwegian lines at Tromnes, between Tretten and Ringebu. From there they were transported by road to the Heidal valley and comparative safety. Many stragglers evaded the Germans and made their way through the snow-covered hills to rejoin their units, or to temporary internment in Sweden. Courageous Norwegian farmers risked their lives to feed and shelter them. The adventures and tribulations of some of the evaders will be told later.

During the withdrawal many instances of gallantry and courage were

*Among the decorations awarded after the war for Tretten was a Distinguished Service Order for Lieutenant-Colonel G. T. German. Colonel King-Salter, who almost died of his wounds, had his leg amputated in a Norwegian hospital.

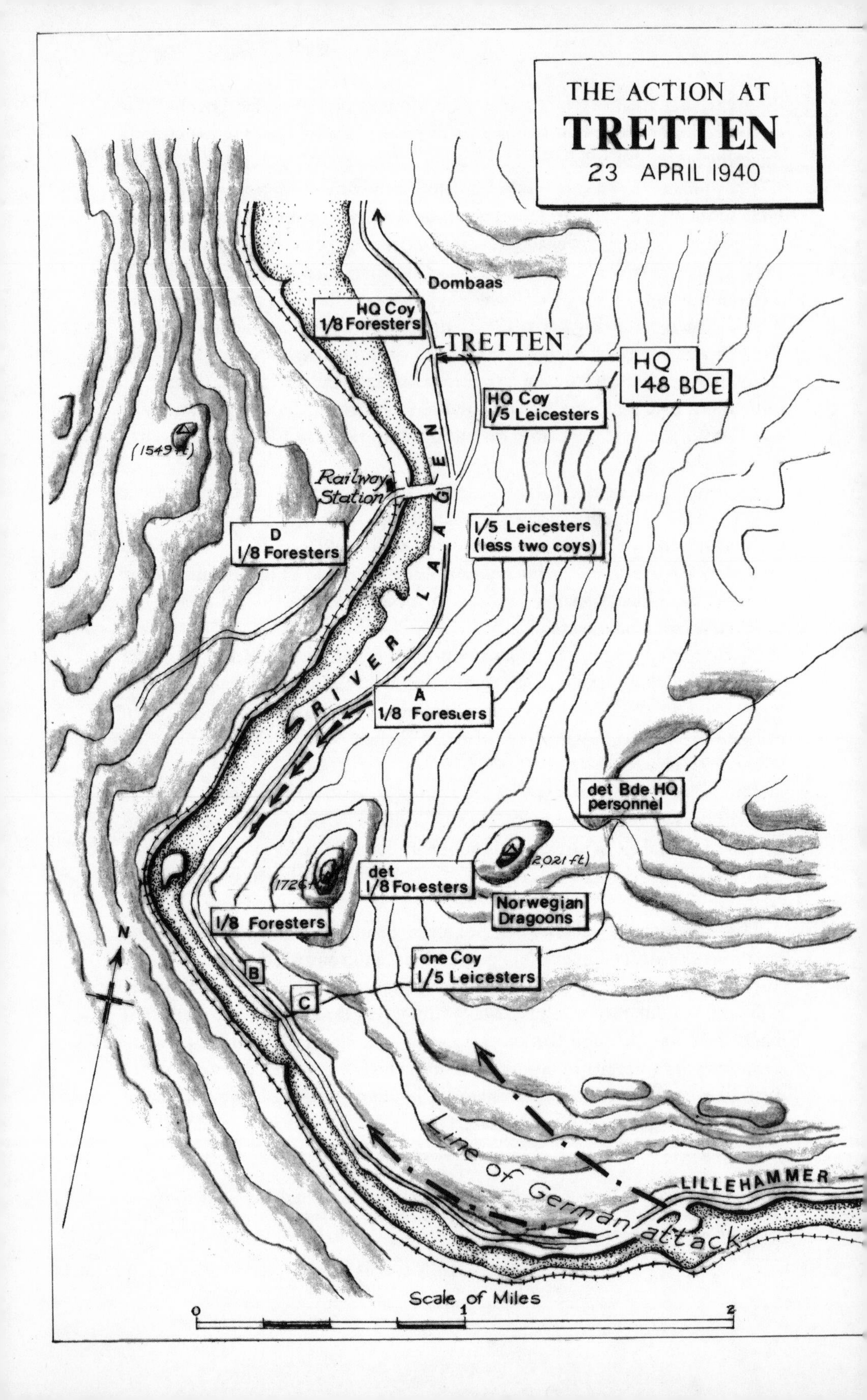

THE ACTION AT
TRETTEN
23 APRIL 1940
Dombaas
HQ Coy
1/8 Foresters
TRETTEN
HQ
148 BDE
HQ Coy
1/5 Leicesters
(1549 ft)
Railway
Station
D
1/8 Foresters
1/5 Leicesters
(less two coys)
RIVER LAAGEN
A
1/8 Foresters
det Bde HQ
personnel
(2,021 ft)
(1726 ft)
det
1/8 Foresters
Norwegian
Dragoons
1/8 Foresters
N
B
C
one Coy
1/5 Leicesters
Line of German attack
LILLEHAMMER
Scale of Miles
0
1
2

seen and recorded. As ever, many went unnoticed. Among the former, the commander of the Leicesters' Mortar Platoon, PSM L. Sheppard, cut off and with his mortars now out of action, refused to retire. Using his men as a rifle platoon, amid buildings blazing from German incendiary bullets, he held his position for two hours in the face of determined enemy frontal attacks. For this PSM Sheppard was awarded the Distinguished Conduct Medal.

For the British the battle for Tretten was costly in both men and morale. Inadequate resources and inept planning had defeated from the start their aim of bolstering the morale of the beleaguered Norwegians. It is clear that Brigadier Morgan did his best to carry out his orders, even when prevented from exercising the direct command of his own brigade. Moulton, in criticizing General Ruge's actions, writes:

> Morgan, in coming south at Ruge's request, placed himself in the hands of the Norwegian command and was left little freedom of choice, so that the responsibility for the destruction of his brigade rests largely with that command (p. 187)

Moulton draws attention to the 'ambiguity of the channels of command' which led to confusion over the withdrawal of Group Dahl, 'which was the immediate cause of the destruction of 148 Infantry Brigade in the attempt to hold Tretten'. This is not to say that Ruge foresaw, or even suspected, the dire consequences of his tactical plans. These were dictated by what he judged to be the best way of delaying the enemy advance towards Trondheim (and ultimately Narvik). The Norwegians fought as dourly and valiantly as the British. Furthermore, General Ruge, as Commander-in-Chief of the Norwegian forces, was led to believe that a much stronger British contingent, with at least one Regular brigade and some air support, would arrive through the Aandalsnes base in time to stem the German advance.

General Massy and others have testified to the 'generally excellent' behaviour of the British soldiers and their leaders, especially their junior officers. Massy, in his despatch (p. 2609), writes of the troops on the ground:

> Brigadier Morgan's 148 Infantry Brigade were young soldiers or Territorials to whom these operations were their first experience of war.
>
> These quite inexperienced troops were rushed into action in an effort to stem the German advance, when the Norwegian forces were already withdrawing. With their flanks turned owing to the fact that the exhausted Norwegian troops had been obliged to withdraw, and their centre pierced by armoured vehicles to which they had no adequate reply owing to the loss of their anti-tank guns at sea, it is not surprising that their casualties in missing were heavy, and heavier than would have been the case with more experienced

troops under more experienced regimental officers' leadership.

Massy goes on to praise Brigadier Morgan's 'capacity for making decisions' under appalling conditions. Enough has been written here to illustrate the general gallantry, (and some individual acts of bravery), of Morgan's soldiers.

Meanwhile, the long-awaited Regular reinforcements for Sickleforce were being disembarked at Aandalsnes and Molde.

On 21 April a War Office telegram confirmed that the Regular brigade to reinforce the Andalsnes expedition would be 15 Brigade, then stationed around Lille, in France. It was commanded by Lieutenant-Colonel H. E. F. Smyth, the CO of the 1st King's Own Yorkshire Light Infantry (KOYLI), who had taken over from the luckless Berney-Fickin. The three Regular battalions in the brigade were the 1st KOYLI, 1st Green Howards and 1st York and Lancaster Regiment.*

Supporting the brigade were 168 Light-Aircraft Battery, (less two troops), 260 Heavy Anti-Aircraft Battery, and 55 Field Company of the Royal Engineers, (less one section serving at Namsos). The brigade sailed from Dunfermline, in Scotland, leaving behind their motor vehicles, including, inexplicably, their tracked carriers, which would have been invaluable in Central Norway. This meant that heavy equipment such as 3-inch Mortars, anti-tank rifles, signal and medical equipment, was now carried by the soldiers, in addition to their normal bulky loads.

On 22 April two of the battalions embarked in naval vessels, the KOYLI in the crusier *Glasgow* and the York and Lancasters in HMS *Sheffield*. The Green Howards, under Lieutenant-Colonel A. E. Robinson, sailed two days later. After an uneventful voyage the KOYLI, now commanded by Acting Lieutenant-Colonel E. E. E. Cass, landed at Aandalsnes, less 'C' and 'D' Companies which were put ashore at Molde, on the northern side of the fiord.

The York and Lancasters, commanded by Lieutenant-Colonel A. L. Kent-Lemon, disembarked at the same two little ports. General Paget sent instructions to Brigadier Smyth on 20 April, despatching almost identical orders to Morgan on the same day. Paget's intention was to secure the lines of communication north and south of Aandalsnes, and also to use 15 Brigade in support of the eastern valley of Österdal, while Morgan continued to operate with 148 Brigade against the Germans coming up the western valley from Lillehammer.

*To avoid confusion we are reminded that Territorial battalions of two of these regiments, the 1/4th KOYLI and the Hallamshire battalion of the York and Lancasters, were already serving under General Carton de Wiart at Namsos.

Colonel Dudley Clarke met Smyth at Aandalsnes on 23 April (St George's Day) and told him of Brigadier Morgan's difficulties at Tretten (which Paget had not been aware of when he drafted his orders). Smyth agreed at once to send 15 Brigade south by rail to reinforce Morgan, then took the first available train to contact 148 Brigade.

Failing to locate Morgan, Brigadier Smyth met General Hvinden Haug near Ringebu. The Norwegian General confirmed that Morgan had lost about 700 men and it was agreed that 15 Brigade should move into the Gudbrandsdal at once to cover the withdrawal of the hard-pressed Norwegians to Dombaas, while the railway was still operating.

General Paget, while en route for Norway on 24 April, learned of the situation at Tretten. He modified his orders to Smyth, so that 15 Brigade could assist Morgan, and made a strong plea to General Massy for immediate air cover to protect Sickleforce against the ever-present Luftwaffe. It was arranged for a squadron of Gladiators to operate from the ice on Lake Lesjaskog, a long narrow sheet of water about thirty-five air-miles south of Aandalsnes. The planes would fly from the aircraft carrier *Glorious* which, with the *Ark Royal*, was due to arrive off the coast of Central Norway on 24 April.

At 4 a.m. on the same date the KOYLI reached Dombaas by train, minus 'C' and 'D' Companies which were still at Molde. They found Dombaas 'utterly wrecked, still smoking dismally in the morning light.' They quickly unloaded the two extra trucks, filled with willingly donated naval rations, hitched to the back of their train.

Meanwhile Smyth had contacted Brigadier Morgan at Heidal, about twenty-five miles north of Tretten. 148 Brigade had virtualy no senior officers and were continually harassed by the Luftwaffe as the intermixed companies tried to reorganize their scant resources.

Morgan was much senior to Smyth and the junior brigadier listened carefully as Morgan outlined the disheartening tactical position. After conferring with the Norwegians it was agreed that the depleted companies of the Leicesters and Foresters should be held in reserve to 15 Brigade while attempting to rest and recuperate.

Meanwhile the train carrying the KOYLI arrived at Otta to be met by a Supply officer who announced that the Germans were advancing on the town. (This information turned out to be false.) The battalion hurriedly detrained and, using tools from a nearby quarry, began to dig defensive positions, watched by an enemy scout plane.

Shortly afterwards the Luftwaffe began a bombing and strafing attack which was to last for ten hours. The fire from the battalion's Brens and the three Bofors guns brought down three enemy aircraft before a direct hit on one of the guns killed or maimed the crew. Three men of the

KOYLI were wounded and the remaining two Bofors guns were put out of action. When the battalion was able to move off they left the little town half-ruined by the enemy's bombs.

They reached Kvam on the morning of 25 April. They found a small village of low wooden buildings where the River Laagen, the road and the single-track railway criss-crossed each other at the bottom of the Gudbrandsdal valley. There they were joined by 'C' and 'D' Companies, whose stories of air attack on the journey fell on deaf ears.

At Kvam the river turns in its course and runs west to east, split in the middle by an island about half a mile long. On either side the hills slope sharply upward, thickly wooded with pines. The river, now thinly covered in ice, ran shallow around the island, with the road and the railway following the left bank.

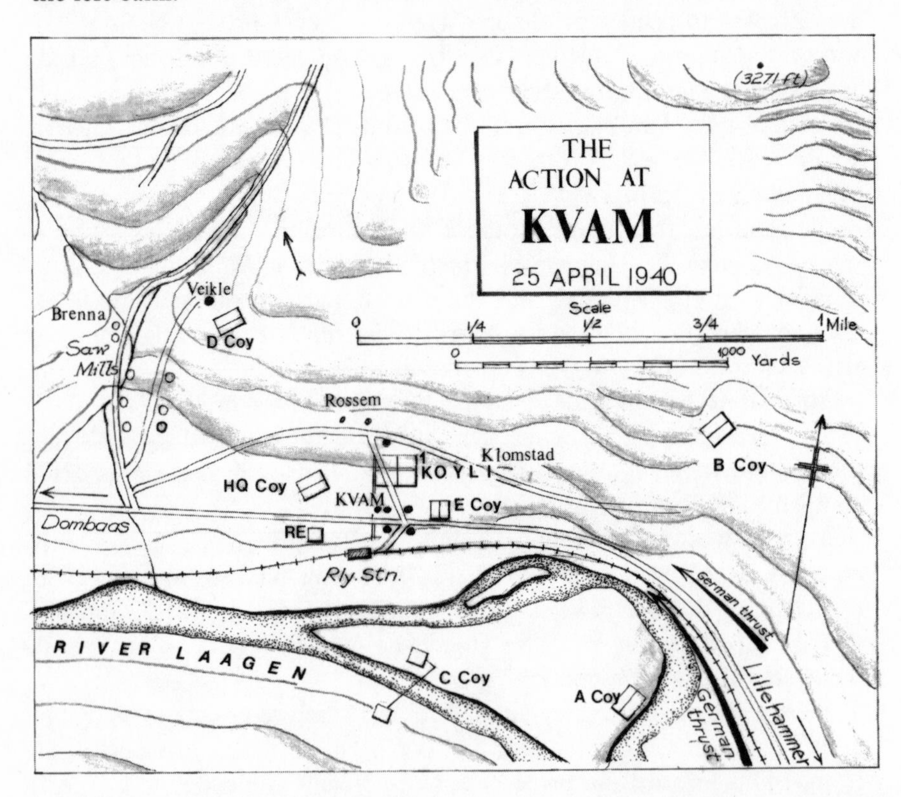

Brigadier Smyth established his HQ at Kvam, considered to be a strong defensive position compared with Tretten, which lay thirty miles to the south. Colonel Cass ordered the men to discard their heavy arctic clothing, deciding to fight the coming battle in light webbing: belt, braces and ammunition pouches. Their weapons, apart from rifles and Brens, were now reduced to two 3-inch mortars backed up by the five 25-mm Hotchkiss guns of the brigade anti-tank company.

Cass sited two companies forward: 'A' on the right, covering the road and the railway, and 'B' on the left flank among the immature silver birches on the valley side. 'D' Company was to the north, near the hamlet of Veikle, while 'C' Company was echeloned back along the river behind 'A'. Both of these latter companies had platoon posts dug in on the island. 'E' Company, which Cass had formed from the dismounted carrier platoon and 'unemployed' drivers, formed a valuable bonus to the KOYLI defences. It was held in reserve at the edge of the village.

General Hvinden Haug had assured Smyth that the Norwegian troops defending the ground south of them could hold on until the night of 25 April. But at 7.30 a.m. the Norwegians, carrying their wounded, began to withdraw through the KOYLI defences. Within the hour, 'quietly and calmly', they had all passed through, leaving the Yorkshiremen to face the enemy. Colonel Cass, an Infantryman of high quality, has described the onset of the German attack:

> First came three tanks and about fifty lightly equipped infantry. Behind came more infantry on foot, motor-cyclists, machine-guns mounted in side-cars and towed guns. Behind again came motor vehicle after motor vehicle – lorries full of infantry, wireless trucks, tanks, tracked carriers, guns and many others.
>
> It was a target that gunners would dream about – three-quarters of a mile of confined road, crammed with troops and vehicles, all clearly visible from the observation post. Just one battery of 25-pounders could have blown the enemy off the road.
>
> But the nearest approach to artillery was the little anti-tank guns. All that could be done was to wait until the enemy came within rifle shot.*

The forward companies were directly in the path of the Germans. With well-drilled discipline the KOYLI held their fire. One anxious soldier, checking to make sure his Lee Enfield was loaded, accidentally pressed the trigger and the battle was on.

At a range of 150 yards both 'A' and 'B' Companies opened fire. The enemy infantry went to ground, leaving several dead on the road. The tanks came on slowly, then ground to a halt at a dip in the road, where their fire was ineffective. But the German artillery moved quickly into position between the road and the river and at once began to shell the KOYLI positions.

The enemy fire was sustained and very accurate. The British soldiers crouched in their slits and waited. At this point Brigadier Smyth was wounded and Lieutenant-Colonel Kent-Lemon of the York and Lancasters assumed command of 15 Brigade. The German infantry attacked along the

*Brigadier E. E. E. Cass, CBE, DSO and bar, MC, quoted by Hingston in the *History of the King's Own Yorkshire Light Infantry* (Vol V, p. 90).

left flank, to be met by the concentrated fire of 'B' Company. The Germans, knowing now that the KOYLI were well dug-in, retired to stage a set-piece attack,* leaving 'B' Company with one soldier dead and one wounded.

'A' Company now faced the next assault, which came from the high ground above the river. They sustained heavy casualties and the survivors were forced back towards the village. To save 'B' Company from being outflanked, 'C' Company was ordered in to restore the line. As they edged forward along the river bank the enemy diverted heavy machine-gun and artillery fire on to them, cutting many down. The company commander was killed as the Germans tried to outflank the KOYLI line by crossing the frozen river.

'E' Company was brought in from reserve to help secure the right flank. Despite repeated enemy attacks, the line was held, and as night fell the more exposed positions were evacuated and a new line established.

'C' Company of the York and Lancasters came forward to replace 'A' Company of the KOYLI, which had lost four officers and eighty-five men. By 2.30 a.m. on 26 April it was light enough for the Germans to open up with small arms fire. A few hours later their artillery put down a heavy barrage and at 6.30 a.m. the first attack of the day came in against the York and Lancaster company. This and subsequent attacks failed until the enemy brought in the Luftwaffe. Kvam village and the defences surrounding it were heavily bombed and strafed.

The Germans now brought up 5.9 cm close-support guns, firing over open sights from about 2000 yards. 'B' Company, who bore the brunt crouching deep in their slit trenches, had few casualties.

General Paget had arrived at Aandalsnes on 25 April. He travelled by car to a small farmhouse just south of Dombaas where he was briefed by General Ruge. The Norwegian Commander-in-Chief again expressed his concern about the inadequacies of the British forces. He had expected two full infantry brigades on 18 April, hoping that his own exhausted troops could pull out of the line, rest and reorganize. He reiterated his complaint that he was never made fully aware of the Allies' plans.

Paget realized the validity of General Ruge's complaints. He agreed that Ruge's troops should be withdrawn, but asked for Norwegian ski detachments to guard the high ground on the British flanks. Ruge promised that his ski troops would operate under British command, and confirmed in writing that General Paget was entirely responsible for the Gudbrandsdal valley, and also for the protection of the railway from Dombaas to Oppdal, forty miles to the north. On 26 April Norwegian troops were withdrawn

*Moulton (p. 196) identifies the German attackers as a battalion of the 196th Division, whose records differ from the KOYLI account by reporting their own casualties as 'very light' (two dead and ten wounded).

from the Gudbrandsdal into rest areas south of Dombaas.*

On arrival at Kvam Paget took personal command. He ordered the KOYLI to withdraw at 11 p.m. on 26 April but was forced to bring the time forward when enemy artillery set fire to the woods in which many of the British positions were concealed. The KOYLI were ordered to pull out, protected by a small rear party armed with Brens and one of the anti-tank guns. The York and Lancaster company failed to get the order to withdraw, but reached safety after a difficult march through the wet snow on the hills.

'D' Company of the KOYLI also failed to receive the order to retire and the company commander, sensing a change in the sound of battle around 7 p.m., sent his runner to contact battalion headquarters. He found Kvam full of Germans and had to shoot his way out. The company commander formed his men into three strong fighting patrols. Covering each other, they fought their way through the woods and marched twelve miles to rejoin the battalion.

Numerous examples of initiative and bravery of this kind could be cited and many are recorded in the regimental histories. If names are to be mentioned, that of Major A. F. McC. Riggs comes to the fore. He constantly ignored danger and inspired his company to beat off enemy attacks time and again. He was wounded by a German tank when clearing a field of fire for a York and Lancaster anti-tank gunner to fire at the enemy armour. Major Riggs was later decorated for his bravery.

The KOYLI retired by transport to the Dombaas area, covered by the York and Lancasters, who had been reinforced by a company of the Green Howards. The enemy sustained heavy losses in the battle for Kvam. The British casualties were the largest incurred in any land engagement in the campaign, either by the Norwegians or any of the Allies.

The Green Howards had disembarked at Aandalsnes very early on 26 April and by 3 a.m. had loaded their train and got under way for Dombaas. While the rest of the battalion unloaded the stores, 'B' Company set off by road to reinforce the York and Lancasters near Kjörem. The newly appointed CO of the York and Lancasters, Major D. C. Tennent, positioned the Green Howards company in support of his own 'A' and 'B' Companies on the south bank of the river at Lien, one mile from Kjörem. 'D' Company of the York and Lancasters was on the left, enfilading the road, and the gap between was covered by the Brens of the Green Howards' Carrier platoon, under command of Captain G. R. Lidwill, and the Pioneers, who had been converted to a rifle platoon. The area was heavily

*Massy, Despatches (p. 2603).

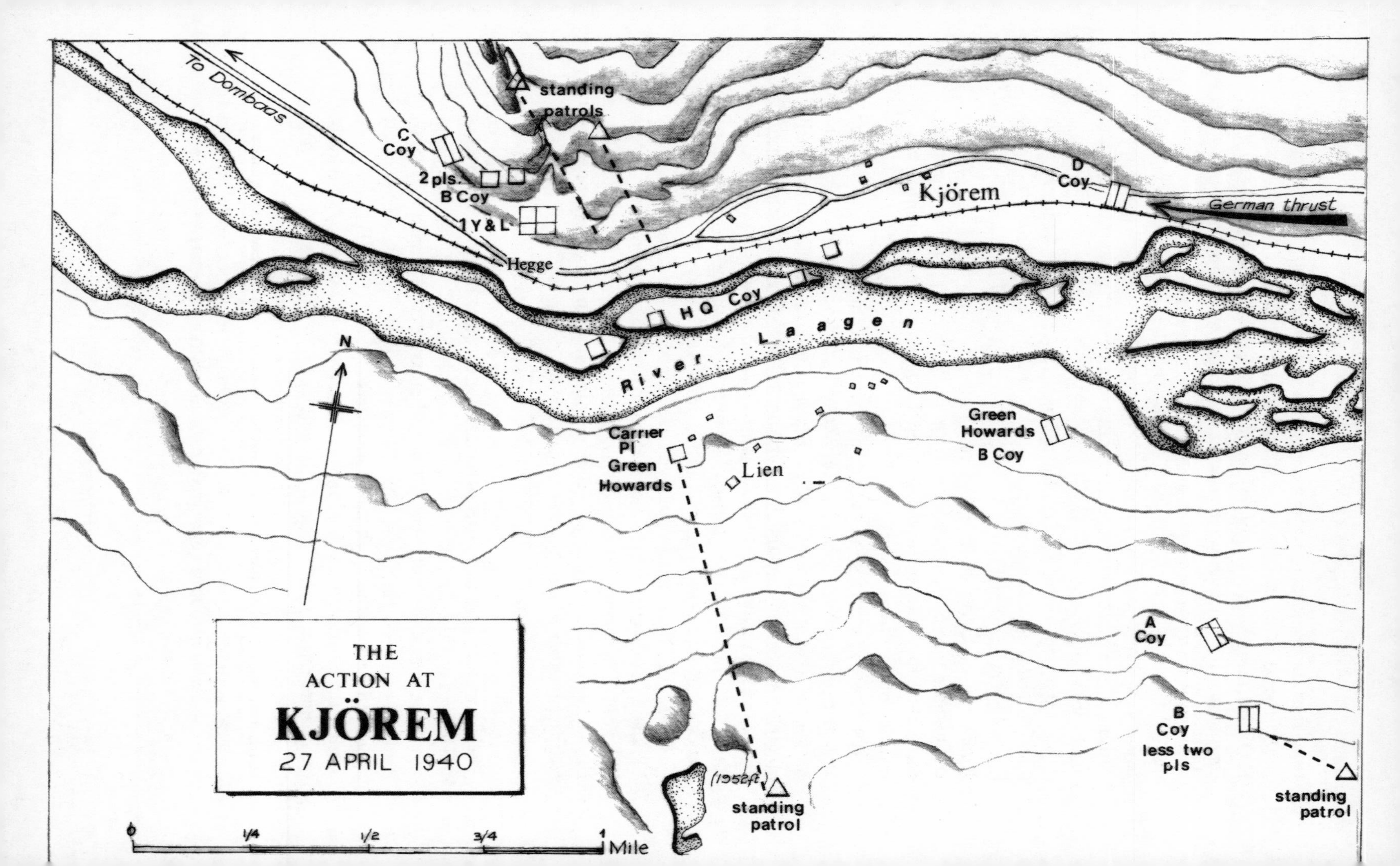
To Dombaas
standing
patrols
C
Coy
2 pls.
B Coy
1 Y & L
Hegge
D
Coy
Kjörem
German thrust
HQ Coy
River Laagen
N
Green
Howards
B Coy
Carrier
Pl
Green
Howards
Lien
A
Coy
B
Coy
less two
pls
(1952ft)
standing
patrol
standing
patrol
THE
ACTION AT
KJÖREM
27 APRIL 1940
0
1/4
1/2
3/4
1
Mile

wooded, restricting the field of fire. Company commanders ordered some of the obstructing trees to be felled and used them to construct sangars camouflaged with snow.

German scout planes immediately pinpointed these positions and, from about midday on 26 April, began strafing along the line of the River Laagen. Then the enemy artillery, with an observation post on the high ground, began intermittent long-range shelling. When the KOYLI had withdrawn through the York and Lancasters' positions, 'C' Company, which had been attached to the KOYLI at Kvam, was dropped off and went into reserve behind battalion headquarters on the left of the road.

Major Tennent ordered strong standing patrols up on to the high ground on both sides of the narrow valley. One of these reported enemy movement along the road from Lillehammer at about 8.15 a.m. on 27 April. The advance-guard of the Germans was stopped by fire from across the river, and from 'D' Company on the left of the railway. The enemy brought up heavy mortars and used machine guns firing incendiary bullets from the hill in front of the British left flank. The familiar German pattern began to develop. Their tanks moved forward along the road to give protection to the infantry, while their artillery and mortars pounded the York and Lancasters' platoon positions.

The Green Howards' company commander, Captain Bulfin, was worried about his right flank, obscured by the thick pine trees above his position. He sent out a standing patrol, who reported enemy movement forward and on the right. Communication with the York and Lancasters had been lost, and, as enemy pressure increased, Bulfin sent No. 10 platoon, under 2nd Lieutenant J. S. Bade, to make contact. After two hours' heavy going through the thick wet snow, Bade found the York and Lancasters' forward companies, who had suffered considerable casualties. Bade's platoon was able to give covering fire while the beleaguered York and Lancasters withdrew to a stronger position. He then made his way back to Captain Bulfin, to find the company under heavy mortar fire. Later, in the confusion of the final withdrawal, the Green Howards' Carrier platoon, who were acting as rearguard to the York and Lancasters, were cut off by the enemy. Only one man, Corporal C. J. Horner, made his way through to rejoin the battalion at Otta.*

Meanwhile the incendiaries had fired the woods and the blinding smoke caused 'D' Company to withdraw to a fresh position at the rear. This exposed 'A' and 'B' Companies to enemy enfilade fire and forced them, in turn, to withdraw through the attached company of the Green Howards. They took up new positions near Sjöa, much weakened by steadily mounting casualties.

**History of the Green Howards*, pp. 12/13.

At about 5 p.m. a German assault threatened to overwhelm 'D' Company and Major R. V. Walters was killed while leading a counter-attack. It was now impossible to evacuate the many wounded because of strong parties of the enemy infiltrating the flanks of the battalion's defences.

A general withdrawal was ordered at 11 p.m. on 27 April and the wounded, with the survivors of 'A' and 'C' Companies, embussed to move towards Otta, where the main body of the Green Howards was preparing defensive positions. As the civilian lorries full of exhausted troops were about to move off, a report came through of an enemy road block between them and safety. A fighting patrol led by Lieutenant M. C. Willis attacked the road block, which was covered by machine-guns from both flanks. In the fierce fighting to clear the road, Sergeant Cully and Private Ryan fought with particular bravery.

The convoy was now able to pass through, while the companies on foot regrouped and cautiously followed. They soon came under heavy machine-gun fire and were forced to scatter and find cover in the thick pinewoods. The brief twilight had deepened and in the darkness the soldiers of 'A', 'B' and HQ Companies fought fierce independent actions to rejoin the battalion.

In the confusion a small group, including Major Tennent, was cut off by the enemy but, after many adventures, reached England via Sweden. When the main body of the York and Lancasters reached Otta the strength of the battalion had fallen by about half to thirteen officers and 300 men. Later the stragglers rejoined the battalion at Otta. But a group from the right bank, who had missed the river crossing, was diverted south over the snowfields of the Heidal and reached Dombass twenty-four hours later.

After a brief rest the exhausted York and Lancaster survivors dug in on the right flank of the line held by the Green Howards. Here they were subjected to frequent strafing by the Luftwaffe until they moved back into reserve at Dombaas. It was now the turn of the Green Howards to attempt to delay the relentless advance of the enemy.

The base at Aandalsnes was under the command of Brigadier D. Hogg. His responsibility was the organization of the base and its anti-aircraft defence. Since the initial landing, continual German air action had sunk several small ships in the fiord and the harbour area, including the Norwegian torpedo boat *Trygg*. On 26 April a Luftwaffe raid ignited ammunition on the wooden quay which, with the houses adjoining, was burnt out.

Molde was attacked on the same day and the power station was destroyed. This was particularly serious as the Norwegian wireless transmitter which provided the base's link with London was no longer usable (although the naval channels were still in use).

A confusing exchange of telegrams now ensued. In the early morning of 26 April Paget sent the following signal to General Massy:

> In view of the rate of enemy advance, arangements to evacuate should be prepared if aerial supremacy is not ensured forthwith.*

Late that night, while Brigadier Hogg was at Molde, his naval deputy, Captain M. M. Denny, signalled the Admiralty on the naval net, warning that evacuation was a possibility. When Hogg returned he held a staff conference and on the morning of 27 April sent a message to the War Office reporting that he was out of communication with the front line troops and that he now intended to plan the evacuation of the Aandalsnes base 'in the first ten days of May'.

General Paget received a copy of Hogg's message later on 27 April and reacted at once by sending a signal to the War Office reiterating his request for immediate air cover and for artillery support. He added that, if these could be provided, he 'could not agree that the situation at the front rendered evacuation necessary'.

On 28 April, while 15 Brigade was preparing to make its resolute stand at Otta, Paget received two messages from General Massy which decisively changed the situation.† The main points arising from the messages were: evacuation had been decided on in principle; it should commence on the night of 30 April/1 May, when ships would be made available; Molde should be the main re-embarkation point, rather than Aandalsnes, with a possible backlog of troops getting away from Molde on the night of 1/2 May. Massy emphasized that the soldiers must have first priority; stores and equipment would be abandoned.

Buckley (p. 77) asserts that the decision to evacuate was taken as early as Friday, 26 April: 'following receipt of General Paget's despatch indicating that this course might have to be considered'. Buckley points out that Carton de Wiart had already reported from Namsos in the same sense. The reason for the War Cabinet's decision is said to be fourfold:

> the overwhelming German air superiority to which we had been quite incapable of making any adequate reply,
> the reversal of the military situation on land in the course of the week,
> the administrative difficulty – itself an outcome to a large extent of the German air superiority,
> the intention to attack Trondheim, an operation which was pivotal to the whole campaign, had been abandoned on 19 April.

*Derry, p. 131.
†The effect of the War Cabinet's decision on Mauriceforce at Namsos is discussed in Part Four.

Dr Derry writes that Paget still maintained the view that he could hold the Dombaas area for a time if reinforcements were landed and significant air and artillery support provided: 'But assuming the decision to be final, his chief concern was the reaction of the Norwegians, since their Commander-in-Chief had so often asked to know, not when the British were leaving but when more of them were coming'. (p. 131)

In fact Paget's last signal requesting help received a flat answer. The War Office signal said. 'The possibility of adequate air support has been fully investigated and it will not be possible to provide this on a scale which would provide you [Paget] with sufficient resources to keep your forces fighting, or even to maintain them'. Paget was asked to assure General Ruge that the Allies would continue to help and would aim at embarking his army so it might fight elsewhere in Norway, properly equipped and supported.

Paget was a man of principle. In formally accepting complete command in the Gudbrandsdal from Ruge, he considered his obligation to regard the safety and welfare of the Norwegian troops as being of the same priority as his own soldiers. It must have been with a heavy heart that he met the Norwegian leader on the morning of 28 April.

At first General Ruge refused to believe Paget's news. He then protested bitterly about the British 'betrayal of Norway', and sent off a signal to General Ironside complaining that the British withdrawal, within a matter of days and without consultation, would constitute a most damaging blow to the morale of the Norwegian Army and people.

But these differences were forgotten as the two professional soldiers considered the best method of holding the Germans at Otta. Paget's mind must at the same time have been occupied with the problems of getting Sickleforce safely back along the single-track railway and narrow, pitted road to Aandalsnes.

In order to get his troops away in safety Paget would have to break contact with the enemy and then ensure that they could be held until the main body was clear by road and rail. Before doing this he was committed to ensuring the safe withdrawal of the Norwegians. Dombass was the critical area here; the safety of General Ruge's troops guarding against an enemy attack from the north depended upon this detachment reaching Dombaas through Hjerkinn.

Paget detailed 148 Brigade to hold the Dombaas area for forty-eight hours, which gave the Norwegians, travelling by night, time to reach the railway. This meant that the British withdrawal beyond Dombaas must be postponed until the night of 30 April.

The flow of military intelligence coming in to Ruge's headquarters was hampered by frequent moves and poor communications. After his discussions with Ruge, Paget was particularly concerned with the rapid advance of the Germans along the Österdal. The French Military Attaché reported that an enemy infantry column, supported by tanks, had passed Alvdal and was heading for Foldal, a mere twenty miles from the Norwegian troops at Hjerkinn. (It seemed at the time that this threat to the British rear was very much a reality but in the event the information turned out to be false. Buckley, p. 79.)

Meanwhile, intelligence reports from the Gudbrandsdal indicated that General Pellengahr's group had been substantially strengthened. The enemy 163rd Division holding Tretten had been reinforced by units from the south. Despite blown bridges and other demolitions their advance was gaining momentum.

Paget had agreed with Ruge that it would need at least two battalions to hold the Germans at Otta. But we have seen that the back-up battalion, the York and Lancasters, were so weakened by their ordeal at Kjörem that they had to be withdrawn to recuperate in the area of Dombaas. The only battalion available to defend Otta was the Green Howards.

When the Green Howards left Dombaas on 26 April they left their 'A' Company, under Major C. W. D. Chads, to take up a position on the road to Hjerkinn. Their role was to support units of 148 Brigade guarding against the reported German column approaching along the Österdal.

As we know, 'B' Company and the dismounted Carrier platoon moved by road to support the York and Lancasters at Kvam. This company, much weakened, rejoined the Green Howards battalion on 28 April as its platoons dug in at Otta. But the Carrier platoon had been destroyed in the German attack on Kvam and this diminished Colonel Robinson's defences.

The small town of Otta lies in the crutch of the Y where the river of the same name flows into the Laagen. The approach from the south is covered by two spurs, each about 1200 feet high. The main road, along which the enemy was expected to attack, follows the east bank of the River Laagen. The railway and a minor road runs along the west bank and crosses the River Otta just above the confluence.

The company commanders had been well briefed and had no illusions about the severity of the imminent enemy assault. Nevertheless, contemporary accounts agree that their morale was high. They held a strong position and they were determined to defend it.

Colonel Robinson put 'D' Company on the spur running south above the right bank of the Laagen. 'C' Company occupied the twin spur, about half a mile forward, on the left of the road. Both companies could enfilade with cross-fire any enemy approach along the valley floor from the south.

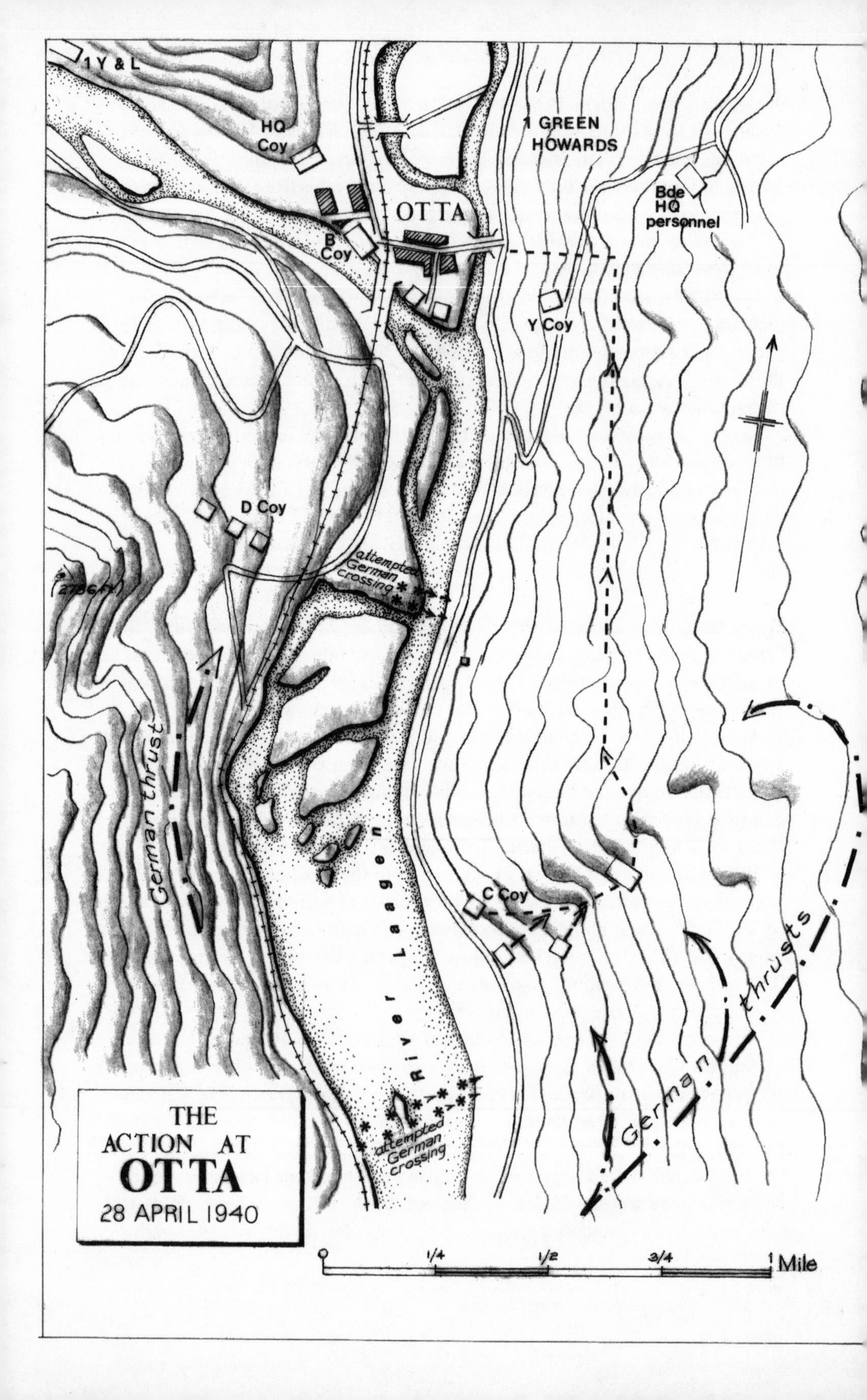

THE
ACTION AT
OTTA
28 APRIL 1940

'B' and 'Y' Companies were in Otta itself, with a platoon from the latter company on the high ground to the east. The mortars, with battalion HQ, were on the northern outskirts of the small town. The five surviving guns of the Brigade Anti-tank Company were tactically sited to cover both roads.

Enemy planes were active from 7 a.m. on 29 April but the first air attacks did little damage. As soon as the light was good enough the German artillery opened up. The Green Howards, well dug in, were little affected by the shrapnel. They got their first warning of the infantry assault when the Luftwaffe strafed the forward positions just before 10.30 a.m.

About 150 enemy troops, supported by tanks and armoured cars, came against 'D' Company, on the right flank. The company commander, Major C. E. W. Holdsworth, let them come within 400 yards of his leading platoon before opening up with every available weapon. The German vanguard suffered heavily and had to retreat. But not for long. The second wave forced 16 platoon further up the slope into the trees, where they lost touch with Company HQ for most of the day.

17 platoon, in the centre, was repeatedly attacked but was able to hang on for several hours. But later in the day the enemy fire intensified and 18 platoon, nearest the railway, was driven back. 'D' Company was forced to leave the spur, but the whole company succeeded in crossing the thinning ice and joined 'B' Company, who had come forward to assist in the withdrawal. The Green Howards' right flank was now dangerously exposed.

On the other side of the river the Germans had worked their way up on to the high ground and were attacking 'C' Company on its left flank. Captain E. R. P. Armitage, (attached from the Royal Scots), had strengthened his platoon positions with wooden sangars and was able to inflict heavy casualties on his attackers.

'B' and 'Y' Companies, nearer Otta, enfiladed the enemy across the river with 2-inch mortar and small-arms fire. The German infantry had not yet reached their forward platoons, but 'Y' Company had knocked out a light tank.

Throughout the afternoon, 'fighting like true professionals', the Germans pressed forward with successive frontal attacks along the west bank of the river. Their comrades on the east side succeeded in infiltrating 'C' Company's positions. Using rubber boats they attempted to cross the river at its narrowest point and were practically annihilated by the Green Howards' crossfire. Throughout the whole battle platoon commanders and other junior leaders showed remarkable initiative and courage.*

As the Green Howards' casualties mounted, Paget instructed their CO to withdraw as soon as dusk fell. Colonel Robinson began issuing his orders

*Green Howards History, pp. 17 to 20.

at 5 p.m.: the forward companies were to pull back at 9 p.m. and the remainder would follow two hours later. The battalion would rendezvous near the railways station at Rudi, from which the move back to Dombaas would be organised by road and rail.

'C' Company's positions had been infiltrated by the German infantry and Captain Armitage did not receive the order to withdraw. As will be seen, he succeeded in getting his company to Dombaas independently.

Fortuitously, there was a lull in enemy activity as dusk fell. The Green Howards' mortars put down a barrage as 'B' and 'Y' Companies, detailed to cover the withdrawal, opened rapid fire. The forward companies passed through safely but 'B' Company, guided by Captain Scrope, (the Adjutant), along the west bank of the river, had trouble in crossing on the thin ice. Captain Scrope and Lieutenant Bade went under in deep water but were hauled out, cold and miserable but unharmed, to continue the hazardous journey across frozen bogland. When they reached the railway station most of the battalion had already left. The Norwegians provided a second train and 'B' Company left for Dombaas. Once the last train was clear of the narrow Rosti gorge a section of 55 Field Company, Royal Engineers, blew up the road and railway bridges, hoping to delay the German advance.

Meanwhile Captain Armitage, cut off with 'C' Company, sent out a fighting patrol under Lieutenant Rawson to attempt to contact battalion HQ at Otta. Rawson, who had behaved with conspicuous gallantry during the day, was never seen again, neither was his patrol. When the patrol failed to return Armitage withdrew to Otta, only to find it in the hands of the enemy. He split 'C' Company into small groups, telling them to make for Dombaas, where they eventually arrived carrying their small arms and as much equipment as they could manage.

The Green Howards were much praised for their stand at Otta.* General Massy's Despatch (Part III, Section 47) states: 'The Green Howards in the Otta position fought splendidly . . . the enemy suffered heavy casualties in this battle and his subsequent actions showed little desire or ability to press home an attack.' This was acknowledged by the German commander, who commented on the bitter fighting at Otta.

Colonel Robinson was awarded the Distinguished Service Order. The citation reads, in part:

> This officer showed exceptional ability in occupying a defensive position at Otta on 27 April 1940 and holding it throughout the 28th. He extricated his battalion on the night of 28/29th from very close contact and succeeded in withdrawing it intact. He set a fine example of courage and devotion to duty which inspired his battalion.

*Two officers and twenty-one other ranks of the Green Howards were killed. Their total casualties for the campaign were five officers and 151 other ranks.

General Paget was now faced with the daunting task of extricating Sickleforce along a narrow valley, using a road and a railway which were prime Luftwaffe targets. His flanks were vulnerable and his Norwegian allies under severe strain after weeks of continual fighting. The immediate problem was how to get the British troops from Dombaas to the embarkation point at Aandalsnes while safeguarding the withdrawal of some 4000 Norwegians.

When Paget met General Ruge on the morning of 29 April it was agreed that the remnants of 148 Brigade would take over the lines of communication to the port of embarkation. Norwegian ski troops would guard the British flanks. Paget's intention was to get Ruge's forces clear of the Romsdal and away to safety by 1 May.

The news from Österdal was discouraging; it was clearly only a matter of time before the reinforced enemy linked up with their comrades driving south from Trondheim.

Paget's forces held Dombaas as the Norwegian detachments from Hjerkinn and Foldal withdrew through 148 Brigade's lines. These were the last Norwegian troops in the area for which Paget held responsibility. General Ruge's offer of a Norwegian Field Battery of four guns was gratefully accepted. These guns were later to prove most useful.

Lieutenant-Colonel Clarke had brought from London the details of shipping expected to be available for the evacuation. In essence this amounted to space for up to 1500 men on the night of 29/30 April, and approximately double that number the following night. Troops left over would be moved on the night of 1/2 May.

This assumed that road and rail transport would be available and effective, and that enemy action would not drastically interfere with the programme. Paget's staff drew up a provisional timetable based on Clarke's information. The York and Lancasters would be withdrawn from Dombaas and embark with base details on the night of 29/30 April. The following night HQ Sickleforce, 15 Brigade and all other British troops would withdraw to Aandalsnes, through the Royal Marine rearguard, for embarkation. It was thought to be too early to make contingency arrangements for the night of 1/2 May. This 'optimistic forecast' was discussed with the Norwegians, who were to provide road and rail transport.

The Military Co-ordination Committee looked upon the evacuation of Mauriceforce from Namsos and Sickleforce from Aandalsnes as one single naval and military operation. But, as Dr Derry points out, the positions of the two forces geographically, tactically and politically, differed significantly.* We know that the shipping schedule, due to bad weather and enemy action, did not run as expected.

Another factor which impeded Paget's provisional plan was the almost complete breakdown of communications between Sickleforce headquarters and the base. The remaining Norwegian telephone network, including the separate railway system, was overloaded and, because of language difficulties, unreliable. The British, particularly in the final stages, were forced to rely on the motor-cycle despatch riders of the Royal Signals, liaison officers, and chance.

On 29 April the York and Lancasters, reduced to sixteen officers and 280 other ranks, left their bivouacs in the woods around Dombaas and entrained for Aandalsnes, (which at that moment was being heavily attacked by the Luftwaffe). Enemy planes were also active along the railway and at Lesjaskog the York and Lancasters were forced to leave the train because of a break in the line. A small number of the battalion was lifted by road to Aandalsnes but the majority were forced to continue on foot. By the evening of 30 April they were concentrated in the woods near the port. They embarked at midnight in the cruisers *Sheffield* and *Galatea*. The York and Lancasters lost in Norway twenty-nine killed, twenty-three wounded and 150 missing.

On the afternoon of 30 April the KOYLI were acting as rearguard for the evacuation of Dombaas. From their positions some three miles south of the town they saw an enemy column, dragging handcarts loaded with heavy mortars and seemingly unaware of a British presence, coming towards them. The leading enemy platoon, marching at ease, came within 150 yards of 'D' Company's concealed platoon positions before the Yorkshiremen opened fire.

Practically the whole of the enemy vanguard was killed or wounded. The Germans mounted a frontal attack against 'D' Company but made no progress. After an hour their assault was diverted along both sides of the road in an attempt to turn the KOYLI flanks.

Colonel Cass had sited his companies in depth with 'B' and 'C' on the flanks and HQ Company and 'A' echeloned to the rear. In addition, 'Y' Company of the Green Howards was positioned far back on the right flank with a field of fire covering the river. The Germans launched an attack across the river but were driven back.

The four Norwegian field guns sent by General Ruge now came into action. After trouble in ranging, when 'B' Company of the KOYLI were in danger from rounds dropped short, the Norwegian gunners dug in their

*The evacuation of Carton de Wiart's force has been discussed in Part Four.

guns. Their aim was now accurate and their fire, greeted with cheers by the British troops, sent the enemy scurrying for cover. For once the enemy had no artillery, and, as the Luftwaffe was busy bombing Aandalsnes, were supported by a single aircraft only, and this was shot down by British small-arms fire.

Cass ordered a withdrawal at 7 p.m., getting his battalion away through the Green Howards' rearguard with few casualties. They reached Dombaas railway station at 10.30 p.m. to join Brigade Headquarters who were already entrained. The Green Howards, following close behind, boarded the same train, with the exception of 'A' and 'D' Companies, who headed for Aandalsnes in Norwegian trucks.

The railway line had been repaired and at 11 p.m. the train pulled out, stopping briefly at Lesja to pick up the Brigade Anti-Tank Company and some 200 Norwegian ski troops who had been guarding the British flanks.

The train made good progress until, at about 1.15 a.m. just east of Lesjaskog, the two engines pulling the train were derailed by bomb damage. The leading coach was telescoped into a crater. The troops climbed out into deep snow amid the hissing of steam and the cries of the wounded, (eight men had been killed and thirty injured). A young Captain of the Green Howards who was a passenger in the last coach describes the scene:

> We got out quickly, each individual making his own way through the thick snow onto the icy road which ran parallel with the track. The Intelligence Officer had produced a bicycle from somewhere and the CO sent him off to the nearest village to find out if there was some place which would give us cover from German aircraft before daylight came, ideally a tunnel.
>
> He returned saying that his informant spoke little English but had said that there was a tunnel up the road, saying what sounded like 'doe meel'. We took this to mean two miles and started off in straggling groups stumbling through the pot-holes in the narrow road.
>
> After several hours it got quite light and we had travelled at least ten miles. It was about 2000 feet above sea level and there was no cover of any kind. We reached the tunnel at Verma at about 9 a.m., actually it was eighteen miles from the scene of the accident. Fortunately for us the Luftwaffe was late on the scene and we were within a mile or so of the tunnel when we were strafed. The casualties were light and about seven hundred of us crammed into the tunnel.
>
> There were two trains in the tunnel, one an ammunition train which seemed to be abandoned. The other train had a long line of empty trucks and an engine with smoke pouring from its funnel.
>
> There was no ventilation in the tunnel, which was more than 400 yards long. We had perfect cover from the enemy but we stood a good chance of being suffocated by the smoke. We sat there all day while the German pilots tried to seal the ends of the tunnel with their bombs.*

*Major-General D. S. Gordon, CB, CBE, DSO, (late Green Howards). From a tape made for the Imperial War Museum (No. 8760/3/2).

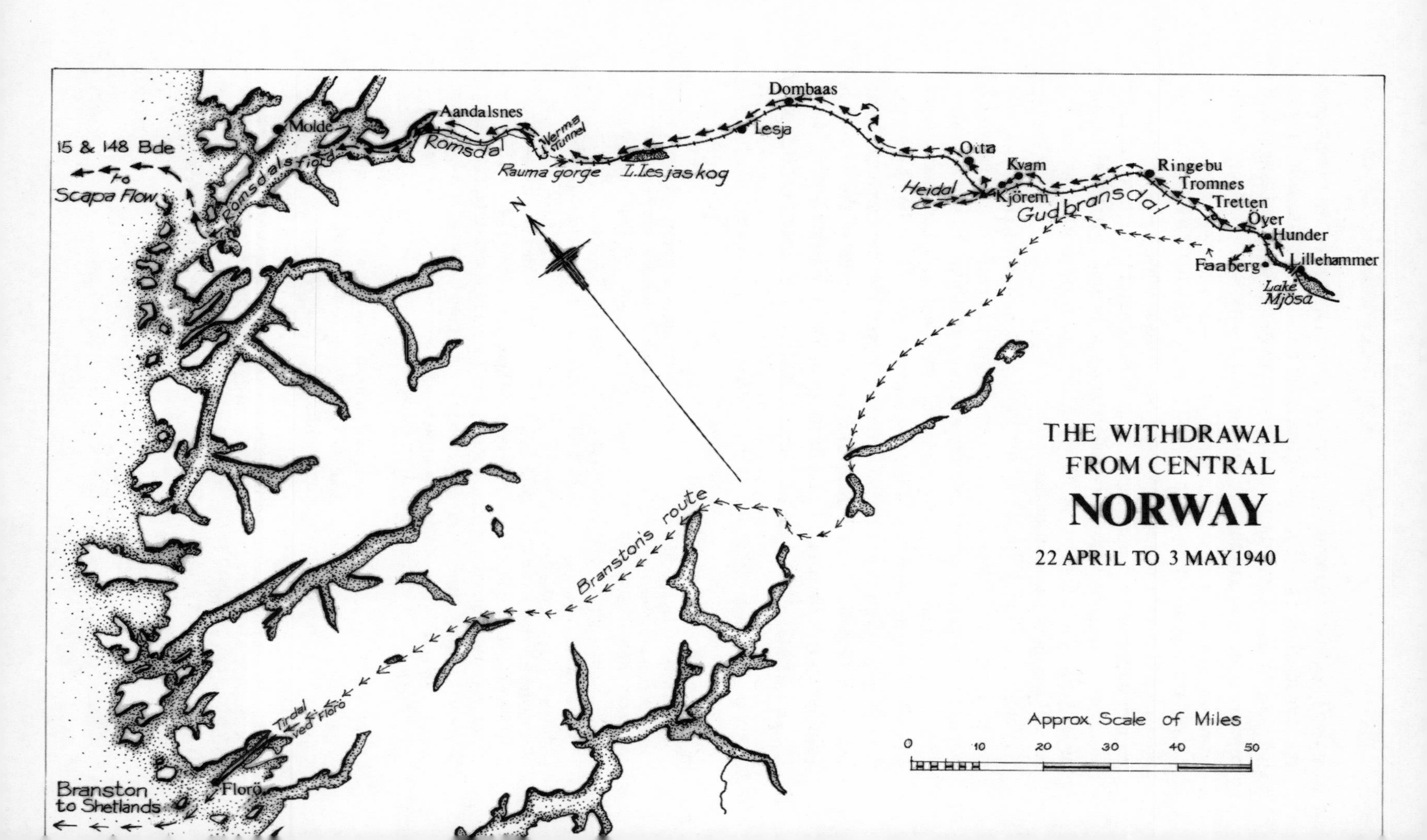
THE WITHDRAWAL
FROM CENTRAL
NORWAY
22 APRIL TO 3 MAY 1940
15 & 148 Bde
To
Scapa Flow
Molde
Romsdalsfiord
Aandalsnes
Romsdal
Verma Tunnel
Rauma gorge
L. Lesjaskog
Lesja
Dombaas
Otta
Heidal
Kvam
Kjörem
Gudbransdal
Ringebu
Tromnes
Tretten
Öyer
Hunder
Faaberg
Lillehammer
Lake Mjösa
N
Branston's route
Tirdal
Ved Florö
Florö
Branston
to Shetlands
Approx. Scale of Miles
0
10
20
30
40
50

Luckily there was a party of Royal Marines stationed near Verma to guard the electric power supply for Aandalsnes. The Marines had hurried to the scene of the accident and took up positions at the head of the Rauma gorge to protect the harassed British troops from attack by the enemy advancing from Dombaas. They were joined by a detachment of Norwegians, and after a brush with enemy patrols withdrew to Verma leaving a rearguard, armed with Lewis guns, to delay the German advance.

Realizing that the Marines were too few to hold the enemy, a composite force of Green Howards and KOYLI was deployed to prevent the Germans getting to the tunnel. This deterred the enemy and it was decided to raise a head of steam on the troop train and leave for Aandalsnes while it was still light. The smoke from the engine began to fill the tunnel and the troops filed out to take up defensive positions around Verma station.

At this critical point (according to Hingston, p. 107) 'the Norwegian railwaymen lost their nerve.' The driver claimed that the train was too heavy to reverse out of the tunnel to the station. But the British had no time to argue about the technical difficulties, they were anxious to get on to Aandalsnes. 'On such an occasion a man of words is at a discount: a man of action is required . . . it is wonderful what a little persuasion and a few stout fellows with rifles and bayonets can do.'

The train crawled slowly out of the tunnel and the soldiers climbed into the trucks. The journey to Aandalsnes was uneventful, although the troops had to march the last mile. The plan to use Molde for embarking having been abandoned, the KOYLI were quickly ferried by destroyers to HMS *Manchester* and *Calcutta*. The short campaign had cost them thirty-nine killed, forty-six wounded and 135 missing.

The Green Howards could see the fires of the bombed villages around the port as they wound down the hill to the quay. Most of them joined the KOYLI in either the *Manchester* or the *Calcutta*, with the remainder embarking in HMS *Birmingham*. The last to leave was the rear party of 55 Field Company, Royal Engineers. They destroyed the abandoned guns and blew up the port installations before boarding HMS *Auckland*, which embarked 240 men in seven minutes. By 2 a.m. on 3 May the quay was deserted and the Gudbrandsdal campaign was at an end.

During the battles in the Gudbrandsdal, and the ensuing withdrawal northwards, groups of British soldiers were separated from their units. Some made for the frontier and escaped into Sweden. Others showed great initiative and evasive skill in getting to the coast, from where they successfully sailed for Scotland. Many, not so fortunate, were captured by the Germans and spent the next five years as prisoners of war. Some were to die in tragic circumstances while attempting to escape.

Among those who reached the coast and eventually sailed to freedom was a group led by Captain P. J. Branston, who commanded 'B' Company of the Foresters at Tretten. The story of his adventures appeared recently in a Norwegian magazine.*

The author of the article, Sverre Hestetun, was a medical student in Oslo when the Germans invaded on 9 April, 1940. He fought throughout the short campaign and was ordered to surrender with the rest of his unit on 1 May. He and several others succeeded in escaping to Hestetun's home near Övre Aardal, from where he devoted his time to helping British Escapers. He writes:

> The story of how the English soldiers managed to escape to England is almost like a fairy tale. England needed these good people, these well trained soldiers, in the period that followed.
>
> It is also with great happiness that I think about all the Norwegians who took huge personal risks in helping these soldiers flee the Germans. They showed great loyalty to their country through their actions against the German invading forces.

Hestetun's article follows the fortunes and vicissitudes of several groups of Britain soldiers as they attempted to evade the Germans. Among them was Captain Branston's party, who eventually came out on the coast near Tirdal ved Florö. On 28 May they 'found' a boat and reached the Shetlands via the Faeroes.

Years later, when Hestetun was a practising doctor, he met on a visit to England a British ex-officer who had served in Norway. Through him Hestetun traced Branston and in 1971 the two met at Skoltegrunn harbour in Bergen:

> On this trip we visited, among other places, Eikefjorden, the house in Tirdal ved Florö, Aardal and Oslo. He [Branston] also gave me the report written about the English soldiers' withdrawal from Gudbrandsdalen in 1940 – Hon. Colonel E. G. C. Beekwith of the 8th Battalion Sherwood Foresters. A copy of this report can be found at the Folk Museum in Sogn. . . .
>
> The joy I felt at being reunited with my old friend was enormous. We visited each other from time to time and kept in touch until he died.

One British group which did not get away was led by Lieutenant-Colonel G. J. German, the CO of the Leicesters. The battalion was split into small parties during the withdrawal from Tretten, and German's group went north to Ringebu. As they came to the village they saw soldiers loading stores. Forming themselves into a squad, they marched into the village

*A translated copy of the article was sent to the author in March 1987 by Lieutenant-Colonel K. G. Allen, the Regimental Secretary of the Worcestershire and Sherwood Foresters Regiment.

street and soon realized that the soldiers were German. Looking straight ahead, they got through the main street undetected. At the outskirts of the village they ran into an enemy outpost and were forced to scatter. The Germans rounded them up and they spent the next five years in captivity.

A tragic incident concerns one small party of survivors from several regiments attempting to get away after Tretten had been overrun by the enemy. They had taken cover along the side of a track north of the village and were waiting for promised transport to return to pick them up. Among the group were Captain J. Lubbock of the Leicesters, Lieutenant Jack Esam of the Foresters, and Lieutenant McConnell, RAMC, who as Medical Officer of the Foresters 'had attended to the wounded with the utmost heroism amid constant shelling'.

At dusk they heard the sound of vehicles and came out on to the road. A German tank appeared around a bend in the track and they dashed back into the undergrowth to crouch down amid the snow. The tank stopped opposite them and a voice in English said, 'Come out, Englishmen, it is all right'.

Lieutenant Esam came forward and was shot down as soon as he reached the road. 'Doc McConnell ran forward to Esam and was also shot down. And then the tank's machine-guns opened up in earnest and sprayed the edge of the wood where they knew full well the remainder lay. Very few escaped alive.' *

King Haakon and his Cabinet had been kept continually on the move by German bombing on the eastern side of Norway. When the road and railway to the coast were cleared the King moved to the vicinity of Aandalsnes. The British withdrawal from the Gudbrandsdal forced another move and the Cabinet voted for Tromsö as their new home. The size of the party was substantial; apart from the King and Crown Prince Olav there were the government politicians and a number of civil servants. With them was the gold bullion which had been brought overland from the Bank of Norway in Oslo.

Molde had been chosen as the embarkation point, and the cruiser *Glasgow* was detailed for the special duty of transporting the Royal party. The town was on fire and an air raid in progress as she berthed, with fire hoses playing, alongside the damaged quay at dusk on 29 April. The voyage north was uneventful and the *Glasgow's* passengers were transferred to a Norwegian vessel at the approaches to Tromsö.

*Colonel E. G. C. Beckwith: Unpublished History of the 8th Battalion The Sherwood Foresters, TA, 1958 (p. 41). Colonel Beckwith, who as a Captain commanded 'A' Company of the Foresters in the Gudbrandsdal, was himself taken prisoner at Hellerud, fifty miles north of Tretten.

Soon after settling in to his new quarters King Haakon issued this proclamation:

> We still have strong positions in the north of Norway and with the help that is now planned we shall continue the reconquering of the country.
>
> It is the numerical and technical superiority of the enemy on land and more especially in the air that has forced us to withdraw. We have reasons to believe that conditions will soon change.
>
> It is not a war the Germans are carrying on in Norway; it is murder and arson. But the morale of the people is unshaken and unshakeable.
>
> I and the Government are firmly resolved to resist until the country has been liberated.*

General Ruge was offered passage to northern Norway on 29 April. Tired and disillusioned, he refused, but on 1 May changed his mind. He asked that his cherished 2nd Division should travel with him but this was considered impracticable and the troops were disbanded to return to their homes. With Ruge, still Commander-in-Chief, went his General Headquarters, soon to play a significant part in the re-conquest of Narvik.

Churchill, in a speech on 2 May, attempted to put the evacuation of Central Norway in some kind of perspective. He pointed out that the Allied intention of cutting off Hitler's supply of iron ore from Sweden had been successfully accomplished, and emphasised that: 'It is far too soon to strike the Norwegian balance-sheet yet, for the campaign has merely concluded a single phase.'†

The Luftwaffe was being challenged in the north. Strenuous efforts were being made to prepare Bardufoss airfield as a fighter base with the help of Norwegian airmen familiar with the site. The aircraft carriers *Ark Royal* and *Glorious* were operating in the area, with two RAF squadrons and units of the Fleet Air Arm flying Hurricanes and Gladiators.

The British Fleet still exercised a tenuous hold over the coastline of northern Norway; the Germans ferried in troops in local boats and steamers at their peril. The main enemy approach to Narvik had to be over the harsh mountainous terrain north of Namsos. And Narvik, so economically important to both the Germans and the Allies, now occupied the centre of the stage.

*Hambro (p. 135).
†Derry (p. 144).

PART SIX

Operations in the Narvik area
The re-capture of Narvik – Final evacuation
12 May to 8 June 1940*

When the evacuation of Central Norway was completed on 3 May, operations in the Bodö–Mo–Mosjöen area had not yet begun. Apart from 'C' Company of the Scots Guards, who arrived at Bodö to protect the airfield on 30 April, Norwegian troops stood alone in the area. As we have seen in Part Three, the Independent Companies arrived in early May. Between 12 and 21 May the 24th Guards Brigade moved down from the area of Narvik. The German threat from the south, protected by the air superiority of the Luftwaffe, developed quickly and on 31 May the last of the retreating Allied troops left Bodö for the island of Hinnöy.

Meanwhile moves to recapture Narvik were in train. General Auchinleck, who was subordinate to Lord Cork, commanded the land and air forces. Auchinleck had at his disposal the 1st and 2nd Battalions of the Foreign Legion and the 27th Demi-Brigade of the Chasseurs Alpins (6th, 12th and 14th Battalions) commanded by General Béthouart. With them, also under French command, was the Polish Highland Brigade of four battalions under General Bohusz-Szyszko.

These were the troops remaining when 24th Guards Brigade moved down to the Bodö–Mo–Mosjöen area. Together with the Norwegian soldiers of General Fleischer, they would form the force to invest and re-occupy Narvik.

Prior to Auchinleck's arrival, Lord Cork had assembled the naval vessels to convey and give close support to the French force, under Béthouart, who were to assault Bjerkvik, at the head of Herjangsfiord. The battleship *Resolution*, which had replaced the *Warspite*, together with the cruisers *Aurora* and *Effingham*, would give weight to the bombardment which would precede the assault. These ships, with five destroyers and four assault craft, embarked two battalions of the Foreign Legion, and their five light tanks, late on the evening of 12 May.

At midnight, in sufficient light for targets to be identified, the bom-

*These operations can be followed on Map No 3 (NARVIK) on page 46.

bardment began. The landing commenced at 1 a.m., when the barrage of shells moved inland. The aircraft carrier *Ark Royal*, whose aircraft were to cover the operation, was out of sight to the west. There was no sign of the Luftwaffe.

The intention was to land 120 men of the Foreign Legion in assault landing craft (ALCs), preceded by the five tanks. But the hoisting of the ALCs out of the *Resolution* took so long that a motor landing craft (MLC) took the lead. It carried the 1st Company of the First Battalion of the Legion, led by Captain Gelat. They were supported by only one tracked vehicle, but once ashore the tank set about silencing the German machine-gun posts with some success. Two more tanks struggled ashore as the remainder of the battalion was rowed to the edge of the fiord by ships' boats. Casualties were remarkably light.

The landing site was half a mile to the west of Bjerkvik, where the snow had cleared on the low ground. The tanks made good progress, followed by the 1st Battalion, whose CO, Commandant Boyer-Resses, 'bawled out his orders in a stentorian voice' from the ship as his *Légionnaires* forced their way eastward.*

In Bjerkvik village an ammunition dump had been blown up by the naval gunfire. Some of the houses were ablaze as the *Effingham* and some of the destroyers opened fire on the enemy machine-gun positions. Lieutenant Peugeot, the 1st Battalion mortar officer on board the *Havelock*, attempted to align his mortars from the destroyer's deck. This unstable base proved to be dangerous and the mortars, with difficulty, were man-handled into a boat and on to the shore, where they proved very effective against the German prepared positions on the high ground.

Two hours after the 1st Battalion had landed, the 2nd Battalion attempted to land at Elvegaard in the face of fierce machine-gun fire. They then switched their attack to the south-east of Bjerkvik, near the Öyjord road. One of their objectives was the Norwegian Army's regimental depot at Elvegaard, now occupied by the enemy. The 2nd Battalion, led by the 5th Company under Captain Puchoix, stormed Elvegaard, supported by their light tanks. The Germans resisted strongly, defending each building. When they were finally flushed out, the French were in possession of a hundred machine-guns and a mass of valuable equipment and stores.

General Béthouart, 'an officer of the Chasseurs, quick and shrewd, wearing an elegant blue cape',† had landed at Öyjord, with his staff, from the *Havelock*. He knew that the 2nd Battalion of the Polish Highland Brigade, (carrying their heavy machine-guns and boxes of ammunition), was on its way from Lenvik. Protected on both flanks by Norwegian ski

*Captain Pierre Lapie, *With the Foreign Legion at Narvik*, p. 32.
†Lapie, p. 35.

troops, they force-marched eighteen miles through thick wet snow in eleven hours.

To their intense disappointment they found the battle for Bjerkvik was over. General Béthouart had earlier sent for two companies of the Polish 2nd Battalion to reinforce the Legion's assault on Elvegaard. They travelled from Bogen in two destroyers but by the time they had landed the Germans had been driven east from Elvegaard. The Poles spent the next two days combing the Öyjord peninsula for enemy stragglers. On the night of 15/16 May they embarked in puffers for the Ankenes peninsula, where they relieved the South Wales Borderers (who had been ordered to Bodö).

Meanwhile on the right, the 14th Battalion of the Chasseurs Alpins, supported by a battery of British anti-aircraft guns, were advancing southwards from the direction of Gratangen. Unfortunately, it was not until 1.45 p.m. on 14 May that they were able to make contact with the Foreign Legion in the Bjerkvik area. This allowed the retreating Germans to escape to the south-east before the Norwegians, coming from the left flank, were able to link up with the 6th Battalion of the Chasseurs and close the trap.

Thus the first amphibious landing of Allied troops under fire in the Second World War had succeeded. The fears of a second Gallipoli among the fiords of Norway had here proved baseless; the Foreign Legion had only thirty-six casualties. At the start of the operation an officer of the Legion said:

> Ah, it is very difficult. We are used to travelling on camels across the desert, and here you give us boats, and we have to cross the water. It is very difficult, but it will be all right. I think so.*

The German grip on the northern side of Narvik had been loosened. General Fleischer's Norwegian troops were moving against the enemy Group Windisch on the heights of the Kobberfjell, operating in nine feet of snow. But General Dietl's men still stubbornly defended two fronts: a northern front against the Norwegians, high in the mountains, and a western front running inland from the Bjerkvik–Öyjord road.

These two fronts met in a right angle at Hartvigvatn, above and to the north-east of Elvegaard. The German defence was centred around the critical area of the Kuberg plateau, against which the Norwegian 1st and 2/16th Infantry were advancing, supported on their right flank by the Alta Battalion. To attempt the encirclement of Narvik, the Polish Highland Brigade now operated on the Ankenes peninsula, relieving the British and the 12th Battalion of the Chasseurs.

On 17 May, as the Poles were in the process of taking over from the Chasseurs, the Germans mounted a determined counter-attack from the

*Moulton, p. 225, quoting Captain L. E. H. Maund RN.

direction of the Beisfiord. The enemy used heavy and accurate mortar fire, and the British 25-pounder guns, now under French control, played a major part in repelling the attack. The Germans had troops along the southern shore of the Beisfiord and on the crest above, with strong points running to the east from Point 295 to the high ground above Beisfiord village.

At the landward end of the fiord a strong enemy infantry company was reinforced by sailors from Group Haussels, rated among the best of the German naval battalions. The ski troops of the Mountain Regiment operated effectively through the high mountains from the Storvatn, where they posed a threat to the Polish right flank.

General Bohusz-Szyszko's orders from the French commander were:

> In the first instance – to hold the position on the Ankenes Peninsula and to prevent the enemy from landing on the southern beach of Beisfiord; to harass the defenders of Ankenes, gain hills 650–773 and harass the enemy to be found in the Beisfiord area, by this means preparing a later attack on Sildvik; to begin preparations for the taking of the Skjom valley with the aim of allowing lighter troops to advance towards Hundalen.
>
> In the second instance – to attack Ankenes, to push through Beisfiord towards Sildvik with the aim of cutting off the German retreat and, in emerging from the Skjom valley, block off the enemy's rear towards Norddalen.*

The Polish General now had under his command the 1st, 2nd and 4th Polish battalions (the 3rd was held in reserve) and a detachment of French ski troops. His battalion commanders were eager to engage the enemy and on the afternoon of 17 May the CO of the 2nd Battalion sent his 2nd Company forward from Hill 405 to try to locate the enemy positions. The leading platoon got to the crest of the ridge overlooking the Beisfiord without opposition. The platoon cautiously descended the northern slopes toward the fiord, covered by the remainder of the company on the ridge above.

When the platoon was well out in the open, the Germans opened up with artillery, mortar and machine-gun fire from well-camouflaged positions on the southern shore of the Narvik peninsula, firing over the heads of their outposts on the Ankenes side. The Polish platoon hastily withdrew under covering fire from 2nd Company, retreating to a small hill about 500 yards beyond the ridge. There they dug in and defended themselves from the German attackers, whose forward troops had made their way skirmishing to the top of the ridge.

The Polish platoon was pinned down on what was now called 'Szasz-

*From a translation of the Official Polish account of the campaign, prepared for the author by Mrs Teresa Mundziel-Staniszewska, Associate of the Institute of Linguists, (October, 1987 – p. 14).

kiewicz Hill' after the platoon commander. With the support of the rest of the battalion they beat off enemy attacks until the late evening of 18 May, when they managed to withdraw to Hill 405. Their casualties amounted to five dead and twenty-one wounded.

The two Polish battalions now extended their positions along the high ground overlooking the Beisfiord. The 2nd Battalion covered the area from Emmenes to Hill 677, while the 1st Battalion ranged eastward as far as Hill 668. One of their companies faced south-east to protect the rear and the right flank. Both battalions restricted their activities to intensive patrolling, attempting to assess the enemy strength prior to the coming battle for Narvik.

The 4th Battalion moved, with the headquarters of the 2nd Demi-Brigade, to the Tjelbotn area, covering the southern approach from Ofotfiord. On 22 May this battalion moved overland to reinforce the 1st and 2nd battalions by holding the high ground in the Klubban – Mattisfiord area. The 3rd Battalion, still in reserve at Ballangen, was to be reinforced by Chasseur ski troops and sent across the mountains from the head of the Skjomenfiord to secure the railway in the enemy rear.

General Béthouart now had control of the Öyjord peninsula. The Norwegian 6th Brigade in its second assault on the Kuberg plateau had pushed the Germans back towards the Jernvatnene on 22 May. British warships in Rombaksfiord had supported the 14th Battalion Chasseurs along the shore towards the high ground in the east, where they linked with elements of the Norwegian 7th Brigade. The Norwegians had full confidence in Béthouart and were certain that Narvik would soon fall.

The German Group Windisch, with the loss of Elvegaardsmoen, had lost their base north of Rombaksfiord and with it the reserves of food and clothing on which it depended. Gone also were the pack transport animals which brought them their ammunition and returned with the wounded. Though weakened from long exposure in the mountains and snow, the enemy was determined to hold the area around Rundfjell and Haugfjell, only three or four miles from their HQ on Björnfjell.

General Dietl had received no reinforcements since mid-April, but on 23 and 25 May the equivalent of two companies of parachutists were dropped in to him. From 22 May the RAF's Gladiators had been flying sortie after sortie against his forward positions and supply lines. His strong personality and leadership kept his men going, but he must have known that the end was in sight.

Because of shortages, mainly of landing craft (especially MLCs, which were busy transporting guns and ammunition to the airfields) the Allies

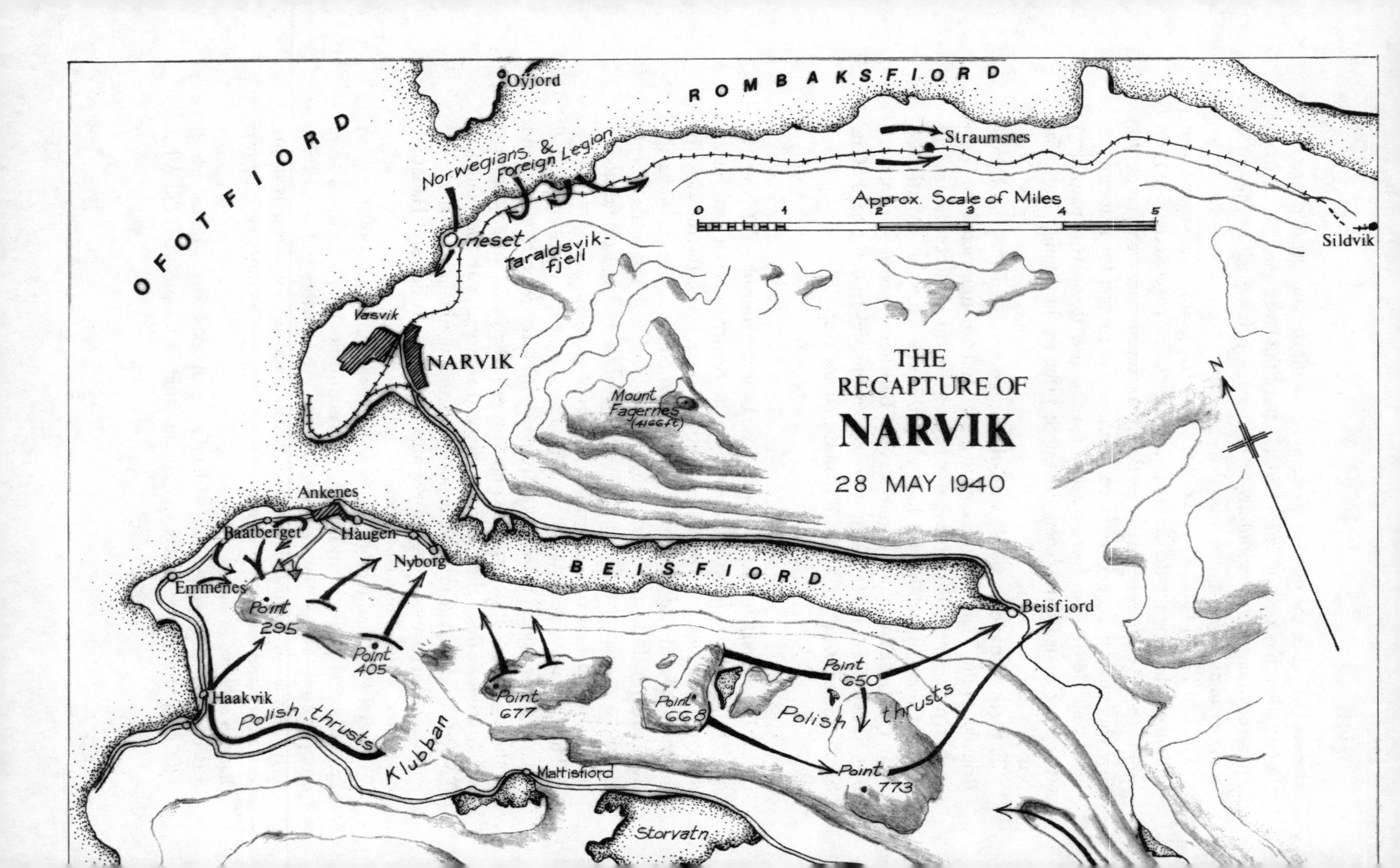
THE
RECAPTURE OF
NARVIK
28 MAY 1940
Approx. Scale of Miles
0
1
2
3
4
5
N
OFOTFIORD
ROMBAKSFIORD
BEISFIORD
Oyjord
Norwegians &
Foreign Legion
Orneset
Taraldsvik-
fjell
Straumsnes
Sildvik
Vasvik
NARVIK
Mount
Fagernes
(4166ft)
Ankenes
Baatberget
Haugen
Nyborg
Emmenes
Point
295
Point
405
Point
677
Point
668
Point
650
Point
773
Haakvik
Polish thrusts
Polish thrusts
Klubban
Mattisfiord
Storvatn
Beisfiord

had twice postponed the final assault on Narvik. A firm date had now been decided upon – 28 May. Thanks to Auchinleck's careful planning, the Allied objective was now reduced to a salient some six miles long and three miles wide, almost surrounded by the Norwegians, French and Poles. The long arms of the fiords were constantly patrolled by British warships which bombarded all but the most carefully camouflaged enemy outposts. All that was now required was sea transport for the assault troops.

Öyjord was chosen for the opening attack rather than Ankenes, which could be enfiladed from the high features adjoining the town of Narvik. The final choice was a small, defiladed beach almost opposite Öyjord, a distance of about one mile across Rombaksfiord. The ground behind it rose very steeply, and many enemy defences there lay open to bombardment from the sea. The initial assault troops were the two Foreign Legion battalions, and a specially selected Norwegian battalion (the 2/15th Infantry) with as many tanks as could be mustered. Once ashore, the attackers could move around the slope of the mountain south-westwards into Narvik. Their landing craft would return at once for the second wave.

Simultaneously the Poles would move against Ankenes (where the Germans had reinforced their troops on the Ankenesstranden) and strike north-east against the high ground at the head of Beisfiord. On the far side of Rombaksfiord the French Chasseurs and the Norwegians would close in to leave the enemy one line of retreat – along the railway through Sildvik towards the Swedish frontier; and this, according to Béthouart's plan, would be cut off by the 3rd Polish Battalion and a detachment of Chasseurs.

Just before midnight on 27 May the naval bombardment began. Four destroyers sailed into Rombaksfiord and opened up on the German defences. At the same time the anti-aircraft cruisers *Cairo* and *Coventry*, with the destroyer *Firedrake*, firing from Ofotfiord, concentrated on known and suspected machine-gun emplacements, including favourite siting-spots at tunnel mouths. The German positions at the east end of Ankenes village and the defences on the opposite side of Beisfiord were bombarded by the six-inch guns of HMS *Southampton.* Two batteries of French 75-mm guns and a Norwegian battery, shooting from behind Öyjord, directed their fire on the beach-head where the Allied troops would land.

Air cover was provided by the Gladiators of 263 Squadron, RAF, commanded by Squadron-Leader J.W. Donaldson, and 46 Squadron, Hurricanes,* led by Squadron-Leader K.B. Cross. These operated from the aircraft carrier *Glorious* and from the partially-completed airfield at Skaanland, (where the RAF had experienced serious runway problems). Bardufoss was also in use, but its aircraft were sometimes grounded by sea fog in the early mornings.

*The Hurricane pilots of 46 Squadron RAF had never previously landed on an aircraft carrier.

Flying often in almost impossible weather conditions, the British fliers established a temporary ascendancy over the Luftwaffe for the first time in the campaign. Their casualties were half those of the enemy.

Remembering the lessons of Bjerkvik, General Béthouart had requested that the naval bombardment should continue until the first wave of landing craft had touched down. The smoke from the bursting shells was rising vertically as the Germans returned fire with mountain artillery, machine guns and mortars.

The Legionnaires embarked, under a two-way arch of shells, shortly after midnight on 28 May. Three ALCs and the last two serviceable MLCs pulled into the tiny harbour of Seynes, in Herjangsfiord, out of enemy sight in order to preserve surprise. As the troops were embarking at Seynes, the second flight embarkation point at Öyjord, in full sight of the enemy, came under fire from the Germans, on whose morale the bombardment appeared to have little effect.

Embarkation was delayed as the second wave was diverted to Seynes, where Norwegian puffers had been brought into use to replace the MLCs (which had been requisitioned to transport the Legion's light tanks).

By 3.30 a.m. 1250 men of the Legion, and the Norwegian 2/15th Infantry, were ashore, enfiladed by German 77s and machine-guns. But casualties were light as the leading assault platoons filtered through the scrubby trees and overhanging rocks towards the high ridge of Orneset. Captain Guillemin of the 1st Battalion of the Legion was among the first fatal casualties, but by this time the troublesome German guns had been silenced.

With the bridgehead established, the Norwegians made for Taraldsvikfjell, which overlooked the western approach to Narvik. Their left flank was protected by the navy's continued bombardment of the line of the railway, down to the station at Straumsnes. A German counter-attack developed from the area of Taraldsvikfjell, and the Allied assault wavered until a British destroyer brought her guns to bear on the German troops. The Norwegians and the Legionnaires regrouped and resumed the attack. But the Germans had been forced to withdraw along the line of the railway and the threat to the Allied landing was over.

The 2nd Battalion of the Legion was prevented from landing initially because their intended beachhead came under the fire of the German counter-attackers. When the position was restored they moved to the right flank and took up a post on a hillock north-west of Narvik railway station. General Fleischer, who had joined his Norwegian soldiers in the landing, now met the French, and with General Béthouart he waited for the latest news of the position of the Polish Highland Brigade.

The commander of the Polish forces opposite Narvik wrote this appreciation of the enemy dispositions south of Narvik:

> The German defence is organized into scattered positions defended by anything from a troop to a platoon, well equipped with machine guns and mortars, and also some artillery platoons. These form a well-organized crossfire system which would easily stop an advance through already difficult terrain.
>
> Beside this, the German positions on the Narvik and Ankenes Peninsulas have been built up and reinforced over several weeks and work has speeded up since 19 May on strengthening the Ankenes positions in particular, and also Hills 650–773, where new defences were created and manning increased.
>
> On the Narvik peninsula, defending its northern and western shore, there are two enemy battalions, one from the 139th Regiment (Mountain troops) and one composite battalion. On the Ankenes peninsula and defending the ridge from Hill 650–773, about two battalions, the 2nd Battalion of the 139th Regiment of Highland Rifles (Mountain troops) with some representation from the 137th Regiment of same and some highland marines (probably part of a naval battalion). They have between one and two battalions in reserve in the Björnfjell area. General Dietl moved his Headquarters on 24 May from Narvik to Hundalen, and the Staff to Sildvik, which does not necessarily indicate that they are about to leave Narvik.*

Other accounts vary, but the Polish report gives a very fair picture of the opposition to be expected from the enemy in the offensive which was to come. General Béthouart had ordered the Polish Brigade (less the 3rd Battalion, in reserve at Balangen) to attack from the south with the aim of gaining control of the Ankenes peninsula. From there they would secure the southern shore of Beisfiord, neutralizing the enemy movement from the opposite shore. The final objective was the high ground to the east of Beisfiord around to Sildvik, with the aim of cutting off the German retreat.

The naval bombardment preceding the Polish assault was supported by accurate fire from the British 25-pounder guns of 203 Battery, located inland from Haakvik. Before midnight on 27 May the leading scouts of the Polish 2nd Battalion had probed the enemy positions near Ankenes village.

To their right, along the high ground running up to the head of Beisfiord, their comrades prepared to move against the strongly entrenched Germans in the vicinity of Hill 405. On the extreme right flank the 1st Battalion were faced with strong enemy defences running south from Point 650. The 4th Battalion were concentrated around Klubban, with a company looking south over Storvatn to safeguard the rear.

Although the 2nd Battalion's commander knew the Germans had

*Mundziel-Staniszewska: translation.

recently reinforced their troops on the Ankenesstranden he was confident that he could oust the enemy from Ankenes. But at 7 a.m. on 28 May the Germans launched a powerful counter-attack which pushed the Poles back towards Emmenes.

The Polish left flank, back to their Brigade HQ in the school at Haakvik, became vulnerable, and their lines of communication for ammunition, stores and food were at risk. As the German attack gathered momentum reinforcements were rushed down from the 4th Battalion. After a heavy fire-fight, the enemy established themselves on Hill 295 at about 4.30 p.m. From there they were able to fire on the Polish positions above Haugen. The Luftwaffe now took a hand and an air strike set fire to the woods immediately behind the First Company's position, which remained critical until the 2nd Battalion troops, with the help of a company from the 4th, had forced the enemy from Hill 295. The Germans retreated to the southern shore of Beisfiord, and the Poles advanced along the ridge to where the First Company had contained the fire. With their comrades on the right (and another of 4th Battalion's companies) the 2nd Battalion fought their way downhill against stiff opposition towards the coastal road.

Nyborg was reached at 9 p.m., when it was still broad daylight. As the Poles reached the shore they saw two boats containing about sixty German soldiers attempting to reach the Narvik side of the fiord. They sank both boats with machine-gun fire before taking cover against the enemy mortars opening up from the north shore.

High above them, and far out on the extreme right flank, the Polish 1st Battalion had been held up by a determined enemy force dug in between Hills 773 and 650. Once more the 4th Battalion provided reinforcements, while a detachment of French 75-mm guns bombarded the German positions. After a three hour fire-fight the enemy withdrew towards Sildvik, pursued by the Poles.

Down on the southern shore their comrades had linked up with Foreign Legion motor-cyclists, who had followed the road around from the Narvik side. The Germans were now in general retreat around Fageness mountain towards Sildvik, and along the line of the railway running north-east towards Sweden. More than a hundred German bodies were recovered by the Poles from the mountainside on their right flank, and along the southern shore of Beisfiord, bearing witness to the fierce Polish assault and the determination of the enemy defenders. The official account gives the Polish casualties as two officers and ninety-five other ranks killed, 189 wounded and twenty-eight missing.*

The naval ships supporting the French and the Poles did not come through

*Mundziel-Staniszewska: translation, p. 35.

unscathed. The Luftwaffe were now using dive-bombers and in the early morning of 28 May the flagship (HMS *Cairo*) was hit by two bombs, causing thirty casualties. When the Allied assault troops were firmly ashore, General Béthouart made it clear that a couple of destroyers would provide sufficient support for his troops. At 6.30 a.m. Lord Cork withdrew his main force, leaving the *Coventry* with two destroyers to support the French.

The last Germans in Narvik, about a hundred men commanded by a Lieutenant, escaped from the town about 12 noon, going south-east towards Beisfiord. Comparative silence followed, while the French and Norwegians regrouped prior to entering Narvik.

The French, with characteristic courtesy, had selected the Norwegian 2/15th Infantry to lead the way. At 5 p.m., followed, on General Fleischer's instructions, by a detachment of Norwegian military police, they entered the town. Behind them came the 2nd Battalion of the Foreign Legion, marching with a careless nonchalance that belied their relief.

> The first blond Norwegian boy that marched into town was the young son of the town baker. We took him in a bannered car to his parents, who embraced him with dough sticking to their forearms. They had had no news of him since the start of the war.
>
> Then we drove to the Judge's house to fetch Consul Gibbs (the British Consul). French, British and Polish flags waved on the car. We drove up and down Street 1. The Norwegian flag again floated above the City Hall and it was more beautiful than ever before.*

The Allied operations on the north side of Narvik resulted in lighter casualties than had been expected: about 150 in all, sixty of them Norwegian. Some 400 prisoners had been taken. The harbour area was badly damaged and the ore quays were destroyed by fire. The large plant which handled the loading of the ore lay in ruins. In the harbour rested some twenty wrecked ships: German destroyers, merchantmen of several nations, puffers and other small vessels. The Allied Chief Engineer reported that the export of ore in bulk would be held up for at least a year.

Narvik was in Allied hands, a victory over the Germans much savoured by the French, whose own country had been overwhelmed by the enemy. But, as Dr Derry points out, the paradox was that 'Narvik, once in our possession, had ceased to count'.

By 30 May the Germans had established a new line on the high ground through Point 1448, some five miles east of Narvik. Their field of fire covered the upper part of Rombaksfiord above Straumen. The irregular

*Broch (Mayor of Narvik) p. 137.

line, breached by large and vulnerable gaps, reached as far as Sildvik, where a stiffening enemy resistance was building up. Most of the German survivors, leaving their heavy weapons, ammunition reserves and stocks of food in Narvik, managed to reach the concentration area by 1 June.

Except among some administrative units, enemy morale was not low, although a small number of deserters fled towards the Swedish border, or allowed themselves to be taken prisoner. But General Dietl had received orders from Hitler that a loss of face caused by defeat in North Norway would not be tolerated. German troops, victorious at Namsos and Bodö, were on their way to relieve Dietl's beleaguered force.

In fact the only effective support the German General received (after the parachutists dropped on 25 May) came from the ubiquitous Luftwaffe. An enemy glider attack on Bardufoss airfield never got past the planning stage. Further paratroop reinforcements were promised but never arrived. Small numbers of essential troops, mainly technicians, were smuggled in by boat from enemy-held ports further south. Fortunately for the German commander, the RAF had their hands full. Their two depleted squadrons had the primary task of defending our bases at Harstad and Skaanland. Enemy long-range bombers, escorted by Messerschmitt 110s, made successive raids on shipping throughout the last three days of May.

The RAF flew seventy-five separates sorties and managed to account for at least nine enemy planes during the heavy raid on 1 June. Over the period 22 May–7 June the Gladiators accounted for twenty-six shot down. The Hurricanes of 46 Squadron claimed eleven, while the British anti-aircraft gunners at Harstad brought down twenty-three.

But the state of the airfield at Skaanland, despite the efforts of Norwegian civilian workers and 229 Field Company, RE, continued to cause serious damage to the Hurricanes as they landed. Consequently, 46 Squadron was diverted to Bardufoss to share accommodation with the Gladiators. Captain Simpson, RE, with one other officer and a squad of Sappers, was given the task of keeping Bardufoss as serviceable as possible for our fighter aircraft before finally denying its facilities to the Luftwaffe. Simpson later wrote:

> The runways for the two squadrons had to be kept going to the very last; that entailed some frenzied work by our small detachment of Sappers from about 2300 hours on 7 June until well into the next morning. The demolitions comprised cratering the airfield immediately after the aircraft had flown off to the ill-fated *Glorious*, the destruction of petrol and ammunition stores and blowing off the breech-sections of the Bofors. The RA gunners dealt with their heavier AA weapons by firing a round with instantaneous fuse. Our RE demolition party was amongst the last troops to embark on the 8th.*

*Stokes (p. 192) who himself met Wing-Commander R. L. R. Atcherley, RAF, at Bardufoss on 8 June to find him 'satisfied with the final arrangements'. Stokes then carried out a last small demolition, which he describes as the final 'act of war' in the Narvik land campaign.

Meanwhile the British public, because of the need for secrecy, knew nothing of the superhuman efforts being made to extricate the Allied force before the enemy was aware of what was going on. Some British newspapers after 28 May gave the impression that General Dietl was on the point of surrendering to the Allies. Such journalistic optimism was never more than wishful thinking. Christopher Buckley wrote (p. 150):

> The capture of Narvik did not lead to any weakening of the German resistance. With dogged determination, from which it is impossible to withold our admiration, this indomitable force retired slowly backwards along the [railway] line towards Sweden. They had been anticipating this moment and had for some days been preparing supply dumps and even an airfield on Björnfjell, close to the Swedish frontier.
>
> Norwegians, French and Poles pressed forward along the railway, but it was soon clear that there would be no wholesale surrender and that the Germans would fight back mile by mile to the border. Time could not be spared for the barren satisfaction of thrusting them into a probably only temporary internment in Sweden, and the Allied command now began to push ahead its plans for evacuation.

Indeed, the Allied plans for the evacuation of northern Norway took precedence over the final military success that the Norwegian Generals hoped for over Dietl's shrinking army. Both politicians and the armed service leaders on the Allied side agreed that the withdrawal could not be delayed, (although General Béthouart had written on 28 May, when evacuation was inevitable: 'I am operating with Norwegian troops whom for reasons of national honour I will not abandon in difficulties on the battlefield').*

Not that the Norwegians themselves were aware of the detailed. Allied plans. As late as 29 May Churchill told the War Cabinet that 'there must still be a few days delay in telling the Norwegians'. Lord Cork and General Auchinleck continued negotiating with the Norwegians over the establishment of a new military base at Tromsö, north of Narvik (from which, presumably, the fight against the Germans would continue).

Rumour had it that the British troops withdrawn from Bodö to the base on Hinnöy were destined to move to Tromsö. The airfields at Skaanland and Bardufoss were being improved and the arrival of additional warships in northern waters also served to further the deception, even after the detailed orders for the withdrawal were issued on 31 May.

Whether justified or not, this was another manifestation of the British government's policy of disseminating information on a 'need to know only' basis. The influence of Quisling and his followers had been much

*Derry, p. 218.

exaggerated by the Press. There had been instances of unintentional leakages of information by the Norwegians (the necessity of postponing the date of the final assault on Narvik arose because of one such leakage). These factors drove the Allies to withhold vital information from the Norwegians for fear that it would fall into the hands of the Germans.

This annoyed and disturbed the Norwegians, particularly the Generals, who regarded the reticence over operational movement in central Norway as a calculated slight. History shows that disagreement between allies is commonplace. It was not surprising that General Ruge complained that an Allied and a Norwegian account of the campaign would never agree, However, as Dr Derry points out, the Norwegian Commander-in-Chief did say in extenuation, 'It always take time to get to know each other's good points as well.' (p. 244).

In the end, on 1 June the Norwegian government was officially informed of the Allied intention to evacuate. General Ruge was told the following day. When offered passage to Britain with King Haakon and the government, he declined, preferring to stay behind with his soldiers.

Also on 1 June, the British Minister in Norway, Sir Cecil Dormer, arrived at Harstad to see Lord Cork. The latter had been asked by the Foreign Office to discuss with Sir Cecil the possibility of reviving the so-called Mowinckel Plan. This dated back to the end of April when the former Norwegian Prime Minister Mowinckel had suggested to the Swedish Foreign Minister in Stockholm the possibility of North Norway becoming a neutral zone. The Norwegian government, wary of being labelled defeatist, dragged their feet in the matter.

The British Cabinet was aware of the plan but apparently thought that it had originated in Germany. The British Foreign Office supported it, seeing it as a manifestation of the enemy's difficulties in North Norway.

In fact the Swedish government had put the Mowinckel Plan to the German authorities in Berlin on 28 May (the day Narvik fell), strongly hinting that Swedish troops should be left in occupation of Narvik.

When Sir Cecil Dormer returned to Tromsö from Harstad he sounded out responsible Norwegian politicians on the subject of Mowinckel's plan. He found no serious opposition and on 2 June the King was told, and, later that day, the Cabinet. After consulting the Swedish Foreign Minister, Dormer contacted Lord Cork and asked for the evacuation to be put back to allow more time for discussion of the plan. Lord Cork agreed to a delay of twenty-four hours, ignoring the Foreign Office telegram, which had said that time for negotiation was very short 'and our evacuation plan cannot be delayed'.* But the Germans by now had other ideas. Negotiations were broken off and the Mowinckel Plan came to nothing.

*Lord Cork, Despatches, 10 July 1947, p. 3177.

The military operations in the mountains now took second place to the evacuation plans, set by Lord Cork to commence on the night of 3–4 June. General Ruge's troops took over the main positions in the French line north of the Rombaksfiord. On Ruge's eastern flank the Norwegian 6th Brigade, operating in rugged mountain country, had been troubled by the thaw which now flooded the valleys. By 7 June they had secured the high ground facing the Rundfjell, hoping to reach the German base at Björnfjell and cut Dietl off from his last supplies. Their final attack was planned for 8 June.

But political expediency demanded that the Norwegian soldiers should be withdrawn and demobilized before German reinforcements arrived in strength. General Ruge met Dietl, who treated him 'with courtesy and generosity'. A preliminary armistice was negotiated for midnight 9–10 June. The following day the Norwegian troops began to pass through the *ad hoc* demobilization centres, pending the signing of a formal armistice.

The Allies were now faced with the task of withdrawing some 25,000 troops from Harstad and several small embarkation points ranging from Ballangen on Ofotfiord to Tromsö in the north. Among the mass of troops on Hinnöy were the three infantry battalions of 24th Guards Brigade. Following the withdrawal from Bodö on 31 May, they were brought to the area of Borkenes, about twelve miles west of Harstad. Amid strong rumours of an impending move to Tromsö, they received orders to dump their serviceable (but unused) motor transport into the sea, as preparations for the evacuation built up.

Further north, at Tromsö, King Haakon, the Crown Prince and the Norwegian government were preparing for departure. They had despatched the few remaining Norwegian aircraft to Finland and nine or ten small naval vessels to the Shetlands. The cruiser *Devonshire* was chosen for the evacuation of this important party, which numbered about 400 passengers, due to sail on 7 June.

Lord Cork had at his disposal fifteen troopships, under the charge of Admiral Vivian in the *Coventry*. In an attempt to reduce the number of ships in the area, one convoy, carrying the French tanks and a variety of stores and equipment, left for Britain at the end of May.

Cork attempted to minimize the danger from the Luftwaffe by concentrating the incoming troopships 180 miles off the Norwegian coast. For fear of marauding enemy submarines, the troopships were allowed into Harstad two at a time. Meanwhile, all available destroyers collected men from scattered fish quays and jetties, while two cross-channel steamers, working alone, shipped men and stores at Harstad itself.

Because of the fraught situation in home waters as Hitler's armies were converging on the French coast, the pool of naval vessels available for escort duty was limited, destroyers in particular being in short supply. The main thrust of the withdrawal was organized into two convoys. The first, escorted by the repair ship *Vindictive* and one destroyer, consisted of six large troopships carrying 15,000 men. This convoy sailed at 3 a.m. on 7 June, to be met half-way down the North Sea by the battleship *Valiant* and four destroyers.

The second convoy, carrying 10,000 men in seven troopships, sailed late on 8 June. The escort was the *Coventry* and five destroyers. Lord Cork, flying his Flag in HMS *Southampton*, sailed in this group, taking with him Generals Auchinleck and Béthouart.

As the first convoy cleared the Vestfiord the enemy were unaware of the mass evacuation. This was partly due to the continued bombardment of the German defences by our destroyers from the Rombaksfiord until late on 6 June. Another factor was the apparent determination of the Norwegian troops to storm the area of Björnfjell. But on 8 June, during the armistice negotiations, General Dietl became aware of the withdrawal. That same evening he re-entered Narvik.

General Auchinleck, in his report of 19 June, 1940, writes:

> The entire process of embarkation, whether from beaches or quays, in fishing boats, destroyers or directly into transport, went with the greatest smoothness and celerity and reflects the greatest possible credit on all concerned. The morale and cheerfulness of the troops remained high throughout, although their destination was not known to them until they were actually on the high seas so well was the secret kept.
>
> The French Chasseurs furnished the final rearguard round Harstad but the actual rear party around the quays was found by the Royal Engineers and Military Police. There was no disorder or unpleasantness of any kind. (p. 3192)

German naval operations in the North Sea and the approaches to Norway had been curtailed by the heavy loss of her destroyers at Narvik and the damaging of her capital ships. Hitler was now very concerned for his troops in the Narvik area. He was also anxious about the security of German supplies through the Leads to Trondheim and other ports, and had spurred on his naval staff to act against the Allies at sea.

The plan, known as Operation Juno, had developed in scope from its inception on 14 May, based on favourable reports from German Intelligence regarding British naval dispositions. The battle cruisers *Scharnhorst* and *Gneisenau*, and the heavy cruiser *Admiral Hipper*, had now been repaired and were ready for sea by early June. Naval Group West appointed

Vice-Admiral Marschall to command the three heavily-armoured ships and their escort of four destroyers.

Marschall's orders were firstly to enter Andfiord and Vaagsfiord, attacking warships and transports in that area. He was then to go on and destroy the Harstad base by bombardment. However, if later air reconnaissance reported better targets in Ofotfiord, he was to go there. His second task was to safeguard the seaward flank of General Feuerstein's forces as they drove northward from Trondheim. To keep the element of surprise, Marschall was told to keep clear of Trondheimsfiord until after his attack on Harstad. That safely accomplished, he should make his temporary base there.

The German force left Kiel early on the morning of 4 June with Marschall flying his flag in the *Gneisenau*. His intelligence reports indicated that there were one or two British battleships in the area of Harstad/Ofotfiord and one aircraft carrier 200 miles off the Norwegian coast. There were a number of cruisers and destroyers on the move around the Vestfiord. The German Naval Command appeared to know nothing of the impending Allied evacuation of Narvik.

By the morning of 6 June Marschall's ships were in latitude 65 north, halfway between Iceland and Norway, attempting to escape the attentions of the Royal Navy. That evening they refuelled from a German oiler, disguised as a Russian merchant ship. In good visibility they steamed slowly north. Marschall had successfully negotiated the North Sea and was now in striking distance of the Norwegian coast, undetected by the British.

The German Admiral had timed his attack on Harstad for 9 June. His earlier information about British naval forces was supplemented by intercepting Allied wireless signals. He knew that *Renown* and *Repulse* were steaming north-west from Scapa. He was able to locate the *Valiant* and the two aircraft carriers *Ark Royal* and *Glorious*, with four cruisers and about fifteen destroyers, off the coast of North Norway.

Then, early on 7 June, German reconnaissance planes reported a lightly escorted convoy of seven British ships steaming south-west about 350 miles off Trondheim. Marschall suspected that these ships were 'returned empties' going back to Britain after delivering reinforcements and supplies. He called a conference of his captains on board the flagship that evening. The Admiral received further information from Group Command West during the conference. This showed that there were three groups of Allied warships in the Andfiord area.

By 8 p.m. Marschall had changed his mind about the attack on Harstad. The intelligence build-up strongly suggested 'that the noticeable westward movement may indicate a British evacuation of Norway, and that the westbound convoys will now offer valuable targets'.* At 3 a.m. on 8 June he signalled his headquarters of his firm intention to attack the convoys. The German Naval High Command reacted in two ways: Group West wanted the battle cruisers to go on with the attack on Harstad; the Chief of Naval Staff thought the convoys would prove a more valuable target. Finally, the decision was left to Marschall (although Group West reminded him that his primary target was Harstad). The Admiral, using short-wave wireless, gave orders for his warships to adopt search formation to find and destroy the convoy.

At this point we may remind ourselves that the pattern for the evacuation required the protection of several distinct groups of ships. The storeships were in a slow convoy of two divisions, escorted by destroyers and trawlers. Then there was Group 1 of the troop transports, which left Harstad early on 7 June to rendezvous with the lightly-armed *Vindictive* 180 miles out. (This convoy was to be met by the *Valiant* and four destroyers late on 9 June). Lastly there was Group 2 of the troopships, more heavily escorted, which had been reported north of Andfiord by German scout planes.

This last convoy was well within Marschall's range. Its escort of the *Ark Royal*, two cruisers and four destroyers, was heavily outgunned by the battle cruisers *Scharnhorst* and *Gneisenau*. The weather was 'changeable', as they say. The Scots Guards history states: 'At 0100 next day [8 June] the appearance of a German recce machine caused some disquiet, but a thick mist came down and hid the convoy.' An entry dated 8 June in the War Diary of the South Wales Borderers records: 'Apart from a visit by a single enemy plane which swooped out of the clouds about 1100 hours, there is nothing to report. *Vindictive* and two of our ships opened fire. Very cloudy about 1500 feet. Misty in afternoon and evening.'

Meanwhile, at 6 a.m. on 8 June, the German heavy cruiser *Hipper* sighted the British tanker *Oil Pioneer* and her escort, the armed trawler *Juniper*. The trawler challenged the enemy warship, which gave her identity as HMS *Southampton*. The *Hipper* immediately opened fire and sank the trawler. The Germans picked up twenty-nine survivors from the *Juniper*, took the crew off the *Oil Pioneer* and sent the latter into the custody of their escort.

Marschall now received information that there was a British cruiser escorting a merchant ship to the south and an armed merchantman and a hospital ship to the north. The *Hipper* sank the armed merchant ship, the 20,000 ton transport *Orama*, at 11 a.m. on 8 June, not knowing that among her passengers were a hundred German prisoners. Some 270 survivors were picked up before the Germans turned their attention to the hospital ship *Atlantis*. Being a non-combatant, the *Atlantis* adhered to the Geneva

*Derry, p. 223.

Convention and maintained wireless silence. She was allowed to proceed unmolested.

The 16,000 ton hospital ship had been taking on Allied (and occasional German) wounded from the Harstad base. Serving aboard her was a Welsh nursing officer of Queen Alexandra's Imperial Military Nursing Service. Sister Emily Jones (now Mrs E. M. Bond) found her service among the fiords both exhilarating and frightening:

> We were a floating hospital with 600 patients. Thirty bombs were dropped around the ship, but we didn't take a direct hit. We thought the Germans were deliberately ignoring the fact that we were a hospital ship, and when a captured German pilot came aboard we asked why they took no notice of the Red Cross.
>
> He said they were not aiming to hit us, but to harass us so that we got out of the way. They succeeded – we moved!*

As the *Atlantis* steamed off towards Britain the *Hipper* and her destroyer escort headed for Trondheim to refuel prior to patrolling the Leads to protect Feuerstein's sea communications. At this juncture, according to General Moulton (p. 253), a mistake in the German communication system took place:

> While the *Hipper* finished off the *Orama*, the two battleships [*Scharnhorst* and *Gneisenau*] steamed south-east at twenty-five knots, in search of a convoy which, with the *Southampton*, had been reported by the *Hipper*'s float-plane. This was a serious error in reporting, due either to a mistake in position or in ciphering. The *Southampton*, the second group of transports and the second slow cargo ship convoy were all well to the north of the Germans at this time. At 1.18 p.m. Marschall gave up the fruitless chase, turned back to a northerly course and released the *Hipper* and his three destroyers to make a start on his second task of clearing Feuerstein's sea communications. Probably on account of exaggerated desire for secrecy, Group XXI had not been fully briefed about Marschall's movements, and wireless communications between Falkenhorst and Marschall were routed through OKH and OKM with a serious time-lag.
>
> Thus Marschall still had no news of the British withdrawal from Harstad and Narvik, and still thought that Feuerstein needed his help to save Dietl. So, deprived of the *Hipper* and destroyers which would have added to their effectiveness in search, the two battleships headed north for the Tromsö–Harstad area.

The events which follow were described in Parliament by Winston Churchill as a 'great tragedy'. Admiral Marschall had still failed in his search for the convoy. His next plan was to attack the group of British warships he knew to be located north-west of the Andfiord. Then, around 4 p.m.

*From the *South Wales Echo*, 27 October, 1987, sent to the author by Mr A. A. Williams of Barry, West Glamorgan, who himself served in Norway with the South Wales Borderers.

on the afternoon of 8 December, a masthead lookout in the *Scharnhorst* sighted smoke on the starboard bow. The smoke came from the aircraft-carrier *Glorious*, making independently for her home port because of shortage of fuel. Escorting her were the destroyers *Ardent* and *Acasta*, some 200 miles ahead of the Group 2 convoy.

As soon as the *Glorious* was identified, the German Admiral ordered battle stations. He steered a north-westerly course which would take him to the windward of the British ship, thus forcing her to turn towards him if she attempted to fly off her aircraft. At about 5.20 p.m. the *Glorious* appeared to recognize the enemy ships and turned away, making smoke. A few minutes later the *Scharnhorst* opened fire with her secondary armament at a range of 28,000 yards. Her first target was the British destroyer escort, but she soon switched to her main guns to shell the *Glorious*.

The German Historian, Professor Hubatsch (quoted by Moulton, p. 254) relates that the *Gneisenau* transmitted a bogus Admiralty message to interfere with the wireless signal from the *Glorious* reporting the engagement. British sources maintain that the aircraft-carrier's initial report (which was not received by the enemy) was cut off when the *Scharnhorst*'s second salvo struck home. No signal was received from either of the two British destroyers.

> What the reason was for the two destroyers in company with the *Glorious* not making wireless enemy reports is baffling. Admirably handled, they did everything possible to fulfil their responsibility of protecting the carrier, and their smoke screens made shooting very difficult for the German ships. German reports are full of praise for the brave and skilful action of the destroyers. (Hubatsch)

One reason given for the lack of communication is that atmospheric conditions in the ionosphere at that time of year would be very difficult with the type of wireless set then in use. This seems to be borne out by the fact that the Germans intercepted no British signal.

The 4.7-inch guns of the *Glorious* were helpless against the enemy. At an early stage the carrier's forward upper hangar was hit, starting a fire which destroyed the Hurricanes and preventing the preparation for a torpedo salvo. Fire from the *Gneisenau* now came down on the bridge of the *Glorious*, causing confusion. The fight had now become a running chase on a south-easterly course, with the range closing and the German ship making almost thirty knots. The two British destroyers which, as we have seen, behaved with exemplary skill and gallantry, laid a smoke screen which for a time hid the carrier from the enemy.

But when the *Glorious* emerged from the smoke, both the German warships reopened fire on her with their main armaments. She was now listing and on fire. The *Ardent* emerged from the smoke to twice attack the *Gneisenau*, narrowly missing with her last torpedo. Both German ships engaged the *Ardent* with their heaviest guns; in four minutes she had sunk. The *Acasta*, now alone, skilfully used the smoke screen to fire a salvo of four torpedos at the *Scharnhorst*,* hitting her on the starboard side abreast the after main turret. She sprang a leak which put her main engines out of action and cost the lives of two officers and forty-six men.

By now the *Glorious* had sunk and the enemy battleships used their secondary guns to sink the *Acasta*. There were 1515 British officers and men on the three ships; only forty-five survived. Among the casualties of the *Glorious* were the pilots of 46 and 263 Squadrons, some of whom had risked their lives to no avail in landing their aircraft on the carrier.

The disaster which overcame the *Glorious* and the two destroyers may well have been vastly greater, had the crowded troopships of the second group been intercepted by Marschall's force. HMS *Valiant*, having escorted Group 1 to safety, returned to sea to meet the second convoy of transports. On 9 June she met the *Atlantis*, who told her by visual signal of the appearance of the *Scharnhorst* and *Gneisenau* in the path of the convoys.

Valiant signalled Scapa Flow with the news, then steamed full speed for 400 miles to meet the second convoy unharmed. Also unmolested was the *Devonshire*† (carrying the King of Norway and his Government) which had been only one hundred miles west of the *Glorious* when she was attacked. Admiral Forbes, warned by *Valiant*'s signal, left Scapa in the *Renown* later on 9 June, with *Repulse* and six destroyers as additional escorts for the convoys. On that day, against the wishes of Grand Admiral Raeder, the German Information Service broadcast the news of their naval victory.

Of the crew of the *Acasta*, just one, Leading-Seaman C. Carter, survived. His account of the last moments of his ship is recorded in Churchill's volume *The Gathering Storm* (p. 589):

> On board our ship, what a deadly calm, hardly a word spoken, the ship was now steaming full speed away from the enemy, then came a host of orders, prepare all smoke floats, hose-pipes connected up, various other jobs were prepared, we were still stealing away from the enemy, and making smoke, and all our smoke floats had been set going. The Captain then had this message

*The damage inflicted on the *Scharnhorst* by the destroyer *Acasta* was such that she had to return to Trondheim for repairs, together with the *Gneisenau*. There on 11 and 13 June the RAF and Naval aircraft attacked the enemy ships without success. In total, eight of our planes were lost.

†The *Devonshire* had received a faint and possibly corrupt message from the *Glorious*. This signal mentioned a previous message (not received) which contained the words '2 PB' (Pocket Battleships). As the signal was not confirmed (and also to safeguard his important passengers) the Captain of the *Devonshire* decided not to break wireless silence by relaying the message. (Derry, p. 226; Moulton, p. 254).

passed to all positions: 'You may think we are running away from the enemy, we are not. Our chummy ship [*Ardent*] has sunk, the *Glorious* is sinking, the least we can do is to make a show. Good luck to you all.'

We then altered course into our own smoke-screen. I had the order stand by to fire tubes 6 and 7, we then came out of the smoke-screen, altered course to starboard firing our torpedoes from port side.

It was then I had my first glimpse of the enemy, to be honest it appeared to me to be a large one [ship] and a small one, and we were very close. I fired my two torpedoes from my tubes [aft], the foremost tubes fired theirs, we were all watching results. I'll never forget that cheer that went up; on the port bow of one of the ships a yellow flash and a great column of smoke and water shot up from her.

We knew we had hit, personally I could not see how we could have missed so close as we were. The enemy never fired a shot at us, I feel that they must have been very surprised. After we had fired our torpedoes we went back into our own smoke-screen, altered course again to starboard. 'Stand by to fire remaining torpedoes'; and this time as soon as we poked our nose out of the smoke-screen the enemy let us have it.

A shell hit the engine room, killed my tubes crew, I was blown to the after end of the tubes. I must have been knocked out for a while, because when I came to my arm hurt me; the ship had stopped with a list to port. Here is something believe it or not, I climbed back into the control seat, I see those two ships, I fired the remaining torpedoes, no one told me to, I guess I was raving mad.

The *Acasta*'s guns were firing the whole time, even firing with a list on the ship. The enemy then hit us several times, but one big explosion took place right aft, I have often wondered whether the enemy hit us with a torpedo, in any case it seemed to lift the ship out of the water. At last the Captain gave orders to abandon ship. I will always remember the Surgeon-Lieutenant [H. J. Stammers, RNVR], his first ship, his first action. Before I jumped over the side, I saw him still attending to the wounded, a hopeless task, and when I was in the water I saw the Captain leaning over the bridge, take a cigarette from a case and light it. We shouted to him to come on our raft, he waved 'Goodbye and good luck' – the end of a gallant man.

PART SEVEN

Comments and Conclusions

The many disappointments and disasters of the brief campaign in Norway worried and perturbed the British government. The Allied withdrawal from Central Norway in early May hastened the fall of Chamberlain's administration. The final evacuation, though submerged in greater events, provoked a storm in Parliament. But apart from those directly concerned, such as relatives of those killed, wounded or missing, interest in events in Norway was overshadowed by Hitler's breakthrough in the Low Countries and the subsequent threat to Britain itself.

Recrimination was inevitable and to be expected. Each political faction defended its own end, while blaming others. Our control of the northern approaches to the Atlantic had been weakened; the Germans held the Norwegian Leads. Churchill's opponents claimed that British strategy at sea had been defensive: 'wars are not won by leaving the initiative to the enemy'. They did not accuse the First Lord of lack of nerve. They blamed him for listening to incompetent advisers who, among other lapses, discounted the effects of the enemy's superiority in the air.

The Prime Minister came in for far rougher treatment. His attempts to conciliate the Führer in 1938, followed by the misleading 'peace in our time' statement to the British people, were revived, and much was made of his unfortunate assertion, as recently as 5 April, 1940, that Hitler 'had missed the bus'. His offer of (false) hope to Norway in saying publicly that the British were coming to her aid in great strength is cited as one of the many political gaffes which were to lead to his downfall.

The planning and execution of the Norwegian campaign showed a fatal divergence between the (military) intentions of the politicans and the collective power of the service staffs and higher commanders to impose their own judgements. This failure, at the highest level, to appreciate the realities of the situation made the already difficult tasks of the field commanders impossible to carry out.

General Moulton (p. 295) lists a number of shortcomings, many of them highlighted in this book: the Chiefs of Staff's belief that German seaborne operations against the western coast of Norway were impracticable; the failure to prepare and to train land and air forces which could be deployed effectively across the sea in Norway; the mistake of sending inadequate forces with large and unattainable objectives, and the frequent changes of plan. These were some of the symptoms of 'a collective breakdown of military judgement'.

Many of these aberrations were soon recognized and overcome; for instance Churchill, with the concurrence of the Prime Minister, curbed the power of the Chiefs of Staff.* On the whole, relations with our allies worked reasonably smoothly, except at the highest level where Anglo-French relations showed some strain as the effectiveness of the Norwegian venture came under serious doubt.

In the field, relations between the British, French and Polish forces worked well, despite an acute shortage of interpreters. General Béthouart's command of his own Chasseurs, the Foreign Legion and the Poles, while co-ordinating the Norwegians in the recapture of Narvik, is an outstanding example of Allied co-operation.

At a lower level, in the medical sphere, the adoption of the international code used by the Foreign Legion to label casualties overcame language difficulties. Where different nationalities worked closely together, as in overlapping areas of defence, there was no friction. In the author's own experience of handover-takeover procedures in very difficult terrain, there was an atmosphere of helpful cameraderie that was heartening. The time-honoured practice of swapping cigarettes and tobacco for food or other useful items was widespread. On rare and memorable occasions an impromptu entertainment was given, such as the accordion 'concert' given by the Foreign Legion while staging at Ballangen with the South Wales Borderers.

In his report General Auchinleck commented on the unsuitability of some of the weapons and equipment issued to the troops. He criticized the wireless sets, comparing them unfavourably with those used on the Indian Frontier. By present-day standards it seems incongruous to read his criticism that 'Personnel were insufficiently trained to get the best value out of heliographs'.

He pointed out that the soldiers were grossly overloaded with clothing, some of which was of little use. The Arctic boots (alleged to be leftovers from the Archangel expedition of 1919) were issued several sizes too large; 'Boots two sizes only above the normal are necessary'.

Other types of footwear came under scrutiny, as this account of a foot inspection after a long march reveals:

* See Part One, p. 3.

Next day was devoted to doctoring inflamed feet for which the rubber ankle boots were largely responsible. For short marches through slush these boots were excellent, while the ordinary leather boots soon became soggy and heavy.

On a long march, however, they [the rubber boots] drew the feet unmercifully and caused them to swell. Men stood in buckets of snow to ease their feet while their wet socks were placed on the backs of cows to dry.* (Hingston p. 77)

Several distinguished students of the Norwegian campaign have attempted to identify the major lesson to be learned from *Weserübung*, the German invasion of Norway and Denmark. Rather than attempt a full re-assessment of this complex matter, the present writer offers a brief summary of different views.

My main source is a paper given to the International Commission for Military History in Washington DC, by Professor Olav Riste† (probably the foremost Norwegian specialist in this subject), in August, 1975. Writing in English, with an academic fluency reflecting his Oxford background, Dr Riste examines two points of view.

Starting with those who consider the undermining of sea power by air power to be a major lesson of *Weserübung*, he quotes General Sir Alan Brooke, Dr T. K. Derry (the author of the British campaign history) and Captain S. W. Roskill (author of the widely acclaimed study of *The War at Sea*). Riste considers these to be a 'compact majority'.

Two dissenting voices are noted, J. L. Moulton‡ who, as a Major-General of the Royal Marines, had wide experience of both land and sea combat, and the famous war historian, Captain Basil Liddell Hart. However, both conceded that the Luftwaffe was the most decisive factor in the German success.

But Moulton considered that a more basic cause of the defeat was the British failure to understand the requirements of a three-dimensional land, sea and air strategy. Liddell Hart, in his *History of the Second World War*, published in 1970, suggested that the German supremacy in the air was more psychological than real as it 'paralysed the Allies' countermoves'. In his view it had psychological effects far exceeding the physical destruction of men and *matériel*.

Looking at the latter view, the author considers himself qualified to comment on the psychological effect on behaviour of prolonged exposure to air attack, having endured (with the rest of 24th Guards Brigade) the constant threat of the Luftwaffe for six interminable weeks. For the soldiers

* Much the same criticism was made about British soldiers' footwear after the recent Falklands war.

† O. Riste: *Sea Power, Air Power and Weserübung*.

‡ Major-General J. L. Moulton, CB, DSO, OBE, was Chief of Amphibious Warfare from 1957 to 1961.

on the ground, exposed in the snow during eighteen hours of daylight, the daunting presence of the Luftwaffe (even high-flying scout planes) became oppressive. This was at its worst in withdrawals like that of 146 Brigade from Steinkjer to Namdalseid, when some soldiers abandoned their steel helmets for fear of being identified from the air.

Frequent entries in War Diaries referred to the unrelenting pressure from the air:

> The 21st [May] was mainly notable for enemy reconnaissance and machine-gunning from the air, and there was no sign of the British fighters whose help had been promised daily. Major Graham was sent to reconnoitre what was said by those at Harstad [the base] to be a good defensive position in the neighbourhood of Viskiskoia, north of the snow belt, and was machine-gunned by low-flying aeroplanes.*

Commanders in the field were only too aware of the German strength in the air. General Auchinleck in his report of 19 June, 1940, put forward, as the first lesson to be learned from the campaign, the effect of the predominance of the enemy in the air. He gives as an example the operations which culminated in the evacuation of Bodö, where the enemy had complete initiative in the air:

> He [the enemy] used it first, to support his troops by low-flying attacks, by bombing, [in the latter stages by dive-bombing], by surprise landing of combat troops by parachute and from seaplanes. The enemy advanced detachments were supplied by air. And secondly, [air power was used] to deny us the use of sea communications in the narrow coastal waters in the theatre of operations.

Yet the actual casualties caused to troops on the ground by low-flying attacks were few. For example, during four weeks spent within a few miles of Narvik, and partly in operational contact with the Germans, the South Wales Borderers lost just three killed and eight wounded by direct air attack.

But the effect on morale of continuous machine-gunning from the air was significant. Troops in forward positions at first went to ground, having learned early on the necessity to dig in. Paradoxically, when they realised that few casualties resulted from the air attacks, some became careless and neglected to keep a constant watch on enemy movement. The Germans also used intensive machine-gunning from low-flying aircraft in replacement of artillery to cover the movement of their troops. It must be said that the enemy on many occasions were thus able to carry out forward and outflanking attacks with impunity, particularly in the Namsos area.

Liddell Hart's contention that enemy air power 'paralysed the Allies' countermoves' is fair comment. Constant harassment from the air forced

* *History of the Scots Guards* (p. 43).

battalion and brigade headquarters to make involuntary changes of location which seriously interrupted the exercise of effective command. Add to this the disruption of supplies caused by low-flying attacks on Allied transport (confined to narrow roads), and it is easy to see that, in some cases, frustration built up to a sense of hopelessness and a serious lowering of morale.

Enemy bombing was most effective at bases such as Namsos, where Carton de Wiart was forced to request London to stop sending supplies to the port, which was heavily bombed on 20 April: 'Enemy aircraft have almost completely destroyed Namsos, beginning on railhead targets, diving indiscriminately.... I see little chance of carrying out decisive or, indeed, any operations, unless enemy air activity is considerably restricted.'*

The German view, according to Riste, did not reveal any overwhelming concern for the 'air power versus sea power aspect of the campaign'. There was, naturally, inter-service rivalry, not least between the Luftwaffe and the Navy. This was personified in the disagreements between Reichs-Marshall Goering and Admiral Raeder. It obviously affected the planning of *Weserübung*, of which Raeder was the main architect.

In early March Raeder told Hitler that, in his (Raeder's) view, the proposed operations went against all the rules of naval warfare. He pointed out that to be sure of success the Germans should have superiority at sea: 'This we do not have; on the contrary, we are carrying out the operation in the face of the far superior British fleet'.

The Admiral counted on surprise as the key to success. He also strongly emphasized the necessity of the naval ships returning to Germany in safety, but could not, at the planning stage, suggest a solution to the problem of protecting German ships operating in Norwegian coastal waters.

At this point Raeder grudgingly admitted that 'the strongest assistance from the Air Force will be needed'. In fact, to achieve surprise, some 2000 men, out of about 11,000 used in the first wave of the invasion, were transported by air, including a battalion of parachutists. Nevertheless, despite the fact that from the Spring of 1939 the Luftwaffe had considered itself to be an independent arm, the German naval planners initially allotted it a supporting role.

But the Germans were well aware of the psychological impact of air power. They had used it in Poland, and in planning *Weserübung* they envisaged the use of threatening 'demonstration flights' for both bomber and fighter planes as a menace over Norwegian and Danish territory. Riste points out that when the expected collapse of Norwegian resistance failed to come about and the Allies entered the arena, a new phase in the contest between British sea power and German air power was introduced.

* General Carton de Wiart: Signal to the War Office, 21 April.

We know the German navy suffered heavily in the days following 8 April. From then on the Luftwaffe was forced to assume the task of controlling Norwegian coastal waters against the expected challenge of the British fleet. Professor Riste stresses that the campaign 'therefore appears to offer an unusually clearcut example of air power versus sea power'.

After surveying the course of events which, after the abandonment of the Trondheim assault, turned the Allied effort into an unsuccessful land campaign, Professor Riste put forward the view that:

> With respect to the impact of air power on land warfare during the Norwegian Campaign it is sufficient to say that, although the psychological effect of total enemy air control was to all accounts considerable, losses due to aircraft action were minimal. The main importance of the Luftwaffe in the land campaign, apart from its disorganizing effect on the defending forces, may therefore again have been to ensure rapidity of movement of troops to Norway, and from south to north inside Norway, enabling the Germans to build up their forces in forward areas very quickly. During April alone, almost 30,000 men were transported by the 582 transports engaged in *Weserübung*.

He concludes that the real lesson of the campaign, as regards the impact of air power on warfare, was not its effectiveness against sea power, but rather the element of speed and mobility which it contributed to land warfare.

Writing from a different viewpoint, Dr Derry points out that Norway had assumed a special importance in the strategy of the Second World War since the invasion of Finland more than four months before the German invasion of 9 April. He finds it very difficult to understand the Allies' lack of comprehensive and precise intelligence and the failure in evaluating what intelligence there was. While assuming that intelligence may have enabled us to foresee much of what the enemy was going to attempt in Norway he writes:*

> But no degree of foresight could at that time have prevented us from suffering the full effects of German air superiority. This was the most obvious lesson of the campaign – or in a sense no lesson at all, since the Air Staff, knowing the insignificant size of the air support which would be available for any Scandinavian expedition, had correctly appreciated in advance the peril to which our lines of communication would inevitably be exposed.

Any reader wishing to follow this up should read Dr Derry's authoritative History. In surveying 'The Campaign in Retrospect' (Chapter XV), Dr Derry ranges widely and comprehensively over other deficiencies in Intelligence work, apart from its bearing on German air superiority. He also criticizes the planning of the campaign and imperfections in the system of

* Derry, pp. 233–4.

command, among 'other deficiencies observed'. When comparing casualties he finds that only in relation to her naval forces did Germany incur any disproportionate losses.

The official casualty list issued by the German General Staff amounts to 5296, small in relation to the results achieved.* Moulton (p. 259) quotes several German sources, arriving at a figure of 5660, of whom 1317 were killed and 2375 lost in sea transport or otherwise missing. This includes casualties in Denmark, which were very small.

British casualties from the land operations amounted to 1869 killed, wounded and missing. A further 2500, mostly British, were lost at sea. French and Polish losses came to about 530 all ranks.

The Norwegian casualties throughout the campaign amounted to 1335, with a further loss of 400 civilians killed. It must be remembered that the Germans occupied Norway for another five years, during which many lives were lost in the Norwegian Resistance Movement, for which the campaign of 1940 had to a considerable extent prepared the ground. King Haakon and the Crown Prince (since 1957 King Olav V of Norway) followed the Royal family's motto of 'All for Norway' and held the nation together from their Scottish base throughout the war.

In the air the Luftwaffe lost some 240 planes, eighty of them transport aircraft. The RAF losses have been given as 112. Number 263 Squadron lost all their planes at Lesjaskog; operations at Bardufoss cost another sixteen, while three Hurricanes were destroyed at Skaanland, without the airfield becoming fully operational. The Fleet Air Arm suffered a much smaller loss.

At sea the losses were proportionately greater, with the Germans suffering the most. The damage to their capital ships on 9 April and in the following week was a grievous blow, as was the torpedoing of the battle cruisers during Operation Juno. Their destroyer strength was dramatically reduced with the sinkings at Narvik and elsewhere in Norwegian coastal waters. Apart from heavier ships, the German naval forces at the end of June amounted to one 8-inch cruiser, two light cruisers and four destroyers. The heavy losses in their merchant shipping seriously impeded the preparations for Hitler's invasion of Britain (Operation Sealion).

The British Navy's major casualty was the aircraft carrier *Glorious*. Among the cruisers, *Effingham* was wrecked and three others damaged. The anti-aircraft cruiser *Curlew* was sunk by bombing. We lost seven destroyers and a further eight were damaged. One sloop, four submarines and many small craft were lost.† The French and the Poles each lost one

* Derry, p. 230. The figure includes those lost in passage to Norway.
† Winston Churchill in *The Second World War*, Vol. 1, p. 574, names all Allied ships sunk or damaged.

destroyer and one submarine sunk, while the French cruiser *Emile Bertin* was badly damaged off Namsos.

Before the war Norway had derived much of her wealth from her large, modernized merchant fleet. As we know, in November 1939, the Norwegian Shippers Association had chartered almost half the fleet, amounting to 1,500,000 tons of tankers and 700,000 tons of other shipping, to Britain. Later the Norwegian government, while being pursued by the Luftwaffe in Central Norway, used its plenary powers to requisition their ships from the shipowners and administered them from a Norwegian Trade Mission in London. The fleet served the Allied cause from Murmansk to the Pacific, losing almost half of its 4.8 million tons, and many of its brave crews, to the enemy.

It is heartening to know that by 1949 the mercantile marine had reached its pre-war tonnage and had again become one of the largest and most modern in the Western world. This is just one factor which shows that the short campaign, traumatic and bitter as it was, changed the course of Norwegian history. As Dr Derry points out:

> In a longer view, however, the events of the campaign, the occupation, and the restoration might be seen also as episodes in a continuing process – in internal affairs, towards an integrated social structure; in external affairs, towards integration in western Europe.*

At the end of the campaign the Germans made strenuous efforts to repair the damage to the port installations at Narvik. By the end of January, 1941, they had made the first shipment of iron ore to Germany and succeeded in importing 600,000 tons by the end of the year. The increasing flow of ore was so important to the enemy economy that Professor Hubatsch believed that 'this made it possible to carry out the great battles of 1942–44, so expensive in material'. But it is to be remembered that, when France was over-run, Germany supplemented the high-grade Swedish iron-ore with cruder minerals from the Lorraine ore-fields.

Derry has pointed out that Germany's strategic gains resulting from the occupation of Norway form no integral part of the campaign itself. The same source† noted three main points in this connection. The first was the acquisition by the enemy of naval and air bases flanking the British Isles. This obviously aided Hitler's plan for the invasion of England while adding to Britain's home defence difficulties in the longer term.

More seriously, as we have noted earlier, it weakened our control of the northern approaches to the Atlantic. German air power, aided by naval defences constructed along the Norwegian Leads, made Allied movement

* Dr T. K. Derry, *A History of Modern Norway, 1814–1972*, p. 407.
† Derry, p. 229.

in that area extremely hazardous. Finally, the Germans' capacity for raiding our merchant ships was increased as their heaviest warships broke out into the open sea to attack our Murmansk convoys two years later, and to raid sea-borne commerce via the North-East Passage.

It would seem that, apart from the economic issue (the necessity of guaranteeing the uninterrupted flow of Swedish iron-ore), the need to protect their own sea lanes, while disrupting their enemies', was indeed a major strategic reason for Germany to launch *Weserübung*. The net results, the true costs and benefits, are very difficult to assess for either side. The author therefore ends with the final words of Professor Hubatsch's lecture at the University of London: 'much remains hidden from the man who takes historical decisions and believes that he can boldly master the future. Whither the journey leads, that no one can tell.'

APPENDIX A

Land Forces taking part in the campaign

I *Allied forces* operating under British command
- **a**: In the area Tromsö–Mosjöen (main base Harstad)
- **b**: Based on Namsos
- **c**: Based on Aandalsnes
- **d**: Air Component (Royal Air Force)

II *Norwegian forces* operating in co-operation with the Allies

III *German forces* operating to complete the invasion of Norway

Ia: *Flag Officer Narvik*
Admiral of the Fleet the Earl of Cork and Orrery, GCB, GCVO
(Appointed Supreme Commander 20 April, 1940)

Commander Land Forces (Avonforce/Rupertforce)
Major-General P. J. Mackesy, CB, DSO, MC
(10 April to 13 May, 1940)

Lieutenant-General C. J. E. Auchinleck, CB, CSI, DSO, OBE
(13 May to 8 June, 1940)
This force was designated North-Western Expeditionary Force with effect from 13 May

Units and Formations
24th (Guards) Brigade (Brigadier the Hon W. Fraser)
- 1st Battalion The Scots Guards (Lieutenant-Colonel T. B. Trappes-Lomax)
- 1st Battalion The Irish Guards (Lieutenant-Colonel W. B. Faulkner, MC)
- 2nd Battalion The South Wales Borderers (Lieutenant-Colonel P. Gottwaltz, MC)

Numbers 1, 2, 3, 4 and 5 Independent Companies (Lieutenant-Colonel – A/Brigadier C. McV. Gubbins, MC – Scissorsforce)
One troop, 3rd King's Own Hussars (Tanks)
203rd Battery, 51st Field Regiment, Royal Artillery

6th Anti-Aircraft Brigade, Royal Artillery (Brigadier F. N. C. Rosseter)
- 55th Light Anti-Aircraft Regiment (163rd, 164th, 165th Batteries)
- 56th Light Anti-Aircraft Regiment (3rd, 167th Batteries)
- 51st Heavy Anti-Aircraft Regiment (151st, 152nd, 153rd Batteries)
- 82nd Heavy Anti-Aircraft Regiment (156th, 193rd, 256th Batteries)
- Number 10 Army Observer Unit, Royal Artillery

229th Field Company, Royal Engineers
230th Field Company, Royal Engineers
Detachment, 231st Field Park Company, Royal Engineers
Detachments, Royal Corps of Signals
Special Increment to HQ 49 Division, Royal Army Service Corps*
(Lieutenant-Colonel H. M. Hinde, OBE)

French units

Corps Expéditionnaire Français Scandinavie
(Général de Division Audet)
27th Demi-Brigade Chasseurs Alpins
(Général de Brigade Béthouart)
- 6th, 12th, 14th Battalions Chasseurs Alpins

13th Demi-Brigade Foreign Legion
(Lieutenant-Colonel Magrin-Verneret)
- 1st and 2nd Battalions Foreign Legion

342nd (French) Independent Tank Company
2nd Independent Group Colonial Artillery
14th Anti-Tank Company (13th Chasseurs Alpins)

Polish Units

Samodzielna Brygada Strzelcow Podhalanskich (Polish Highland Brigade)
(Brigadier-General Z. Bohusz-Szyszko)
First Demi-Brigade (Colonel B. Chlusewicz)
- 1st Battalion (Major W. Kobyliński)
- 2nd Battalion (Lieutenant-Colonel W. Dec)

Second Demi-Brigade (Lieutenant-Colonel J. Kobylecki)
- 3rd Battalion (Lieutenant-Colonel M. Maćkowski)
- 4th Battalion (Major A. Jackowski)

Ib: *Operations based on Namsos*

North-Western Expeditionary Force, Central Norway
Lieutenant-General H. R. S. Massy, DSO, MC
(19 April to 6 May, 1940)

Commander Land Forces (Mauriceforce)
Major-General A. Carton de Wiart, VC, CB, CMG, DSO

* Detachments of the Royal Army Service Corps were also responsible for servicing all French and Polish units throughout the campaign.

Units and Formations
146th Infantry Brigade (Territorial Army)
(Brigadier C. G. Phillips, DSO, MC)
- 1st/4th Battalion The Royal Lincolnshire Regiment (Lieutenant-Colonel R. W. Newton)
- 1st/4th Battalion The King's Own Yorkshire Light Infantry (Lieutenant-Colonel W. S. Hibbert)
- The Hallamshire Battalion, The York and Lancaster Regiment (Lieutenant-Colonel C. G. Robbins)
- One Section 55th Field Company, Royal Engineers

French Units (Général de Division Audet)
5th Demi-Brigade Chasseurs Alpins
(Général de Brigade Béthouart)
- 13th, 53rd, 67th Battalions Chasseurs Alpins
- Detachments, Anti-Aircraft and Anti-Tank Artillery
- One Section Engineers

Ic: *Operations based on Aandalsnes*

Commander Land forces (Sickleforce)
Major-General B. C. T. Paget, DSO, MC
(20 April to 3 May, 1940)

Units and Formations
148th Brigade (Territorial Army)
(Brigadier H. de R. Morgan, DSO)
- 1st/5th Battalion The Royal Leicestershire Regiment (Lieutenant-Colonel G. T. German)
- 1st/8th Battalion The Sherwood Foresters (Lieutenant-Colonel T. A. Ford)

15th Brigade (Regular Army)
(Brigadier H. E. F. Smyth, MC)
- 1st Battalion The Green Howards (Lieutenant-Colonel A. E. Robinson)
- 1st Battalion The King's Own Yorkshire Light Infantry (A/Lieutenant-Colonel E. E. E. Cass, DSO, MC)
- 1st Battalion The York and Lancaster Regiment (Lieutenant-Colonel A. L. Kent-Lemon)

168th Light Anti-Aircraft Battery, Royal Artillery
260th Heavy Anti-Aircraft Battery, Royal Artillery
55th Field Company, Royal Engineers, (less one Section)

Id: *Royal Air Force* (Air Component)

Officer Commanding: Group Captain M. Moore

Number 263 Squadron, Gladiators (Squadron-Leader J. W. Donaldson)
Number 46 Squadron, Hurricanes (Squadron-Leader K. B. B. Cross)
Number 11 Observer Screen, Royal Air Force

II *Norwegian Land Forces* operating independently or in co-operation with the Allies

Commander in Chief

General Otto Ruge

Because mobilization was almost completely disrupted by the German seizure of the main centres of population on the morning of 9 April, a formal hierarchy of command is difficult to reconstruct; much of the military organization had to be improvised to meet a rapidly changing tactical situation. In studying the list which follows, it should be borne in mind that the total number of Norwegians serving under the colours did not at any point in the campaign amount to more than 25,000 men.*

Divisions

2nd (Central Norway, under Major-General Hvinden Haug)
3th (Southern Norway, under Major-General E. Liljedal)
5th (Trondheim area) Its commander, Major-General Laurantzon, fell ill in mid-April and the effective command of Norwegian troops in North Tröndelag became the responsibility of Colonel Getz.
6th (Northern Norway, under Major-General Fleischer)

Groups

Colonel T. A. Dahl (The Toten group), north of Oslo and west of Mjösa
Colonel H. Hiorth (The Österdal group)
Major-General Hvinden Haug (The Hedemark group), north of Oslo and east of Mjösa
Colonel C. Mork (The Hönefoss-Hadeland group), north-west of Oslo
Lieutenant-Colonel Roscher-Nilsen (The Haalogoland group), northern Norway

Brigades

4th Brigade – Colonel Östbye
5th Brigade – Colonel J. Jensen
6th Brigade – Colonel K. R. Löken
7th Brigade – Colonel W. N. Faye

Units

2nd Dragoons
3rd Dragoons
2nd Infantry (1st Battalion)

* Major-General O. Lindbäch-Larsen: *Krigen i Norge 1940* (Gyldendal, Oslo, 1965) p. 48.

3rd Infantry (1st, 2nd Battalion)
4th Infantry (1st, 2nd Battalion)
5th Infantry (1st, 2nd Battalion)
6th Infantry (1st, 2nd Battalion)
9th Infantry (1st Battalion)
10th Infantry (1st, 2nd Battalion)
11th Infantry (1st Battalion)
12th Infantry (1st Battalion)
13th Infantry (1st, 2nd Battalion)
14th Infantry (1st, 2nd Battalion)
15th Infantry (1st, 2nd Battalion)
16th Infantry (1st, 2nd Battalion)
The Varanger Battalion
The Alta Battalion
The Guards Battalion
The Torkildsen Battalion

Regiments
3rd Artillery
3rd Infantry (Telemark)
7th Infantry (Agder)
8th Infantry (Rogaland)
14th Infantry (Sör-Haalogoland), Lieutenant-Colonel Nummedal
15th Infantry (Nord-Haalogoland), Colonel B. H. Sundlo

Hans Majestet Kongens Garde, (King's Guard)
It should be noted that some units in the above list, e.g. the King's Guard, found only a relatively few men for actual operations in co-operation with the Allies, while most of General Fleischer's 6th Division fought continuously in the North throughout the entire campaign.

III *German Land Forces*

Overall Commander
General N. von Falkenhorst.

Divisions
2nd Mountain (Major-General Feuerstein)
3rd Mountain (Major-General Dietl)
7th Flieger Parachute (under Luftwaffe command)
22nd Airlanding (not used, withdrawn for Holland)
Panzerabteilung
69th Infantry
163rd Infantry
169th Infantry
170th Infantry
181st Infantry

196th Infantry
198th Infantry
214th Infantry

Groups
XXI and XXXI (operated initially in Denmark)
Fischer (the eastern group, going north)
Laendle (Lake Mjösa, going north)
Pellengahr (operated in Gudbrandsdal)
Hausells (Narvik and Ankenes areas)
Windisch (north and east of Narvik)

The two latter groups consisted partly of sailors from the German warships sunk in the fiords around Narvik. Professor Hubatsch reports that some 2100 of these 'fighting seamen', armed, equipped and clothed from the captured Norwegian Army depot at Elvegaardsmoen, were formed into three naval battalions.

In common with other groups they took their name from their commanders; Erdmenger and Bey served in the Narvik area, while the Kothe battalion fought with Windisch. Their value to General Dietl has been underestimated. The two northern groups were supported by a battery of mountain artillery, one half-battery with Hausells and the other with Group Windisch.

Regiments
1st Parachute (under Luftwaffe command)
11th Motorized Rifle
137th Mountain
138th Mountain
139th Mountain
193rd Infantry
310th Infantry
340th Infantry
345th Infantry
362th Infantry
General Goering (Motorized)

Not all the German units shown above saw active service in the field. Some were committed to the ever-lengthening lines of communication. Others guarded the ammunition depots or garrisoned the large towns and vulnerable ports.

APPENDIX B

List of Sources

ANDENAES–RISTE–SKODVIN: *Norway and the Second World War* Johan Grundt Tanum Forlag, Oslo, 1974

AUCHINLECK, Lieutenant-General C. J. E.: Report – see Lord Cork's Despatch, *London Gazette* No. 38011, 10 July, 1947

BECKWITH, Colonel E. G. G.: *The 8th Battalion Sherwood Foresters, T A* (Unpublished)

BROCH, Theodor: *The Mountains Wait* Joseph, 1943

BUCKLEY, Christopher: *Norway – The Commandos – Dieppe* HMSO, 1952

CARTON DE WIART, Lieutenant-General Sir Adrian: *Happy Odyssey* Cape, 1950

CHURCHILL, Winston S.: *The Second World War,* Vol. 1 Cassell, 1948

CLARKE, Brigadier Dudley: *Seven Assignments* Cape, 1948

CORK AND ORRERY, Admiral of the Fleet, the Earl of: Despatch, *London Gazette* No. 38011, 10 July, 1947

DALZIEL, Peter: *The 'Puffers' at Narvik, Army Quarterly,* April and July, 1965

DERRY, T. K.: *The Campaign in Norway* (History of the Second World War, UK Military Series, edited by J. R. M. Butler) HMSO, 1952

DERRY, T. K.: *A History of Modern Norway 1814–1972* Clarendon Press, Oxford, 1973

FEN, Aake: *Nazis in Norway* Penguin Books, 1943

HAMBRO, Carl J.: *I saw it happen in Norway* Hodder and Stoughton, 1940

HINGSTON, Colonel A. C.: *A Territorial Battalion in Norway* (King's Own Yorkshire Light Infantry) *Army Quarterly*, 1949/50

HUBATSCH, Professor W.: Problems of the Norwegian Campaign 1940 *RUSI Journal,* August, 1958

LAPIE, Captain Pierre O.: With the *Foreign Legion at Narvik* Murray, 1941

MACKESY, Major-General P. J.: Report – see Lord Cork's Despatch, *London Gazette* No. 38011, 10 July, 1947

MACKESY, Piers: *Churchill on Narvik, RUSI Journal,* December 1970

MASSY, Lieutenant-General H. R. S.: Despatch, *London Gazette* No. 37584, 29 May, 1946

MOULTON, Major-General J. L.: *The Norwegian Campaign of 1940: A study of warfare in three dimensions* Eyre and Spottiswoode, 1966

POLISH MINISTRY OF INFORMATION: *Polski Sily Zbronjne* (Polish Armed Forces) Vol. 2 Overseas Campaigns – Narvik. The Polish Institute and Sikorski Museum, London 1959. Translated into English by Teresa Mundziel-Staniszewska, Associate of the Institute of Linguists, June, 1987

POLISH MINISTRY OF INFORMATION: *Polish Troops in Norway*, A photographic Record of the Campaign at Narvik. M. I. Kolin, (Publishers), London, 1943

RISTE, Professor Olav: *Sea Power, Air Power and Weserübung* Paper given to the International Commission for Military History, Washington, D. C. August 1975 (ACTA No. 2)

WAAGE, Johan: *The Narvik Campaign* Harrap, 1964

ZBYSZEWSKI, K. and NATANSON, J.: *The Fight for Narvik* Lindsay Drummond, 1940

REGIMENTAL HISTORIES AND WAR DIARIES

Extracts from the Histories and/or War Diaries of:

The Royal Engineers
The Scots Guards
The Irish Guards
The Royal Lincolnshire Regiment
The Royal Leicestershire Regiment
The Green Howards (Alexandra, Princess of Wales's Own Regiment)
The South Wales Borderers (24th Regiment)
The Sherwood Foresters (Nottinghamshire and Derbyshire Regiment)
The King's Own Yorkshire Light Infantry
The York and Lancaster Regiment
The Royal Army Service Corps

TAPED INTERVIEWS

Tapes (or transcripts of tapes) made by the following for the Imperial War Museum have been referred to and/or quoted from:

Lieutenant-Colonel J. Q. Adams (Author)
Tape 9103/3
Mr J. R. Drury (Ex-Corporal, 8th Foresters)
Tape 9313/4/1
Mr T. Flower (Ex-Colour Sergeant, 2nd Bn. South Wales Borderers)
Tape 8990/3
Major-General D. S. Gordon (late The Green Howards)
Tape 8760/3
Mr H. Meltzer (late Norwegian Army, IR 3)
Tape 9159/2
Captain S. H. K. Spurgeon (late Royal Australian Navy)
Tape 4773/1

In addition to the above:

Brigadier D. M. L. Gordon-Watson (late Irish Guards) was interviewed by the author in November 1986.

Mr Kenneth Williams (Ex-Private, 2nd Bn. South Wales Borderers) taped his recollections of the campaign for the author in September, 1987.

INDEX